MRS. GANDHI'S GUEST
Growing Up with India

by
David Baily Harned
and
Elaine H. Harned

RESOURCE *Publications* · Eugene, Oregon

Resource Publications
A division of Wipf and Stock Publishers
199 W 8th Ave, Suite 3
Eugene, OR 97401

Mrs. Gandhi's Guest
Growing Up with India
By Harned, David Baily and Harned, Elaine H.
Copyright©2010 by Harned, David Baily
ISBN 13: 978-1-62564-733-7
Publication date 2/11/2014
Previously published by Ultra Publications, 2010

Previously pubished as
Strange Bedfellows: Growing up with India.

MRS. GANDHI'S GUEST
Growing up with India

TABLE OF CONTENTS

PREFACE

Professor David Baily Harned is a well-known scholar of Christian Thought, the author of many books and a strong advocate of the study of world religions. Much of the credit for building the Department of Religious Studies at the University of Virginia, Charlottesville, VA goes to him. The present work, *MRS. GANDHI'S GUEST: Growing up with India,* tells something of his times in India at work and at play during almost forty years, sometimes alone and at other times with his wife and children. His first weeks in India in the Sixties left him with overwhelming impressions of crowds and beggars, but in a short time things changed. That trip, he says, "profoundly altered my life and me." Some events outside Jaipur and in the midst of the Varanasi bazaar transformed his perspective and taught him that "divine grace is not mediated through one tradition alone." He returned the next year with his family and served as a research professor at Punjabi University, Patiala. One of his books was first published in India during that visit. During several later trips he helped to establish a University of Virginia semester in India program, but also found ample time to pursue his fascination with Indian sacred architecture - not only Hindu, but also Jain, Buddhist, Parsi, Sikh, Moslem and especially Moghul. He made a number of trips to Ellora and Ajanta and became particularly interested in the 12th and 13th c. Hoysala temples at Belur, Halebid, and Somnathpur. Mahabalipuram and Pattadakal, in Tamil Nadu and Karnataka respectively, furnished remarkable laboratories for the study of South Indian sacred architecture over the course of many centuries. The religious architecture and sculpture are everywhere presented in terms of their own time and place, history and political and social contexts.

The final chapters deal with the Harneds' impressions upon returning to India in 2005 and 2006 after an absence of many years. He observes that "so many sites in India are too rich to be grasped in a single visit and need to be seen time and again." That is true enough, but it is equally true that many things in India changed with lightning speed during their absence of twenty years. He sees

India throbbing with new life rooted in her own culture, but enriched by the traditions of the Middle East and England; indeed, he gives particular attention to the monuments of Moghul and Islamic culture as well as to the Jain and Parsi communities. He emphasizes that the genius of India has never been exclusive; the country has been hospitable to other religions and cultures for thousands of years. It has accommodated all peoples within one dazzling syncretistic household. He draws our attention, for example, to the Jewish synagogue in Cochin where there has been a community of believers for more than 1500 years. This openness reflects the Indian understanding of secularism as protection of and respect for other religions and cultures.

The differences the author notes between the Eighties and the present are numerous and important, especially in the socio-economic realm since Manmohan Singh became finance minister in 1991. For the author, perhaps nothing is more revolutionary and exciting than advances in the status of women. In any event, the West will have to run fast to keep pace with the dramatic changes in contemporary India. The work includes interesting reflections and helpful suggestions on Indian life, art, architecture and culture. It is very readable.

I think that this book would appeal to academics as well as to the general reader. It could be especially valuable to students of architectural history. It will be of great help to visitors to India from the USA and Europe. It will be most useful to non-resident Indians(NRI's) who visit India yearly in great numbers. It tells them "where to go, where to stay and what to see in India." It emphasizes the many positive points about India today, but it also cautions about the difficulties tourists might encounter. The book deserves wide attention and appreciation.

Dr. K. L. Seshagiri Rao
Professor Emeritus, University of Virginia
Chief Editor, Encyclopedia of Hinduism
Co-editor, Interreligious Insight, World Congress of Faiths

ACKNOWLEDGEMENTS

Human life is indebtedness. Many debts spark much gratitude. I want especially to register these debts of mine:

-to my wife, **Elaine H. Harned**, who provides the reasons to write and do all other things and who is my co-author;

-to Professor **K.L.Seshagiri Rao**, my Indian brother without whom neither these experiences nor this book would ever have occurred;

-to **Dr. M.S. Nagaraja Rao**, former Director General of the Archaeological Survey of India, who introduced me to many of the country's treasures;

-to **Dr. and Mrs. Dudley Rochester**, most supportive of neighbors and invaluable transmitters of our photographs to India.

CHAPTER ONE

An Unexpected Gift

How did it all happen, to make my life so different from what I had planned? As is so often the case, the relation between causes and effects is not at all transparent. But it is accurate to say that if I had not come to Charlottesville, Virginia, I would never have been so frequently in New Delhi, India. So I think I must begin by writing of what took me to Charlottesville, a town of which I had never even heard until four months before I uprooted my little family and transplanted us there. In the spring of 1967 I was in my fourth year as an assistant professor of religion and Biblical literature at Smith College in Northampton, Massachusetts. I had just been promoted to associate professor for the next year and, even though a decision on my tenure would not be made for another twelve months, we had already purchased a lovely home on a hilltop less than three miles from the campus. We were very happy there and had no thoughts of moving anywhere else.

Then lightning struck. I received an invitation to join the faculty of the University of Virginia as a tenured full professor at a salary that far exceeded what I could ever expect at Smith. I was to be the chairman of a new department that would be my own creation and so I would not be bound by any precedents set by other people. I was 34 years old. I am sure that in its long history the University had appointed others no older than I as full professors and chairmen, although I never met any. I was dazzled by the whole prospect, all the more because I knew I had not earned or deserved such an offer. From untenured assistant one day to tenured full professor the next, from apprentice to master without even one day spent as a journeyman associate professor – I would never forget how premature the invitation had been. The University asked me for a speedy decision but, of course, there really was no decision to be made. And so off we went from Northampton to Charlottesville to become Southerners, whatever that might turn out to mean.

The reasons why the move to Virginia required little reflection or discussion with family or colleagues -- every colleague seemed in favor of our departure! – had less to do with personal advancement than with a fundamental change in American higher education that I was given an extraordinary chance to pioneer. At the beginning of the 1960s the United States Supreme Court delivered its opinion that classroom prayers violated the traditional understanding of the separation of church and state when they were offered in American public schools. The fourth paragraph of that decision, however, encouraged the study of religion in a public context just as strongly as the first three paragraphs had discouraged the practice of religious rituals there. Many people of all religious persuasions were dismayed by what seemed to them the action of a thoroughly secular Court. Few people recognized the potential the opinion provided for the development of religious studies for the first time as part of the curriculum of public colleges and universities across the nation. Now the study of religion would not be confined to private institutions and the wealthy young people who could afford them but potentially available to everyone who pursued higher education no matter whether in a public or private school.

There was another side to the coin that I found equally exciting. A department supported by the taxpayers of the Commonwealth of Virginia could not focus on a single tradition. In the Virginia suburbs surrounding the District of Columbia there were residents from every country in the world and practitioners of every living religious tradition. My department would have a duty to be inclusive, perhaps more so than any other one in the land. Then religious studies could provide fertile terrain for the development of concentrations in China or Japan, India or Africa or elsewhere, as well as offer encouragement for study abroad. In various ways the inauguration of religious studies affords impetus for the internationalizing of the curriculum in a public school. There are few better remedies for the insularity and provincialism that have frequently been evident in American culture and that much of our educational system has done little to ameliorate. When I came to Charlottesville I knew of two other departments which had been created in the wake of the Supreme Court decision on prayer, one in Florida begun in 1965 and the other in Indiana a year later. Both were founded by friends of mine, fellow students at Yale and then colleagues at

Williams or Smith. But their interests certainly did not coincide with mine and so I thought we would be different in some fundamental ways.

I decided to bring a visiting professor with me to Charlottesville so I would not be entirely alone during my first year. The person I chose was K.L. Seshagiri Rao, a freshly minted Harvard PhD who was a year or two older than I. This was certainly a gamble, because we had never met, but he was greatly praised by Wilfred Cantwell Smith and other friends of mine at Harvard. He was teaching at Santa Barbara but would be free to join me for the 1967-68 academic year. Then he was scheduled to return to India to assume a prestigious post as the senior professor of Hindu studies at Punjabi University in Patiala. There he would be a charter member of the first ecumenical center for the study of world religions to be established in any Indian University. Seshagiri was himself a Hindu, a Gandhi scholar, a specialist in interreligious dialogue and the author of a recent book on Hindu - Christian encounters. I said I would meet him and his family on their arrival at the Charlottesville train station. He walked sedately down the platform carrying a neatly furled umbrella. His wife, clad in a brilliant sari came a few steps behind, clutching many bundles that kept threatening to elude her grasp. She was followed by three very large ambulatory plastic plants, self-propelled trees really, through the dense foliage of which I eventually glimpsed the breathless faces of three Rao boys—Ranjan, Nandan and Santosh. It was impossible not to like Seshagiri Rao; he quickly became a very popular figure at the University and he was an extraordinarily successful teacher. He and I got on well from our first day; it was as though we had grown up together and had known each other all our lives. I am not aware that I have ever had a better friend or known a wiser colleague.

It was the absence of any inhibition or constraint between us that led me one day to tell Seshagiri that while I knew interreligious dialogue was his field it certainly was not mine and I would be a very unwilling partner in any ventures in that area. I had many miles to go before I would feel familiar with important aspects of my own tradition, such as Greek and Russian Orthodoxy; I was not about to go haring off after other faiths about which I knew nothing at all. It seemed to me the best thing I could do for any sort of religious dialogue was simply to cultivate my own garden. I interpreted Seshagiri's nod and smile to indicate acceptance even if not enthusiasm. It was not until a year later that I realized how utterly wrong I had been. His nod and smile expressed his acceptance of the challenge my lack of interest represented. Thanks to him, eighteen months later I was up to my ears in interreligious dialogue, where I was certainly way out of my depth but seemed to have no options except to sink or swim.

Seshagiri's presence with me in 1967 was a great blessing because our conversations clarified what I wanted to build in Charlottesville. First, we should be roughly half and half, Western and Eastern. On the one hand, America was in some sense not at all easy to specify a Christian nation, and so this tradition deserved special treatment. On the other, we were not alone; we had to do business with many other nations and who was to say their traditions and faiths were less interesting than ours? Second, religion and culture are inseparable. It is not possible to study a tradition in thin air, so to speak, as though it could be understood in isolation from its practitioners and their daily lives. In other words, our teachers must be well trained in area studies. All of which is to say, third, that field experience would become more often than not a sine qua non for appointment to the faculty. At the end of the 1960s, unfortunately, field experience was in very short supply. Finally, we needed scholars who were acquainted with different methods and perspectives: sociological, psychological, textual, historical, linguistic, philosophical, cultural. All this would require a large department and I was confident the University would support my aspirations. But it would certainly require at least a decade because more rapid assimilation of new faculty could expose us to problems it would be better to avoid. I knew that my ideal of area studies and diversity of methods would founder on the rocks of reality. It did, time and again. But we still made extraordinary progress and we did have what was a more or less distinctive profile because of my commitment to a balance of Eastern and Western traditions, even though other new departments began to proliferate across the nation.

The date for the departure of the Raos came and went. But even though I missed my Indian brother both of us were absolutely certain that we would see one another again. What we did not know was how soon that reunion would occur and how little time would elapse before we were colleagues again. For the moment, however, Seshagiri was in the Punjab, the great fertile plain that stretches across India and Pakistan below the foothills of the Himalayas, and where I had never been. Until Independence in 1947 the Punjab was an assortment of princely states, some small and others large that had been ruled for generations by Sikh families. Today India's share of the Punjab is still religiously, politically and culturally more or less a Sikh state. Its language is Punjabi rather than Hindi, which is one of the country's two official languages and is spoken in the capital. So this was an unfamiliar and somewhat alien context for a Hindu scholar from the southern state of Karnataka, and whose first tongue was Kannada. Even so, he had been appointed to a highly visible and prominent position. Seshagiri was barely settled at Punjabi University before he was confronted with a considerable challenge--organizing the 500th birthday party of the Sikh religion or, more properly, hosting a large international congress to commemorate the quinquecentenary of the birth of Guru Nanak, the founder of the Sikhs. This was to be a great national event with dimensions that were political as well as religious. But Seshagiri was a born politician and an expert in all the Indian religious traditions. This task might not prove much fun but he surely had the political skills to accomplish it.

Now lightning struck again and this time the bolt came from the hand of Seshagiri. We were spending our summer as always in Northfield, Massachusetts, when I received a large envelope from India. It provided me for the first time with all the details of the impending celebrations and contained formal invitations to a dozen receptions and parties. A host of people from the West as well as the East would be there, including some acquaintances and friends of mine. Then I was astounded to discover that I was one of a handful of Westerners invited to attend as guests of the Government of India. Mrs. Gandhi had allocated funds not only to cover our international airfare but also to pay all expenses for extensive individual travel throughout India either for research or for recreation for as long as we were able to stay in the country. Half a dozen eminent scholars and me? Me? Lecturing in three months time in India about Sikhism to an audience of Sikhs. The idea was bizarre. I had never even met a single Sikh in my whole life. And all this was recompense for saying that I had little appetite for interreligious dialogue! In response to a request for the title of my address, I chose "Secularization and Guru Nanak." I had worked on the idea of secularization for a year or so. I thought I would see whether Nanak would fit or could be jammed into this context. My address was very long on secularization and very short on Guru Nanak. When I received the invitation I had never even once in my life heard the name of Guru Nanak. But eventually my paper was well received by a large and appreciative audience. It was published hither and yon and finally, or so I was told, even in Danish. Without much knowledge at all, I was suddenly regarded as an expert by those who knew even less than I.

As a young man I had traveled rather extensively, mainly in Europe and always in the West. The East seemed much too far away and I had never wanted to go there because I knew nothing about it. Did I want to go there now? I wrestled indecisively with the question. I had not been out of the United States since Elaine and I were married. First there had been the kerfuffle of the marriage itself, then the births of our two sons, then completion of my doctoral dissertation, then our moves to Smith and later to the University of Virginia, as well as buying and selling two houses and superintending the publication of my first two books. Life had become delightfully complicated. Did I really have time for this? The only people I knew going to the East in the late 1960s were on their way to Vietnam or else some hippies wanting to hibernate in the Himalayas. But some inner voice told me, If you throw away this gift which you certainly have not deserved, you are a coward and a fool. So I tried to pretend that I had no great qualms and off I went, cowering in my seat on the plane in the face of the longest journey I had ever made, remorseful at the prospect of leaving my family for perhaps as long as three months when I had never left them until now for more than two nights, quite unable to imagine what lay before me, utterly alone and holding only a single certitude about my future: I would be a stranger in a strange land.

When your plane lands in New Delhi and the door is opened, it would be difficult to mistake the country you are in. The spice laden and flower scented air from the nearby city washes over you, mixed with the less pleasant smell of automotive pollution. In later years, after the pollution was finally gone, the sudden inrush of that fragrance always brought tears to my eyes, saying to me,

Welcome home. I was quickly disabused of my poor thin preconceptions of India. I had expected dirt. I found standards of personal hygiene not often matched in Christian cultures and an astonishing absence of litter that certainly would put to shame American cities and rural areas as well. I had expected to see appalling need. Instead, I found foods in remarkable variety and abundance, fruits and vegetables and grains in such multihued profusion they would have caught the eye of any artist. I did see poverty as well as affluence, certainly, but usually at a distance, protected by the thickness of my wallet, thanks to the largesse of Mrs. Gandhi. Money has many uses; one of the most important is the insulation against reality it affords, even if that means we are disconnected from the struggles and small triumphs of ordinary life.

Because it seemed that I did not have to watch my pennies, my initial acquaintance with the city was very superficial and unsatisfying. I went everywhere by car, instead of on foot or by motor rickshaw. So I had few contacts with ordinary Indians. I saw everything at a distance, from behind the closed window of my car. From this perspective, so remote and disengaged, what I saw in New Delhi was not squalor and decay but enormous beauty, beauty everywhere. There was the grandeur of the broad and leafy avenues and the overwhelming and majestic facades that were the legacy of the British Raj, the reminiscences of the Mughal Empire in 17th century Shahjahanabad, the fascinating bustle of the goldsmiths' and silversmiths' and jewelers' streets in the neighborhood of Chandni Chowk, and the eloquent simplicity of the Mohandas Gandhi memorial. So I lingered in Delhi, bent on savoring the old city and the new. But even though I looked carefully at many sights, nothing seemed really to touch my heart.

By the end of my week in the city my first impressions had yielded to other ones that were entirely different. The beauty that first struck me had been created by the British when they moved their seat of power from Calcutta to New Delhi. They had designed the flower-bordered grand avenues for themselves. Now I knew that the chief architect of all this, Sir Edwin Lutyens, had intended his most important buildings to intimidate the native populace. Lutyens had nothing but ill-concealed disdain for the natives and all their works. The Raj's palace—now called Rashtrapati Bhavan and the residence of the president of India –has 340 stately rooms which required a staff of more than 2,000 servants. It was designed to be a Colossus that would dwarf all that was Indian and display to the natives their insignificance before the Titan that was the British Empire. On the columns of the palace portico are carved many bells, fated never to ring because they are stone, signifying that no bell would ever toll for the demise of the Empire. This is not India but anti-India, except for the irony that 18 years after the palace was completed the Viceroy left it, never to return, and it became the property of the new republic of India, imperial trappings passing to common folk.

The crowds that had once seemed so exotic and colorful now were a constant source of irritation, so claustrophobic I yearned for any way to escape them. The Chandni Chowk area in picturesque old Delhi was perhaps the worst place to be; one went with the crowd, for its surge was too hard to resist. It seemed impossible to go anywhere without a taxi, for a Westerner on foot was vulnerable to all sorts of intrusions. The most annoying aspect of the human density everywhere was the beggars. There were legions of them and they were never deterred no matter what I did. I had the sense that I was surrounded by thousands of them, each one with a hand held out in supplication. My first impression was that there was little poverty to be seen; I knew much better now. Poverty was everywhere; India seemed to have no middle class at all. A few people were rich and most of the rest had virtually nothing at all. There was one beggar in particular outside my hotel who literally haunted my dreams for weeks. He was handless and seemed to sense how much he repelled me. So he would come as close as he dared and wave the stumps of his arms in my face. By the time I could call a policeman or someone from the hotel he had melted once again into the crowd. There was not a single day while I was in Delhi that I was not his target.

I wanted to escape the crowds and catch a breath of fresh air but even if I could have taken refuge in some garden there was no fresh air to be found in New Delhi. The pollution, most of it automotive from diesel taxis and buses and trucks, was simply overwhelming. It was impossible to go out of doors without choking. But worst of all was simply the otherness of this city, its alien and foreign character. I felt that I understood nothing. During the three months since I had received my invitation to attend the conference in Patiala I had worked very hard to learn something of Guru Nanak and the history of the Sikhs, and to write a paper that would not be an embarrassment. But that had left me with no time to discover anything about contemporary India, its politics and economics and culture. I was woefully unprepared for this trip; it was clear to me that I should not have come. I was lonely, homesick and quite convinced that wherever I should be it was not in New Delhi, nor anywhere else in India. So I decided I would abbreviate the trip. I was committed to remain in India until after the conference, and then I had been scheduled to travel to two other sites, Khajuraho and Varanasi, to see tenth and eleventh century temples at the former and the holy Ganges River at the latter. But I decided that I would cancel those visits. My acquaintance with India thus far had been a complete disappointment; nothing here had really engaged my attention and caused me to pause in wonder and astonishment, except perhaps the plethora of beggars and the claustrophobic crowds. So after a week in New Delhi it was more than time to move on to Jaipur, about which I knew nothing. But, whatever else it was, at least Jaipur was not Delhi.

I was surprised to find that Jaipur is all dressed in pink. The buildings in the city center are painted pink because this is thought to be an especially welcoming color. I was delighted by the Rambagh Palace Hotel, which had just been converted from a royal residence two or three years earlier because the Maharaja of Jaipur wanted to encourage the development of tourism in Rajasthan. Jaipur has four main tourist attractions. One is the huge and imposing City Palace. Another is the so-called Wind Palace. Scarcely more than an extremely decorative façade because it is only one room deep, it provided a place where the ladies of the royal court could watch whatever was happening on the road outside without themselves ever being seen. A third is the Jantar Mantar, an 18th century astronomical observatory built by Maharaja Jai Singh II, the founder of the city. The last and perhaps the most interesting is Amber, about six miles outside Jaipur.

It is a forbidding fortress long deemed impregnable and it was the capital of Rajasthan until Jai Singh built himself a palace in his newly planned capital of Jaipur. The interior of the fortress evokes much astonishment because

JAIPUR, Cenotaphs of Gaitore
The most imposing of the Cenotaphs of Gaitore is devoted to Jai Singh II, the founder of the new capital city. It is a place of astonishing tranquility that is frequented by no one.

it is so different from the dour exterior. This is a light and airy palace with murals and other decorations painted in lovely pastel shades and carved marble walls that are simply breathtaking because they are done with such exquisite delicacy. I visited all four of these places and found them genuinely memorable and interesting.

I went somewhere else as well. I do not know why. It was not mentioned in any of the tourist literature I had. I was not accompanied by any guide. I simply hired a taxi and after a drive of a few miles I was in front of the cenotaphs of Gaitore. I wish I knew what had led me here but I do not. This is a place of mesmerizing splendor and serenity framed against a sere and unwelcoming rock strewn hillside. I spent the entire afternoon here and came back two other times during this brief visit to Jaipur. I never saw one other person here except for the distant figure of my driver. These white marble memorials all date from the 18th century and honor the maharajas of Jaipur and other male members of the royal household. A cenotaph is unlike a tomb or mausoleum because they contain human remains while a cenotaph is a memorial to someone whose remains are elsewhere. The royalty of Jaipur were all cremated and eventually their ashes were scattered on the waters of the Ganges. The simplest cenotaph consists of a marble platform on which there are four columns supporting a small dome. In Rajasthan the word for such memorials is <u>Chhatris,</u> which means canopies. More elaborate cenotaphs can have dozens of columns and ceilings and walls that are elaborately carved. This was the most beautiful place I had yet seen in India. The white marble reflected the midday sun so that I was dazzled both literally and metaphorically by such astonishing beauty. By late afternoon the marble had mellowed greatly and was even more welcoming. Dusk had fallen before I reluctantly took my leave.

Gaitore is wonderful nourishment for the soul. I felt more at peace than at any time since I had left home but I also felt a strange sense of exhilaration. Suddenly I felt that this trip I had been so ill-prepared for was introducing me to my future; it was something I could not have rejected because it was my destiny. The stones themselves seemed to speak to me, or so I thought. Their message was very simple: This is where you were meant to come and what you were meant to see. But your pilgrimage is not done, it has barely begun. Now you cannot see its design but one day it will be clear. Be patient, for all of this needs time. Accept that you are a pilgrim and that for you everything is ordained. Sit here and be still; look and learn. Of all the cenotaphs at Gaitore, the

JAIPUR, Cenotaphs of Gaitore
Detail of the intricate carved bands around the base of the Cenotaph of Jai Singh II.

most delicate and elaborate is the memorial to Jai Singh II. It includes several dozen slender and graceful white marble columns and has a wonderfully carved ceiling. Around the interior walls are carved hordes of charging horsemen and many war elephants, vases of flowers and troupes of dancing girls. But the virtuosity of the master artisans who labored here is perhaps best displayed in the exquisitely detailed peacocks that adorn many walls. Nearby and shaded by old trees there is a cenotaph in remembrance of the male children of the royal household who died in infancy. Ignorant and untraveled in this country though I was, I knew that I was standing amidst one of the glories and wonders of India. I was simply overwhelmed. A few miles away there are other cenotaphs memorializing the maharanis of Jaipur and other ladies of the court. These are also beautiful but much less impressive. My three visits to Gaitore in as many days caused me to cancel my plans to leave India immediately after the conference in Patiala. Somehow I felt that I had been counseled to stay the course.

From Jaipur I flew to Udaipur in southern Rajasthan, a small city of great charm. For the first time on the trip I was able to take long walks through the byways and alleys of an Indian town where there were no beggars and no crowds. I had a splendid time. I stayed at the rather legendary Lake Palace Hotel which is precisely that, an 18th century palace in the middle of Lake Pichola which looks as though it is afloat. There is no access to it except by launch. I was greatly impressed by the Jagdish Temple, the first Hindu shrine I had found an opportunity to explore with any care. It is adorned with splendid carvings and was a bustle of activity while I was there. Then it was time to turn north, far north, and take a plane from New Delhi to the city of Srinagar, the capital of conflict riven Kashmir. When I arrived there I ran straight into the Muslim-Hindu strife that had been endemic in Kashmir since the days of Partition in the summer of 1947. There was a curfew enforced in the city, sporadic gunfire in the streets, and few crowds except for the occasional knots of tourists who, like me, had little sense of what was going on, or why. But this did not bother me very much because my hotel, yet another maharaja's palace, was away from the center of the city and set amid tranquil and secluded gardens on the shore of Lake Dal, a place of awesome natural beauty.

A Mughal emperor once said, "See Kashmir and die." What he meant was that no natural beauty in this world surpasses the beauty of this place and so when you have seen Kashmir there is nothing else for which to search. You have found paradise on earth. My own next destination would be the town of Patiala and the Guru Nanak convocation, where there would be no mountains and no lakes. So I followed the sage advice of the emperor who, had he known Latin, would undoubtedly have counseled, Carpe diem. I gave myself up to pure vacation. I spent much time on the lake and I did much hiking and even a little climbing. I was fascinated by the Mughal Charbagh gardens that I was able to visit because of their use of fountains and watercourses as principal elements in garden architecture. A charbagh garden is perfectly geometrical, designed in quadrants which are usually separated by lovely watercourses. I had never seen anything like this anywhere else. But soon it was time to turn south again, first by plane to Delhi and then by car to Punjabi University, a drive of approximately ten hours through the immensely fertile North Indian plain.

Punjabi University is new and large and handsome, with very extensive grounds and beautiful gardens, the focal point of which is the Guru Gobind Singh Bhavan, which houses the Center for the Study of World Religions and the department of religious studies. It is a remarkable example of contemporary architecture, a great white concrete tepee topped by an eternal flame and surrounded by a large reflecting pool that nearby villagers thought was sacred and so we sometimes found them wading or even bathing there. Above the pool are four concrete 'boats' projecting from the tepee and they contain offices for the staff and professors as well as Western-style bathrooms. All of this seemed truly awesome to the inhabitants of the surrounding villages from which our stewards and many other employees had been recruited. There was a small bridge across the pool and on the first floor a large and pleasant lecture hall where the later sessions of the conference would be held. The political aspects of the Guru Nanak Quinquecentenary could not have been more obvious at the opening sessions, held under a vast tent that intensified the effects of a temperature that twice exceeded 120 degrees. Before the monsoon rains begin, this verdant northern plain is an oven, despite the proximity of the Himalayas. Everywhere around me there were groups of soldiers, aged Sikh grandees, bureaucrats from the

Punjab and Haryana governments in Chandigarh, politicians and newsmen from New Delhi as well as scholars from four continents. But when we finally moved for the academic sessions into the Guru Gobind Singh Bhavan, the conference became truly fascinating. By and large the papers were excellent, and the questions and discussion focused and interesting.

All day long young stewards circulated through the hall bearing glasses of cool water and cups of hot sweet tea to assuage the dehydration caused by the intense heat. Their immaculate starched white jackets contrasted vividly with the more muted clothing of the delegates. Late one morning I left the conference hall to go to the lavatory. There I discovered two stewards who had just found the only place in the bathroom where they could flush clean the cups and glasses. One boy neatly placed glasses and crockery in the bowl; when everything was ready the other pressed the lever and flushed. Then he flushed a second time just to make sure everything was quite sanitary. I followed them back to the conference hall as they offered the delegates more cool water and hot tea. I asked another steward if he could bring me some Coca-Cola in a bottle and he hurried off. I was very grateful. As we all know, water has been one of the greatest killers in the so-called Third World since time immemorial. There is a simple but important lesson here: Modernization travels at a different pace in different places and when it touches the lives of some people that surely does not mean it has touched everyone—or that it ever will. Modernization must be taught; it cannot simply be thrown at people like a baseball.

The conference afforded ample leisure for me to spend time in several of the neighborhood Sikh churches, called gurdwaras, as well as in their schools and the attached langars or free kitchens that provide food and drink for any passerby who wants them, whether Sikh or not. These practical encounters complemented our academic sessions and instilled in me a lifelong admiration and affection for the Sikh community. Sikhism is a very young religious tradition, being today not quite 550 years old. There are approximately twenty million Sikhs (the word means disciple) in the world today, the vast majority of whom live in the Punjab, a prosperous agricultural state that lies north of the national capital, New Delhi. Their founder was Guru Nanak (1469-1539) who was heir to strains of Hindu and Muslim mysticism that were current long

14

before his birth. But the message that Guru Nanak began to proclaim at the age of thirty was not a mere amalgam of motifs drawn from those traditions; it was genuinely new and soon commanded a considerable audience. Nine gurus succeeded Nanak. A guru is someone who banishes the darkness and offers the possibility of enlightenment, but only if the grace of God prevenes and opens the heart so that one is empowered to believe.

The tenth guru, Gobind Singh, died in 1708; he decisively influenced the whole subsequent history of Sikhism. First, after the assassinations of his four sons, he declared that he was the last human guru and that with his death the mantle of the guru would fall on the Sikh scriptures, the Adi Granth. Sikhism has no priesthood, no intermediaries of any sort between the believer and God. So Sikhs are "a people of the Book" in a stricter sense, perhaps, than any other religious tradition. Second, in 1699 Guru Gobind Singh created a community within the community, a spiritual elite of unusual commitment which he called the Khalsa, the community of the pure. All the men in the Khalsa are now named Singh or lion and all the women are called Kaur or Princess. Every male Sikh, however, no matter whether Khalsa or not, is expected to honor the "Five Ks." The acronym stands first of all for unshorn hair worn in a bun atop the head where it is held in place by a comb and all this is covered by a turban which is made from about 22 feet of cloth. The uncut hair represents vitality or virility and the comb means discipline and order, control over oneself. Third and fourth, a Sikh must wear a knife or sword and also a steel bangle on his wrist. The knife or sword stands for strength and courage, the bangle for restraint; the might of Sikhs can be exercised on behalf of widows and orphans but never in acts of aggression. In the contemporary world many Sikhs prefer to wear a small ornamental dagger or sword around their necks. Finally, there is underwear, which demonstrates a need for and achievement of control over physical desires. The faith is strictly monogamous.

Guru Nanak was very skeptical of all talk about religious and sacred things; his focus is consistently upon the Holy, Sat Nam, an omnipotent and omniscient Lord who is best described as sovereign, loving will. Because divine transcendence is understood in moral rather than spatial terms, the transcendent Lord is free to be immanent within his creation; Sat Nam indwells the souls of believers, whose Godconsciousness is a gift of grace that grows through the disciplines of meditation, prayer, hymns and the reading each day of the Adi Granth. Guru Nanak's understanding of God certainly emerges from the Bhakti tradition in Hinduism, the way of devotion, but it becomes something quite different in his hands. Apart from grace, the human condition is characterized by egotism and blindness, the latter being the consequence of the former. Because we think of the self as the center of the universe, we can no longer see how all things point beyond themselves to Him who is the true center. So our world becomes maya, a realm of seeming and shadows. It is all a delusion now, but this is not to say that it is an illusion; the world is real but our perception of it is warped. Grace reorients us and fills our hearts with a new love so that we can see again. In his discussions of both the Holy and the human there is the same stress on the priority of the will, the importance of love, and the cruciality of divine initiative and grace.

Some Gurdwaras (which means the home of the guru, the Adi Granth) are grand, others are very modest, but all fly the bright yellow flag (the Nishan Sahib) that is the Sikh emblem. Many gurdwaras include schools and kitchens, but their largest room is always reserved for the Adi Granth, which usually rests on some ornate base. Everyone, male and female as well, is invited to recite from the holy book. From its beginnings, Sikhism has been a protest against the Hindu caste system, especially the notion of a Brahminical priestly caste. Its holiest shrine, the Golden Temple in Amritsar, has a door on each of its four sides, signifying that the four great caste divisions or Varnas are equally welcome to come into the presence of Sat Nam. Who is a Sikh? The question is not difficult to answer. A Sikh is anyone who believes in God, adheres to the teachings of the ten gurus, and accepts the Adi Granth as the Word of God. Sikhism is far more influential than its numbers would suggest. For example, the late Lt. General Jagjit Singh Aurora, the liberator of Bangladesh in 1971, was a Sikh. So is the Prime Minister, Manmohan Singh, who as Finance Minister in 1991 began the great transformation that has brought India to where it is today.

Unfortunately, I saw very little of Seshagiri in the course of the convocation, for he was always busy overseeing some aspect of the conference. But I did manage to persuade him to agree to return to Charlottesville as a visiting professor again in another year. I was content with this because I was confident that then I could convince him to return with his family and remain permanently in my department. One of the final events for some of the Westerners at the conference was a lavish reception given by the Maharaja of Patiala at his palace. It was a memorable occasion but also bittersweet because, not to my surprise, I was not at all ready to leave Patiala. I wanted more time with my new friends in the Guru Gobind Singh <u>Bhavan</u>: Harbans Singh in Sikh Studies, Lal Mani Joshi in Indian Buddhism, Sundararajan in Hinduism, Avtar Singh in Sikh ethics, and of course, Seshagiri. But I was grateful for all I had received.

After Patiala I had only two more destinations in India before turning north for Nepal and its capital, Kathmandu. The first of my remaining targets in India was Khajuraho, scarcely more than a hamlet in an isolated location in the state of Madhya Pradesh in central India. But this little agrarian town boasts two dozen temples constructed in the 10th and 11th centuries during the reign of the Chandela dynasty, when Khajuraho was an imperial capital. They are in the Nagara or North Indian style and they are among the finest examples of sacred architecture in the land. Every shrine is lavishly decorated with sculptures that are not often rivaled and rarely bettered. All of this represents a cosmic dance, a union of human beings with one another, of the human with the divine, and of the earthly with the heavenly, in a universal act of regeneration that renews and recreates the world and sustains it against the threat of chaos. Khajuraho is a sermon in stone, a sculptural encyclopedia of Hinduism, and so it was a fitting stop to prepare me for my last visit in this introduction to a few of the riches of India. I was dazzled here again, just as I had been at Gaitore, although in an entirely different way.

The most notable of all these wonderful and unweathered temples is Kandariya Mahadev. It sits atop an extremely high plinth or platform that I had some difficulty climbing. Its central tower or <u>shikhara</u> soars 31 meters into the air above the plinth. It is built from 84 subordinate towers each of which is higher than the one before it. It is amazing how every aspect of the whole edifice gives the impression of ascent, aspiration, soaring up into the realm of the gods. All the walls of this temple dedicated to Siva are covered with carvings of gods and goddesses and avatars, hunters and their quarries, loving couples here and there captured in sexual union, soldiers and musicians, celestial maidens or apsaras, and a host of other beings. The quality of all this workmanship is consistently breathtaking. It is at Kandariya Mahadev that the erotic carvings celebrating the rhythms of nature and the fecundity of life reach their zenith. The internal carving is just as elaborate as the exterior. But there are many treasures at Khajuraho, not one only. The Lakshmana temple is especially important. Lakshmi is the goddess of wealth and the wife of Vishnu. In the central shrine she stands flanked by Brahma, the lord of creation, and by Siva, the lord of destruction, in a fine and arresting tableau. The sanctum is adorned with carvings of the life of Krishna, perhaps the most appealing of all the incarnations of Vishnu. There are many loving couples here in highly erotic poses. The Vishvanath temple is also worthy of special mention. It has two staircases, one guarded by a pair of lions and the other by a pair of elephants. Everywhere one turns there are voluptuous figures of women engaged in the daily tasks of 10th century life: fondling a child, dressing, playing music. The Devi Jagdamba temple has a three-headed, eight-armed figure of Siva that is very powerful. The Varaha temple has a huge boar-faced figure, another incarnation of Vishnu, that is quite remarkable. And there is a most appealing Nandi, the sacred bull that is Siva's mount. There is much more of great interest than I can begin to describe.

Varanasi, Benares as it used to be called, is Siva's town. It would have been swept away long since if he had not intervened to break the fall of the waters of the Ganges from heaven so that they nourished the plain of Bengal instead of overwhelming it in a murderous inundation. Siva is everywhere acknowledged as God the destroyer, of course, but here he is also known as patron and protector, and that is why Varanasi is the holy city of the Hindus. It is also arguably the longest continuously inhabited place on earth. It is said that every devout Hindu wishes to die in Varanasi and to be cremated on the banks of the Ganges, the river of life that bears away whatever remains after life is gone. But it is also true that every day there are countless signs of the vitality of those who remain in the city. I have never seen another city bazaar like the one in Varanasi, where everything that human beings have ever devised since the beginning of time can be purchased any day.

As I flew into the city I was aware of one small cloud across my personal horizon. I had exhausted my supply of pipe tobacco; I needed more, and it had to be the variety of Amphora that comes in a light brown pouch. So after we landed I asked my taxi driver to take me straight to the city bazaar and then return later to drive me to Clark's Hotel. It took only a few minutes to locate a well provisioned tobacconist, even though darkness had fallen. Because my taxi would not yet have returned, I yielded to the movement of the crowd and passed one stall after another, amazed by the incredible variety of goods on display, constantly jostled by the surging crowds. I had never seen such astonishing human density, all of us touching and pressing against our unknown neighbors, and yet no one seemed to mind in the least. It was as though we were all one family. All of us walked at the same pace because our movements were dictated by the crowd and not by individual volition. Despite the vast multitude there was an eerie silence in the bazaar, all of us bent on different and mysterious errands, no one uttering a shout or an imprecation or a complaint or calling to a friend, all of us countless bits of flotsam and jetsam carried ineluctably on by the rhythms of the whole toward the embrace of Mother Ganga, the holy river. Eventually the bazaar ended at the bathing ghats where the populace comes each day at dawn to wash bodies and clothes and scrub their souls. This is a very holy place and has been since time immemorial.

Siva the destroyer is also the Lord of the Dance, the one whose cosmic dance awakens the world from its sleep and brings animation to it. I stood on the stone steps of the bathing ghat leading down to the river, walking no more. Suddenly I realized that I was weeping and that my cheeks were covered with tears. Part of the reason was joy. Somehow in this bazaar the carapace of my Westernness was cracked; no, shattered. My sleep was interrupted and at last I could begin to see. All the images and all the impressions from these many weeks that had lain fallow somewhere in the recesses of my mind flooded into the light of consciousness and I was simply overwhelmed. Some of my tears had to do with the fact that finally I could grasp some of the diversity and density, the alien and exotic and mysterious panorama that is India. What had seemed so foreign and incomprehensible to me was not threatening now but beckoning. My walk through the bazaar had been one of my roads to Damascus and this had been one of the most important nights of my life. I was overcome by the sense of the presence of God as I stood on the steps of the ghat, this holiest of all places in India that was not even a stone's throw from the commercialism of the most thronged bazaar I could ever have imagined. I had reached my last destination on this first trip to India and as I looked back at the bazaar it struck me as somehow an inauguration, an initiation, a rite of passage, and the fulfillment of the intimations that had come to me at Gaitore.

So I wept in gratitude for all I had received. But some of my tears also had to do with the fact that just as I thought that I had encountered the life of India it continued to elude me. Just as I reached out it managed to escape my grasp. The figures in the bazaar confronted me anew with the transcendence of the human, its elusiveness, its sometimes enigmatic face, its depths that resist all attempts to fathom them. Sometimes this can be ignored or pass unnoticed in familiar surroundings but it is inescapable in a land as foreign as India. The correlate of human freedom is an element of chance or caprice or accident in a world where now so much is imprevisible. As soon as a person enters an otherwise static universe there is caprice and chance and the presence of Siva, the Lord of the Dance. Did Siva's town turn me into a Hindu? Of course not. But I did feel that there were ways in which I had been changed forever by this journey. Certainly I had received the gift of another place that would draw me back and educate me time and again.

Thoughtless and shallow as I may have been, I had come to India to see the sights. It had never occurred to me that this trip would be more than that. But the Westerner who came to look finally stayed to listen and learn, although not at my own initiative but because I had been touched by the hand of God at Gaitore and in the Varanasi bazaar. I had come as a spectator but left as a participant because I had learned that all those who venture into Siva's domain are summoned to the dance. I was not prepared for this; it was not my choice. Only in retrospect, only months and years later, did I come to recognize how greatly I had been blessed at Gaitore and Varanasi. But I knew by the time I left the holy city that my days there had expanded my vision in a way I would never forget; my views of my own self and of other selves and of all of us together had been permanently altered. The God whose presence I felt so strongly in Varanasi, however, was none other than the Lord to whom I had committed myself during my days in the Faculty of Divinity at the University of Edinburgh more than a dozen years earlier. But now I knew full well that his grace was not mediated through one tradition alone. His sovereign love was much too expansive and embracing to be restricted to such narrow confines.

The next morning, soon after dawn, I was in a small boat in the middle of the Ganges. It was a beautiful day and the river was so calm it seemed to have no current. Even the birds were silent. In the distance I could see the smoke from the cremation ghat rising straight into the still air, and nearby a great crowd of people at the bathing ghats, washing themselves and their clothes in the sacred river. But their voices were too distant to intrude upon the serenity that surrounded our little boat. This was perhaps the most coveted place of all for those of the Hindu faith, to be floating in the embrace of the mother of life, the Ganges. It seemed that all nature conspired to sanctify the moment. It was impossible not to reflect upon the events of the previous evening. But I could not fathom then and I do not know today all the reasons why I wept as fiercely as I did. The tears taught me one thing beyond all doubt, however: the life of David Harned and the life of India would be bound up for many years to come and this was only the first of the trips I would make to the subcontinent. Seshagiri's generous and gentle joke had achieved its purpose, for I had come here and learned and would return. And Mrs. Gandhi had won her bet, at least in my case. The rupees given to me had been well spent, because I would be back in India with my family in a matter of months.

※ ※ ※

CHAPTER TWO

Family Life in the Punjab

One morning soon after I had returned from India my friend Fredson Bowers telephoned to say that he wanted to nominate me for a National Endowment for the Humanities fellowship. I told him that I was most grateful. Fred was sitting in for ten months or so as our interim dean of the faculty of arts and sciences. Then he said he would need to have a completed application, including a research proposal, on his desk the same afternoon. I told him that I could comply with his wishes, of course, but he should not expect anything much if I had to cobble together the whole application in an hour or two because we had a looming deadline. Then I forgot about the whole thing. Some months later I received a letter from Washington informing me that I had been awarded a NEH fellowship for the 1970-71 academic year. This sent me hastily in search of a copy of my proposal, because I could not remember the details of what I had written then. What had I committed myself to try to accomplish?

The proposal stated that I would take myself and my family to rural India where I would serve as a research professor at Punjabi University in Patiala. I would be the first person to serve as professor of Christian studies in its fledgling Center for the Study of World Religions, the first such ecumenical venture to be established in any university in India. During my tenure there I would prepare a series of lectures on topics for interreligious dialogue and these would be delivered both at the university and elsewhere. The lectures would then be published in India under the imprint of Punjabi University and perhaps an American publisher would also be interested. Me and my family? Our boys were then five and seven. Me and interreligious dialogue? Just what I had told Seshagiri Rao I did not ever want to do. But my little family was thrilled-- and I was too, because I had never expected a favorable response to such a hastily crafted proposal. Punjabi University responded to the news that I could return with infinite graciousness and the members of the department seemed quite pleased. Sardar Harbans Singh, the head of religious studies, wrote to say that I would receive the salary of a senior full professor for as long as we could remain in Patiala. We would be housed in one of the two suites in the sparkling new university guesthouse, rent free, where a splendid chef would prepare our meals and I would have a handsome office in one of the four "boats" of the Guru Gobind Singh Bhavan and as much secretarial assistance as I could use. What more could I possibly require?

The boys were very excited, perhaps most of all because this would mean their first rides in an airplane. I wanted our trip around the world to be great fun for them, but also as easy as possible. So first we flew to Edinburgh for a week, where I could show them where I had lived during my days as a student at New College and introduce them to the beauty of the Highlands, which they have loved from that day to this. Then to London, where I had first become acquainted with a culture other than my own. There, as a Winant Volunteer and ADC to Tubby Clayton, I had learned for the first time of the bias toward the poor and downtrodden that lies at the heart of Christianity. And so to Paris, a city that had seduced me as a young man just as successfully as it defeated all my attempts to master its language. After exploring one or two other cities we flew from Beirut to Istanbul, our last stop before New Delhi and a place I had never visited until now.

I was awed by the architectural grandeur that we found in Istanbul. Perhaps most overwhelming of all was Hagia Sophia, a church built in 537 that boasted the largest dome in the world until the Renaissance, when Brunelleschi trumped it and created a still larger one for the Duomo in Florence. Istanbul was good preparation for India in a way, because of the Islamic architecture of the Caliphate, notably on view in the Blue Mosque, Topkapi Palace and the Grand Bazaar. One day we spent on the water, catching a steamer through the Bosphorus and far out into the Black Sea. These were the times when plane hijackings were not infrequent, and so security at the Istanbul airport was very tight and the soldiers on duty were heavily armed. When it was time for us to embark on our way to New Delhi we were asked to walk across the tarmac between two lines of troops with automatic rifles and then stop beside the plane for a thorough body search. Eager to board for what would be only their second really long flight, our boys had wormed their way to the head of the line. They were very ticklish. When the searches began they writhed and wriggled and screamed with laughter. Eventually the officer in charge just motioned to us all to board the plane, unsearched. Our sons received many grateful smiles from their fellow passengers after that.

The situation in New Delhi was utterly different. The fragrance of flowers and spices filled the plane when the doors were opened and the atmosphere in the airport seemed almost festive. As we neared The Imperial there were millions of blooms along the wide avenues. The clerks at the reception desk seemed to remember me well from my earlier visit. In 1970 The Imperial advertised itself as "the best Indian Hotel in New Delhi." So we decided to spend a week there to acclimatize the boys a bit to India before the nine or ten hour drive to Patiala. To my great surprise and chagrin, there were two young and unkempt American hippies also staying at the hotel. One wore a quite soiled and disreputable turban. When the two of them returned from somewhere one afternoon, both bare-headed, I happened to be standing in the lobby as they asked for their laundry. A few minutes later one of them ran up to the concierge's desk with a package in his hand and shouted at the startled man, "You ruined it! You ruined it!" As the concierge later explained to me, the boy thought that turbans came from turban stores where all of them had been already wound. He simply had no idea what to do when his laundry package from the hotel included about 22 feet of immaculately laundered and carefully folded white cotton cloth--but no turban. I was amused and rather pleased by the story and even more so by the scruffy boy's obvious discomfiture and dismay.

Our hotel was only a few blocks from Connaught Circus, the shopping center for the modern city, so we had much time to wander in the shops and bazaars as well as to visit most of the main tourist attractions. I soon saw my nemesis from the first trip, the beggar with no hands, but even though I passed him on numerous occasions, he seemed to have forgotten all about me. There was another beggar, however, a boy scarcely older than my son Kit, of whom I was very wary. We encountered this gypsy child--if that is what he was--every time we walked to Connaught Circus. Timothy had a remarkable gift for mimicry as a little boy and each day that we saw the beggar child Tim would mimic with uncanny skill his stance, his gestures and the whine in his voice, despite all my warnings not to do it. In the eyes of the little beggar boy there was such blazing hatred that I feared what he might try to do to Timmy. So from then on we walked to Connaught Circus by a different route and I tried to teach my sons that even these infuriating professional beggars were also human beings who were trapped in a dreadful life from which there was no hope of escape, and all of this was through no fault of their own.

When we reached Patiala after a long day's drive Punjabi University did not disappoint us. The buildings were new and spotless and of some real architectural merit. The grounds were very spacious and the extensive rose gardens were in profuse bloom. Our own quarters delighted all four of us; we had more than sufficient space and two large Western-style bathrooms, as well as a large terrace to share with some other residents, if any ever appeared, and two balconies of our own with interesting views. The other suite in the building, I learned, was usually reserved for the governor of the Punjab. There was one small cloud on our horizon: our handsome accommodations had no electricity. I duly reported this to the university as we fumbled around in the darkness and an electrician was dispatched to us. He verified that we actually had no electricity. Then he squatted in front of one of the outlets and began to pray. He prayed for a very long time. Then he tried the light switches again. They still did not work. He looked very crestfallen and soon departed. I telephoned the university again and asked if they could please send us a less religious electrician. Soon a whole bevy of them arrived, although they might actually have been gardeners or plumbers or social workers for all I knew. But eventually the problem was identified. There had been two sets of electricians employed in the construction of the new building. The first set was responsible for installing the wiring in the guesthouse walls. The second came along later and placed the outlets where they were most aesthetically pleasing. Unfortunately, there was no third set charged with relating the work of the first set to the labors of the second. After a few hours, however, the connections were made and then there was light! There is a lesson here: whatever the efficacy of prayer might be, it does not do much by itself to generate a flow of electrical current. It does not bring light, it brings enlightening, which illuminates in a very different way.

Our chef, Parakram, was a Hindu and so our food was vegetarian, but the variety of dishes he served was simply astonishing. None of us in fact missed meat or fish because Parakram always had a new treat in store for us. We have never encountered a finer cook and all four of us became very fond of him. Our routine was quickly established: the boys were enrolled in an English-speaking school in Patiala town; they were the only foreign students there. A bus took them to and fro each day and there were always a good many other children from the university on the bus, including Nikki, the daughter of the Harbans Singhs, who always kept a friendly eye on our boys. I left for the Guru Gobind Singh Bhavan after breakfast and returned in the late afternoon; then all of us walked around the university grounds for most of an hour. We enjoyed drinks on our balcony and then Parakram brought us dinner at eight. During our first several months we were the only occupants of the guesthouse and so nothing distracted Parakram from his usual attentiveness to all our needs. The students at Punjabi University were all Sikhs, remarkably tall and lithe and athletic. They were a very masculine but gentle lot, many of them destined to be officer candidates in the Indian army. Most Indian olympic athletes are Sikhs. On our evening walks we were greeted by many young men holding hands and also holding a freshly plucked rose from the communal gardens to their nostrils. Men held hands with men and women with women but especially outside the big cities it was extremely uncommon to see men and women holding one another's hand. There were very strong cultural inhibitions about this.

During the day I much enjoyed my conversations during our tea breaks with some delightful colleagues, especially Seshagiri, Harbans Singh, Avtar Singh and Lal Mani Joshi. The latter two were hard at work completing major book manuscripts, Avtar Singh finishing a systematic exposition of Sikh ethics, the first one ever to be written by a real moral philosopher, and Joshi concluding a massive study of the decline and virtual extinction of Buddhism in India more than a thousand years ago. We had long discussions about their work and what they had found during their research that had particularly excited them. I have rarely had more interesting professional conversations. Both men were absolutely first-rate and their presence would enhance any department of religious studies I knew of in America. They were also genuinely interested in the small book I was committed to writing on the themes of grace and play; both of them were eager to suggest parallels between their traditions and my own. Avtar Singh and his wife invited us one evening for dinner. They served roasted goat, a rare delicacy in the Punjab which is offered only to most honored guests. We were very touched. They had no children of their own and they absolutely doted on ours.

It was really an idyllic life, here on this peaceful and verdant northern Indian plain, surrounded by caring colleagues. Several months into our sojourn in Patiala, however, two events befell us that briefly disturbed our tranquility. First, I came down with a near-fatal case of amoebic dysentery which required medical attention in New Delhi and then a bit of convalescence at the Gandhi Peace Foundation there. It reduced me quite literally to nothing but skin and bones and months passed before I could walk normally again. Second, Timothy suffered a playground accident at school. We were told he was hurt but not where to find him. So Elaine took a taxi through the town in one direction and I took a motor rickshaw in another. Soon I could hear him screaming and I tracked the sound to a dilapidated little house on a nameless street on the outskirts of the city. As I burst through the door a very old man, without raising his eyes from my son for an instant, said, "You know I am doing this better than it would be done in the United States of America." I was relieved to see that Tim was not screaming because he was in pain but because he wanted his parents. The old man would not accept any money from me for dealing with Tim's broken wrist. I tried to insist but to no avail; all he would accept was a simple word of thanks. The next morning I took Timmy to the medical unit of our embassy in Delhi and I told the American physician there what the old man in Patiala had said. He remarked that what I had been told was probably accurate because the old Indian set broken bones morning, noon and night all year round and American physicians simply did not have comparable experience. In any event, the rather complex triple break healed perfectly and caused no discomfort after it was set. The cast stayed on Tim's wrist three weeks longer than it would have at home, however, because his daily glasses of buffalo milk provided much less calcium than milk from American dairy cattle. All in all, our two small setbacks seemed of very little importance.

There was something else, though, that threatened to interrupt our busy and pleasurable life and cause us no end of distress. When I received a bill from the university for the cost of our guesthouse meals over a period of two months in residence it was clear that I was being cheated very badly. The sum was so large that I could not possibly overlook it and so I had to take the matter to Harbans Singh. He had a long talk with Parakram and--as I learned only much later--even suggested the possibility of dismissal, which would have ruined our cook's life. That evening when Parakram brought dinner he was as cheerful as ever, but the meal was inedible. Every dish was laced with fiery little chili peppers, scores and scores of them. The boys burst into tears and Elaine looked as though she wanted to do the same. I ran down to the kitchen to confront Parakram and I told him that I was going to murder him. Then, to my annoyance, I completely lost control of myself and burst out laughing. He did the same. We threw our arms around each other and embraced. But I warned him that while he was always free to cheat me a little bit he was never again to try to cheat me by such a very large amount. This accommodation satisfied us both. After all, India was India, not Kansas.

FARIDKOT
Sardar Harbans Singh, Elaine Harned, H.H. Former Maharaja of Faridkot and others on palace grounds.

We had two thoroughly enjoyable trips which each took us away from the university for a week or so. The first was due entirely to the kindness of Harbans Singh, who took us to Faridkot, a former princely state to the west of Patiala and located next to the Indo-Pakistani border. We were guests of the Maharaja and our quarters were, to say the least, sumptuous. His sea-green palace reared up from the brown plain like an apparition from some alien, grander world. Many years earlier he had employed Harbans Singh as a tutor for his only son. His Highness knew that I wanted to learn more about agrarian communities in the Punjab and so he told the senior officers of the palace guard to take us to several villages inhabited by their relatives, neighbors and friends. Everyone turned out to greet our little caravan. We had wonderful, festive and very instructive times, for the officers proved to be very able interpreters.

We were offered most gracious hospitality everywhere and this gave us a chance to be in a good number of homes. The men talked about farming and village life in the front room and the women clustered together in the kitchen. Few Westerners in 1970 had been as privileged as we were in Faridkot. Our boys enjoyed this socializing almost as much as their parents did. I was surprised and gratified at how easily our boys fit in with the village children. They behaved as though they were all familiar neighbors. They smiled and played with each other and went running off hand in hand to explore the surroundings. At the end of the day, however, not all of my questions about farm practices were satisfactorily answered. On the drive from Patiala to Faridkot I had seen a number of farmers plowing behind two animals yoked together, one a camel and the other a buffalo. This seemed to me a very odd pairing and I could not imagine why it was done with such apparent frequency. I must have asked 20 people for an explanation but no one had an answer. Then someone answered my question with a question of his own: who would have two of one when he could have one of two? In other words, who would be satisfied with repetition when he could have variety? There is an aesthetic side to the Indian psyche that is so strong I could not dismiss this answer to my question as entirely far-fetched. All I know today is that I still know nothing more than I did then.

Sadly, everywhere we turned there were signs of the decline of Faridkot, despite all of its agricultural abundance. Some of the former rulers of the princely states received huge privy purses from the central government but the majority were granted only a pittance and Faridkot was very much among the majority. Our Land Rover drove us by his shuttered distillery, his boarded up bottling plant, and even his once excellent but now derelict hospital--the list of closures ran on and on. Of his 60 vehicles the Rolls Royces and Daimlers and Bentleys were long since gone, and now only a few Land Rovers remained. His Highness was adored by his former subjects but he refused to appear any longer in public. He who had given his people so much for so long now had nothing left to give; he was simply too proud and too embarrassed to appear among them any longer. So he came out from the palace only to drive at high speed to his home in Delhi, a long day's journey away. But His Highness did give us one very formal dinner, served close to midnight after a cocktail hour that no one could ever have described as abbreviated. Every single item on the banquet table except for the crystal goblets was solid gold, all very heavy solid gold, cutlery and plates and serving dishes too. So many relics of days of power were spread before us, now testimonies to the evanescence of all human grandeur and glory. We said goodbye to His Highness with rather heavy hearts, for in the short space of a week we had become quite fond of him, this man so like and yet so very unlike everyone else. We would miss him and we knew that he would miss us very much. He kept asking us when we could come to visit again.

There had been another guest at the palace with whom we had enjoyed drinks and dinner each night, and who was an exceptionally charming and intelligent man, Lt. General Jagjit Singh Aurora, the commander of the Indian Army for the eastern sector of the subcontinent. His Highness told us when we first arrived that while the children were certainly welcome visitors to the palace, he really did not care to be around them very much. I never discovered whether this was true or merely an affectation. But General Aurora certainly did enjoy small boys; he beamed whenever they came into the room and invited them to jump up in his lap. Each night he would bounce the boys on his knee and regale them with tales of life in the military. He also told them that very soon, in order to safeguard the vulnerable eastern flank of India, he would invade East

Pakistan, scatter the army arrayed against him, liberate the populace and encourage the formation of a new government that would be less hostile toward the people of India. Four or five months later our boys were glued to their television screen as they watched "their" war unfold exactly as the General had told them it would, except that it required even less time and less bloodshed than he had anticipated. General Aurora taught Kit and Tim a memorable lesson, that sometimes people in high places do speak the truth, and sometimes they are even willing to share it with small boys.

More than 15 years later I gave a talk on contemporary India to an audience of about a thousand people in Baton Rouge, Louisiana. There were a great many Indians among those who had come to hear me. General Aurora had a prominent place in what I said that night, for it would have been difficult to discuss India's relations with Bangladesh with no reference to the Indian who was celebrated by many people as the liberator of that land. After my talk and a reception I was stopped in the corridor by two young turbaned Sikhs, both not much short of seven feet tall, who wanted to shake hands. Then they told me they were General Aurora's nephews. They promised they would telephone their uncle that

FARIDKOT
Village and American boys halt their games to pose for a moment.

31

night and tell him everything I had said, but meanwhile they wanted to renew family ties and chat with me. We had a splendid time, then parted amid many expressions of best wishes and avowals of enduring friendship. I have very happy memories of that evening. To coin a phrase, it's a small world.

The other trip took us in the opposite direction, up into the heavily forested foothills of the Himalayas. In Chandigarh we caught a tiny train which puffed and panted and eventually carried us from sea-level to 7,000 feet, more or less, where it deposited us at a station with much whistling and many sighs of relief before expiring there for the night. We were now at India's premier hill station, Simla, which once seen can never be forgotten because it is surrounded by such breathtaking beauty, cradled in dense pine forests and guarded by the Himalayan peaks. The town cascades down steep hillsides. The railroad station is nearly at the top of Simla, but we still had to walk higher to a pine-covered spine which overlooks the whole town. One end of the spine is anchored by the Anglican church and its cemetery, the other by the buildings that once were the summer palace of the British Raj. This was our destination, a vast architectural anomaly which after India's independence became the Indian Institute for Advanced Study. We walked most of the length of the spine through fine pine woodland inhabited by countless chattering monkeys until suddenly we emerged in front of the daunting more or less Victorian Gothic edifice that had become the IIAS. I had never before seen anything like Simla; it was as though we had been suddenly transported back a hundred years. This was a museum where the colonial era had been preserved in Amber, just as once it was. The Anglicanism, the architecture, the social round of the many expatriates and even the uniforms of the police all seemed to be reminiscences of the heyday of the British Raj, when the great and the good and their servants had fled the baking summer sun of the plains for the bracing air of Simla.

We had come here at the invitation of Dr. V.K. Gokak, the director of the Institute for Advanced Study. He was a thoughtful and fascinating and extremely genial host. He had been the vice chancellor of the University of Bangalore, one of India's largest and finest educational institutions, until his appointment to the directorship in Simla. He was also widely acknowledged as the greatest poet there had ever been in his own native tongue, a South Indian Dravidian language called Kannada which in 1970 was spoken by about thirty million people. But he told me, with a rueful smile, that here in the far north of India there might not be anyone within hundreds of miles who could read his poems in their original language. Even though he was very sociable I think there are not many intellectuals who have found themselves so isolated and alone. At Independence India had 15 official languages and many hundreds of dialects that were unintelligible to anyone who was not a member of the local tribe, so to speak. Now, nearly a quarter of a century later, the situation seemed to be little better. The two languages that were most widely used now were English and Hindi. But the latter was a regional tongue, the medium of discourse in the capital area but almost unknown in some parts of the South. And to the north of the capital, in the Punjab, speaking Hindi can provoke unpleasantness and on occasion even physical violence. To the Punjabi-speaking natives, long covetous of their own independent state, it can seem an act of aggression. As for English, though widely used by the bureaucracy everywhere, after all it is still the language of the conquerors.

Human identity is partly a linguistic creation. We are defined by the words we speak to others and their language to us offers further definition. All thought requires a language that shapes the way we see the world and determines how much of it will elude our sight. Words are not cyphers, not neutral things, but part of the material from which our identity and character are fashioned. So what does it mean in India to talk about national character or identity when you have 15 official languages and more dialects than you can count intelligible only to your friends and neighbors? Dr. Gokak and I spent much thoroughly enjoyable time discussing language and national character without reaching any firm conclusions. We also had some long conversations about the manuscript I was working on because he was greatly interested in comparative religion and thought there were many parallels between Hindu and Christian notions of play and grace. All too soon, however, it was time to leave Simla. I said goodbye to my new friend in the gardens of the viceregal lodge in front of a low stone wall on which there was affixed a very long weathered brass plaque, a relic from the days of the Raj, with a score of names engraved upon it and lines from the names pointing toward the high peaks they designated which rose in front of us. Mt. Everest was far off to the right, a bit dwarfed by some of the heights nearer at hand. There was nothing at all to obscure the view from where I stood of the whole massive range in front of me. Here were the high Himalayas in all their glory, snow-capped, unmatched in their way by anything else on earth.

Back in Patiala life was not quite as carefree as once it had been. I had a number of speaking engagements to fulfill in the Punjab, although my audiences were sometimes more interested in the white blond hair of my sons than in anything I had to say. White blond hair was a marvel that very few Punjabis had ever seen and they were endlessly curious about it. As a member of the editorial board of the Journal of Religious Studies (India) which Seshagiri had recently founded, I felt obligated to contribute a number of reviews and some articles as well. I was also asked to evaluate a good number of the unsolicited manuscripts that the journal received. The department was also receiving early contributions to the massive projected Encyclopedia of Hinduism which was another Rao project. All of us shared the task of evaluating these submissions. I was pleased to feel that at least to some extent I was earning my salary. Our social calendar also expanded considerably as we came to know more and more people in the university. But I grew more and more concerned about the completion of my little book because the deadline for the typescript was no longer comfortably far in the future. I already had a title, Grace and Common Life, but that did not mean I already had a manuscript. Far from it. I still had much to do. My work was not greatly advanced on the days when I turned up at the Bhavan after breakfast only to find its doors firmly locked. All religious holidays of the traditions represented by all the professors were observed by the closure of the Bhavan. This meant that some weeks the building would be shut for two or at least on one occasion for three weekdays. I remarked to someone, with more than a trace of irritation, that if we added a Parsi, a Jain and a Jew to the staff none of us would ever again have to come to work in the Bhavan at all. But no one paid much attention to me.

If I pointed out on occasion that our endless procession of religious holidays was not doing much to further the advance of scholarship the answer was always the unvarying reminder, this is a "secular" state. It is described as such in the Constitution that was written three years after the Republic of India finally achieved its independence. But the meaning of "secular" on Indian soil is not at all what the word denotes in the West. Secular is derived from the Latin word saeculum which simply means "world" or sometimes "mere world." So it often has an irreligious cast to it, or at least an areligious significance. There is no religion in the saeculum or at least there is not supposed to be. The religious and the secular are juxtaposed. In India, however, secularity simply means tolerance and the absence of any partiality. Secular people can be and usually are profoundly religious. Secular men and women welcome all religions and treat every one of them with respect. Secularism is never in any way preferential. Of course one is free to choose one's own faith but in the marketplace of ideas every faith must be treated with equal respect. So even though something like 82 percent of the population of the subcontinent is Hindu, it can not be called a Hindu state. It is a secular republic hospitable to all religions. Has this dream of equality and fairness been realized since Independence? Yes, to an amazing and wonderful degree. Why is Easter a four-day national holiday every year when every government office in the whole country is shut tight? Any Indian knows the answer to that: Because India is a secular state.

On Sikh holidays we usually went to the neighborhood gurdwara with the Harbans Singhs and I sometimes went there alone as well. I felt very much at home there and participated in the worship as well as I could although I could not understand the language. One had to be careful to walk around the Adi Granth only in a clockwise fashion and, when leaving the chamber, never to turn one's back on the Scriptures but to back through the doorway. To my eyes the atmosphere was very similar to low-church Protestantism. I found especially affecting a rite in which the worshippers pass one another a ball of fragrant sweetmeats and everyone takes a pinch of the delicacy and eats. The rite binds together the members of the community and reminds everyone of the beneficence of Sat Nam, the Lord, from whom all good things come. This corporate worship was very meaningful for me and far different from the individualism that characterizes worship in a Hindu temple. I always felt I was truly welcome when I attended the gurdwara. I wish one could find the same sense of welcome in many Christian churches.

I eventually described my little book on grace and play as an essay in "natural theology," which in a sense it was, but only if that discipline were stood on its head. Traditionally, natural theology was thought to lie within the domain of reason, while revealed theology had to do with matters of Christian faith. The first, which dealt with "proofs" for the existence of God, came before the second, which was concerned with the saving activities of God. In my eyes, this traditional understanding had everything backwards. In fact, God's being is disclosed in God's acts, not the reverse. We know that He is because of His actions toward us, because of what He has done. Therefore, natural theology is not a preface or introduction to revealed theology but is wholly dependent upon it and is best seen as a postscript to it. But if this is true, then why talk about it at all? What is the point? From my perspective, its function is to demonstrate to people that Christian images and stories have limitless power to define and illuminate, to sort out and organize the ambiguities and confusions and opacities of our daily experience. This has nothing to do with proofs of God's existence or with empirical verification of Christian claims. It has to do with "empirical fit", if you will, with expressive power that can capture this good earth and our ordinary commerce within it. We want to nudge people toward acknowledging the persuasiveness of this vocabulary.

Grace is a dominant refrain in a number of religious traditions, the Christian and the Sikh and the Hindu among them. In Christian eyes, divine grace has three primary dimensions: building community, accepting and forgiving the sinner, and strengthening or empowering, not least of all by unshackling us from parts of our past. Always, although sometimes in ways it is difficult to discern, it means liberation. Grace is not a specifically religious notion, however, for intimations of it abound everywhere in the dad daily and quite ordinary experience of most of us; so little there is that we have not received from others. Grace simply means a gift, one that surprises us because it is unexpected and undeserved. <u>Grace</u> <u>and</u> <u>Common</u> <u>Life</u> examines grace in two areas that are perhaps the most important for the formation of a sense of identity, the family or household and play, especially playing with peers. The two are inseparable not simply because the family is the context in which our play begins, but also because they say the same thing about the unity of freedom and order, the essential interdependence of liberty and structure which, when they become disjoined, lose their true significance and creativity.

This was the first time in my writings that I had argued that the notion of play is the best metaphor for the whole fabric of the Christian life. I had a host of reasons for this, but the two most important ones concerned the ideas of self-seriousness and justice. If there is a God, we are called to be absolutely serious about him and not absolutely serious about anything else whatsoever, lest we fall into idolatry. The opposite of faith in God is self-seriousness, because it displaces God from the center of things and puts the self in the center instead. That is why self-seriousness is our primal sin, from which all others spring. But if we can imagine ourselves as players there is no possibility of such self-seriousness: "All the world's a stage, And all the men and women merely players; They have their exits and their entrances." The second reason, justice, has to do with other selves, who always deserve from us the same fair play we hope to receive from them. Without justice as fair play no society can long thrive or even endure. The exercise of my freedom requires some sort of order or framework for its every creative expression, that is to say, the rudiments of a just society. Playing with peers expands the freedoms we first find within the family in new and more sophisticated ways that deepen our sense of the inseparability of rules and liberty. We learn more subtly that rules and regulations are not devised to stand in our way; they exist so that we can find our way. Most simply stated as an axiom: You have to play by the rules or you cannot play at all. Freedom without guideposts is anti-human surrender to chaos.

To write of play as a basic category for understanding the Christian message somehow seemed far easier on Indian turf than it might have been in America because the notion of play figures so prominently in Indian stories of the gods and is so familiar to every Indian audience. The preface to the Indian edition of my book was written by Seshagiri Rao and Harbans Singh together and they declared: "Grace is a dominant theme in all the theistic traditions of the world. In Hinduism and Sikhism, the motifs of grace, prsada, Kripa, raza, Nadir, and play, lila, Krida, figure very prominently. In the Var Majh, Guru Nanak says: 'Thou alone knowest how thou didst originate it (the universe); it is thy play.' In the Hindu scriptures, creation of the universe is regarded as the play (lila) of the Lord; he is seen as nitya lilanurakta, ever engaged in play." Siva, god of destruction and renewal, is the most widely worshipped divinity in the Hindu pantheon, and he is most often portrayed as Siva Nataraja, the Lord of the Dance. It is his acrobatic play that brings the universe to life and endows it with movement.

But if Siva is the best-known personage in Indian myth and religion, the most significant figure in Indian history is the great third century B.C. emperor, Ashoka. On a hillside at Dhauli a few miles south of Bhubaneshwar on the road to Konark and Puri, the warrior king surveyed the corpses strewn across the landscape in front of him one day in 272 B.C. The carnage signalled his overwhelming victory against the native Kalinga forces mustered to fight against his invasion. Suddenly Ashoka was sick of death and stricken with remorse. He never raised his sword again. He became a Buddhist and proclaimed that all men were his children and therefore brothers of one another. It is said that during his later years he erected more than 80,000 small stupas or cairns, stone mounds, to honor the Lord Buddha all the way from the Bay of Bengal to the Aegean Sea. He also ordered the erection of stone tablets on which were carved his Ashokan Edicts, detailing the rules of right conduct. These efforts to honor the Buddha and to proclaim his message everywhere sparked a profound moral and spiritual revolution several centuries before the birth of the Christ.

Religion and history, Siva and Ashoka, the lifebringer and the lawgiver, the player and the architect of the playground, the dancer and the arbiter of the rules of the dance--always the two together at the very heart of the Indian vision, never one of them alone, for in isolation they wither and bear no fruit. The Republic of India today has two symbols that are especially prominent and important. One is the four-headed lion column that Ashoka erected at the site of the Buddha's first sermon in the deer park at Sarnath and subsequently also at Sanchi. The lions are seated on the wheel of the law, Dharma, duty and right conduct. This image of its nationhood appears on all Indian coinage and currency. But the second is the even more ancient figure of Siva Nataraja, the symbol of Indian cultural creativity and possibly even better known than the lion pillar. In its wisdom, India has tried since Independence to hold the two together in an Ashokan spirit of toleration of diversity and dissent. That is what I too tried to do in a small way with a different vocabulary and for a different culture: to insist upon the inseparability of freedom and order, which are the essence of play.

As it happened, my manuscript met its deadline. The New Delhi publisher chosen by the university was most competent and accommodating. Even though his typesetters knew not a single word of English, the book appeared in a handsome edition that was entirely error-free. I was amazed because the page proofs I had seen had been littered with mistakes. I was very pleased upon our return to Charlottesville when a neighbor, Walker Cowan, the director of the University Press of Virginia, told me that he would like to publish an American edition. It appeared only a few months thereafter. I recently reread it, though with some trepidation because it had been written in a foreign culture where I was half a world away from my own library and much distracted by all the novelties and challenges of living in India with small children. I was rather astonished to find in it some of the tightest argumentation and most economical prose that perhaps I have ever written. I am embarrassed by some of the big words that I used in 1970-71, but by and large I would write the book no differently now than I did then.

We made two other excursions during our months in Patiala. The first was a visit to Jaipur, a long trip from the Punjab. I wanted it to be a special treat for the family midway through our months in Patiala, and I was certainly not disappointed. I thought everyone would enjoy staying at the Rambagh Palace, which in 1970 was one of the most interesting and elegant places to stay in all of India because it had been so recently converted from a maharajah's country residence into a hotel. I was sure the boys would enjoy the large indoor swimming pool with its trapezes and other athletic equipment hanging from the ceiling above the water. I wanted Elaine to see the palace inside the fort at Amber which contained some of the best art and architecture I had yet seen in India; I thought the boys would relish the elephant ride to the entrance of the fortress so long as their parents were with them. I was sure that Elaine would be impressed by the beauty of the wide boulevards of the Pink City and the splendid architecture of the Wind Palace, the Observatory and other public buildings.

Most of all, of course, I wanted Elaine to see the cenotaphs of Gaitore. Although I had seen little of India I was convinced nonetheless that these must be one of the real treasures of the country. Elaine found them breathtaking and could not tear herself away from the scene. We stayed there for hours. Even the boys at their young ages seemed awed by the beauty of all this glorious white marble so intricately carved, gleaming in the noonday sun. I was very pleased because I felt myself such a debtor to Gaitore. When we arrived I was sure I heard the cenotaphs breathe a word of welcome. I am not sure in my own mind whether I had come to show the cenotaphs to my family or my family to the cenotaphs. There were no visitors except us just as there had been no one the previous year except me. But if I had not come to Gaitore then I would not have remained in India after the Patiala conference. If I had not remained I would never have seen Varanasi or had the transformative encounter there in the city bazaar. If I had not had that encounter, my time in India would have changed my life very little if at all and I would certainly never have brought my family to India in the autumn of 1970. The designs of our lives are very subtle and elusive sometimes; I had never had any plans of my own to visit Gaitore and, indeed, had never even heard its name.

Our other excursion took us no farther afield than New Delhi on a trip intended to combine business with pleasure. The business was the renewal of our 90-day visas for temporary residence in India, which were about to expire.

When I went to apply for their renewal a clerk told me that I had come too early. I explained that this was a Friday and the visas would expire on Sunday but he told me nonetheless to return on Monday when the office reopened. I complied with his request only to be told by the very same clerk on Monday that now the visas could not be renewed because I had come too late. Our visas had already expired. I told the clerk in a very colorful fashion what I thought of him personally, of his whole extended family and, for that matter, what I now thought of the entirety of the woefully corrupt and bureaucratic Indian civil service. He simply stared at his shoes with a somber expression on his face and uttered not a word. So for the rest of our days in India I suppose we were illegal aliens. But it did not matter; no one ever asked to see a valid visa, not even when we left the country to return to the States.

We went to Delhi for Christmas and stayed at the India International Center, which we had discovered on a previous visit was a wonderful place to stay with children, for its grounds lead into the Lodi Gardens. These are the site of a number of 14th and 15th century tombs of kings and other members of the royal household from the Lodi dynasty, unfortunately no longer very well maintained. But the gardens are a splendid place to walk and play games and there is much shade cast by many fine old trees. The Christmas service at the American Church was very festive and high-spirited and jammed with small children. We had been shopping and had bought two brightly painted wooden Christmas tree ornaments but we had nowhere to hang them. We had not bought a tree for ourselves because the few we found were very scrawny. So we decorated our rooms with balloons. On Christmas Day the boys were ill; they had worms and lay twitching and bouncing on their beds in obvious discomfort. Even so, we had a lovely walk in the Lodi Gardens. I cannot remember another Christmas since childhood when I felt a greater sense of peace and joy. This was Christmas stripped down and bare, yet it outshone everyone's expectations.

When it finally came time to leave India we all found it very difficult to say goodbye. We were leaving so many dear friends-Seshagiri and Sarasa and all their sons, Harbans Singh and his lovely family, Joshi, Parakram and the Avtar

Singhs and so many others. We would miss Patiala, a wonderful place to work, where we had always enjoyed good food, good times, and good company. I would miss the Punjab more than any of the other places I had visited in India, this quiet and fertile plain that seemed to stretch out to the ends of the earth, with its inverted blue bowl of sky cloudless by day and studded with countless stars by night, this haven where I had enjoyed greater peace than anywhere else I could remember. Sad though I was to leave, I promised my friends that I would not stay away for long and that I would surely never forget about them and India while I was away. The second part of that promise I kept; the first, to my disappointment, I did not.

❁ ❁ ❁

CHAPTER THREE

Caves and More Caves

My third lengthy trip to India was postponed several times, partly because two different years we were in Scotland where I served as a visiting professor in New College at the University of Edinburgh, where I had once been a student, partly because my own responsibilities increased in Charlottesville. We were now adding two new positions every year since I had been so quickly summoned back to the chairmanship. But in the late summer of 1978 I finally left for Bombay, although this time my family remained in Virginia. In a way, this was to be the most important of my early visits. It was funded partly by the Smithsonian Institution and partly by the University of Virginia and had a large and exciting business component, but my other emphasis would be on the memorial and religious art and architecture of the subcontinent. This seemed to me a natural extension of the interests that sparked my doctoral dissertation and eventuated in my first book, <u>Theology and the Arts.</u>

This would be my first visit to the South, where I would spend at least half my time, much of it in Mysore. I would stay there as long as necessary until all the arrangements for our University of Virginia Semester in India program had been finalized to my satisfaction. It had taken Seshagiri and me several years to complete our preparations on the American side, mainly because the university had no international programs at all at this time, no experience whatsoever with them in the past, and so many reassurances were necessary before we received final authorization. I hoped that this visit would enable me to conclude what was still unfinished on the Indian side. I anticipated nothing except much good will and enthusiasm, but I was also prepared for all sorts of bureaucratic delays because in 1978 India was specializing in bureaucratic delays. Our program would be based in Mysore for many reasons. Seshagiri was born and raised in this area. His brother-in-law lived here and would be very important to us. Mysore is a small and safe city, beautiful and tranquil and blessed with a fine climate. It has an excellent university where we would be welcomed. It is on a main railroad line and an easy three hour drive to the international airport at Bangalore.

Seshagiri would be our senior resident professor and he would be accompanied by two of our doctoral students specializing in Asian studies. As an adjunct professor we would enlist his brother-in-law, Dr. M.S. Nagaraja Rao. Although not related by blood, they are very close friends and married two sisters. Nagaraja was the long-time director of art and archeology for the state of Karnataka and also the senior curator of the Mysore City Palace, perhaps

MYSORE, City Palace
This is perhaps the grandest palace in India today.
This silver door with exquisite workmanship is at the entrance to the Private Audience Hall.

the finest and most impressive palace in all of India. No one else knows as much as he does about the antiquities of Karnataka. He would teach one course and lead a number of field trips to the most important sites in the state. In addition, our students would be able to elect whatever courses they chose at the University of Mysore upon payment of a most nominal fee. At the close of the semester they would be free to travel for two or three weeks wherever they wished within India, although we would not allow them to travel alone. The group would be limited to forty students. We were not interested in germinating future India specialists, but simply in giving prospective lawyers, physicians and businesswomen a sense of what this great land is like. Now the task before Nagaraja and me was to arrange for meals and lodging and develop satisfactory relations with the administration of Mysore university.

The other focus of these months would be the sacred buildings and sculptures of South India and for this, too, Nagaraja could provide invaluable counsel. I was well aware that I could only begin most of these

MYSORE, City Palace
Lavishly decorated brick and limestone columns welcome guests to the enormous expanse of the Durbar Hall.

explorations after our business in Mysore was done but at least I could begin. I had promised Seshagiri that even before going to Mysore I would visit the so-called "cave temples" at Ellora and Ajanta, two rather remote sites northeast of Bombay. He assured me they were both essential destinations in any survey of the sacred architecture of India. So this visit would begin in Bombay instead of New Delhi, although it would end once again in Patiala. I had been present more or less for the inauguration of the Center for the Study of World Religions there and I felt I had an obligation to return for at least two weeks whenever I was in India and to participate in whatever projects were underway. It would be good to be in Patiala again.

My Air India flight touched down quite early at Santa Cruz Airport. When the doors of the plane were opened, we all knew we were in India again. There is no fragrance like the bouquet that is India, the odors of blossoms and spices gentling the acrid smells of the automotive pollution that in 1978 was a part of every Indian urban experience. By noon I was already being driven through the streets of Bombay on my way to the Taj Mahal Hotel. This legendary place was built in 1903 for Indian guests because all the luxury hotels of the day were for whites only. Today the Taj Mahal flourishes while all the others of the same vintage are gone. My room and balcony were directly above and in front of Bombay's greatest monument, the Gateway of India, commemorating the 1911 visit of King George and Queen Mary, no less imposing in 1978 because of all the beggars, snake charmers, soothsayers and pimps huddled beneath it. I arrived in the midst of Diwali, the Hindu festival of lights, which we had much enjoyed earlier in Patiala. The streets were very festive and everyone seemed carefree and merry.

The next morning having breakfast on my balcony I noticed that part of the Indian navy had anchored just behind the Gateway of India—a large aircraft carrier, two heavy cruisers, a number of destroyers and a squadron of smaller ships. With all their flags flying, they made a colorful show that added to the holiday spirit of the city. My first destination of the day was Crawford Market and its hordes of shoppers combing through hundreds of food stalls intent on buying treats for the evening meal on this last night of Diwali. From there, at the suggestion of the hotel concierge, I went to the fascinating Chor Bazaar or Thieves Market, but I soon had all the clamor I could stomach in a single day. I was eager to see two Parsi fire temples and they were nearby. So I went there and even though I was not allowed inside I could stand in the open doorway and survey the whole spartan interior and the sacred fire and its attendants. Then I took a taxi to the top of Malabar Hill, where there are wonderful topiary gardens and spectacular views of the great teeming city far below.

We had stopped on our way up the hill so that I could visit a very busy Jain temple. The worshippers and attendants were all clad entirely in white and some of them were wearing surgical masks over nostrils and mouth so they could not accidentally ingest some tiny insect. Jains are perhaps best known for their adherence to the principle of reverence for all life. The serenity and quietness in this place were a notable contrast to the hubbub that is so frequently found in Hindu temples. Jainism began far more than two millenia ago, first as a non-theistic sect within the embrace of Hinduism but at least during all of the Christian era it has been an independent faith centered about 24 Tirthankaras or spiritual pioneers and guides. A hallmark of Jainism is its ascetic and renunciatory character. Another is its resolute opposition to the Hindu caste system.

But the principal reason I had come to Malabar Hill today was to visit a different destination: the high-walled compound of the "Towers of Silence" where the Parsis disposed of their dead. Because the four elements of the universe--earth, air, fire and water--are sacred to this tradition. So Parsis could not bury their dead either on land or at sea; nor could corpses be cremated. The dead are most reverently carried to the tops of these towers and there they are quickly and silently devoured by vultures that roost nearby and their skeletons are soon reduced to powder. Rich and poor are all reunited in a common death which does not pollute our good earth. The Parsis are a tiny but thoroughly admirable religious community mainly clustered around Bombay. They are the last surviving remnant of the ancient religious tradition of Zoroaster; a millenium ago they were forced to flee their homeland because of Moslem persecution and eventually they found refuge in Bombay. There they prospered greatly under the British Raj and today possess a sizable proportion of the riches of the subcontinent.

The Hindu New Year festivities caused the city to sleep late, or at least its usual frenzy was rather subdued the next morning as I walked quite early down to the Gateway of India, in search of the ferry that would carry me in about an hour's time six miles or so across the harbor to the small island of Elephanta with its renowned "cave" temple. Bombay is one of the world's great commercial seaports. The Navy ships were still at anchor, ocean-going tankers and freighters from many countries plowed back and forth in front of us, and there were were myriad fishing boats, grey-painted and most of them with three sails, quite similar to Arab dhows. Elephanta has only one important shrine and it is not a "cave temple" at all, although that misnomer is often used to describe it. This is a rock-cut shrine built--or, more properly, excavated and carved during the 7th century. It is approximately 250 feet above the jetty where the ferries deposit their passengers and it is a long and somewhat demanding trek from jetty to cave entrance. Wide stone steps flanked by two wonderful carved stone elephants lead to a spacious mandapa or pillared veranda.

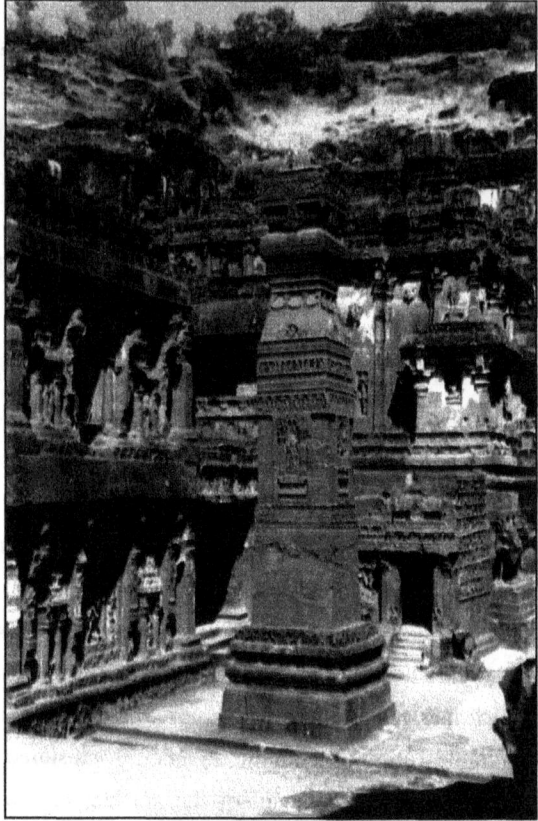

AURANGABAD, Ellora
If there is one Hindu work of art that surpasses everything else, this is it. Site 16 at Ellora, Kailasa, the replica of Siva's mythical home in the Tibetan Himalayas.

From the temple entrance the visitor has his first sight of the principal image, the Trimurthi or Maheshwara, a column surmounted by three emormous and awesome heads. An earlier generation of scholars understood the heads as representations of the Hindu trinity, a rather androgynous figure of Brahma the Creator to the right, Vishnu the Preserver facing the visitor and to the left the terrifying visage of Siva the Destroyer, who is beyond doubt the dominating presence and to whom the temple is dedicated. But this Shaivite dedication of the shrine has been even more strongly stressed by more recent interpreters, who regard all three heads as representations of Siva in his different roles. I find this latter interpretation much more persuasive and I think that now it is commonly accepted. In any event, this raises a fascinating question in

AURANGABAD, Ellora
*Verses from the two great Hindu epics, the Mahabharta and the Ramayana, are carved
into the living rock of the world's greatest monolithic sculpture.*

interreligious dialogue which perhaps only the Maheshwara himself, the Lord
of the universe, can adjudicate. Some versions of Hinduism emphasize the
distinctness of the members of the trinity and the irreducible polytheism of the
tradition. But there are also other trends, some of them more philosophical, that
incline toward some sort of monism or at least a Shaivite henotheism. In the
Christian tradition we can see something not at all dissimilar: a trinitarianism
that emphasizes the distinctness of the three persons and on the other hand
a stress upon their absolute unity. All this is to say that it is difficult to hold
threeness and oneness together in the imagination at the same time. Some
Hindus and some Christians recognize that they share a common task and can
benefit a good deal from interreligious dialogue. I am very much inclined to
believe that we have more in common with some versions of the alleged
polytheism of the Hindus than we do with the strict monotheism of Islam.

On each side of the great Maheshwara there is a quite formidable
Dwarapala, a giant doorkeeper or sentinal perhaps 15 feet tall. There are many
more dwarapalas, including two at each of the four entrances that lead to
the center of the temple where the sacred lingam stands. There are no other

adornments at all except for eight friezes or panels carved in the living rock of the temple walls. For me, at least, they fall naturally into four pairs. First, there is Siva Mahayogi or Lakulisa, and opposite him is Siva Nataraja, the Lord of the initiates and the Lord of the Dance. Second, there is the wedding of Siva and Parvati, where lesser divinities shower them with flower petals. Brahma and Vishnu are present as well as Parvati's father, Himalaya. This is paired with a picture of domesticity with the married couple playing with dice. Third are two panels in which Siva is portrayed vanquishing the demons of darkness. Finally there is Siva the androgyne, half feminine and half masculine, the unity that signifies wholeness and the completion of human togetherness, the androgynous dream of perfection. This is paired with the depiction of Siva bringing the Ganges from heaven to earth, directing the inundation of water upon his own matted hair, where mother Ganga and her two daughters, the Yamuna and the Saraswati Rivers, divide in order to soften their impact when they fall on down to earth. So the cosmic destroyer brings the water of life. The supreme male warrior has three women dancing in his hair, and why should he not, for he is the Lord of the Dance? Once again the masculine and the feminine coalesce in a moment of unity and fulfillment.

Elephanta is a fascinating compend of Hindu theology and a quite successful instance of the reconciliation of opposites. More than 1,300 years ago some of the most proficient and gifted sculptors of their age bequeathed us a legacy of astonishing beauty. What is most remarkable about it is that everything is in motion, fluid, dynamic, dancing. Everything in the shrine was fixed in stone more than a millenium ago and yet nothing here is fixed at all, nothing is static, least of all the stone. Centuries ago Portuguese soldiers vandalized the temple but that does not really matter because in some sense the shrine lives outside the bounds of time; the serenity and joy and confidence of the figures on its walls are in no way dimmed. This is indisputably great art and Elephanta alone justifies a visit to Bombay. I thought at the time I would probably never see any Hindu art better than this. I was very wrong, as I learned within three days. But I spent an entire day very happily on Elephanta Island and then caught the last ferry back to the mainland, watching the returning fishing boats outlined against the setting sun, which seemed to turn the whole Indian Ocean into old molten gold.

After Elephanta perhaps the most engrossing tourist attractions are the Victorian Gothic public buildings. Apart from Glasgow and London, the cities in the world with the most dazzling Victorian Gothic buildings are in Australia and India, and especially in Calcutta and Bombay. Among the landmarks in Bombay is Crawford Market, the huge wholesale and retail outlet for vegetables and fruit and flowers all arranged in the most aesthetically appealing way, as well as meats and poultry and fish and anything else imaginable that might appeal to the human palate. It is an incredible and fascinating technicolor display. The external friezes by the main entrance to the market, which portray farmers at work, as well as the design of the internal fountains were all created by Lockwood Kipling, the head of a local art college and the father of Rudyard, who was born in Bombay and spent his childhood here until he was sent away to school in England. Rudyard returned to India after his schooling and worked as a journalist before his career as a prolific novelist and poet began to blossom. He was the first English novelist to receive a Nobel Prize. His long poem "The Ballad of East and West" begins, "East is East and West is West, and never the twain shall meet." The poem ends, however, on a strongly affirmative note, as the son of a British colonel and the son of a native brigand chief swear their undying friendship and loyalty to one another. No one could have been more a child of the West or more indifferent to the East or less concerned about whether the twain would ever meet than I was. But then I came to India and my life was changed for good.

Crawford Market has one distinction that it does not share with any other Victorian Gothic building in Bombay. In 1882 it became the first edifice in the whole country to be electrified. But the other great buildings of that period have their own distinction, too. Among them are the Flora Fountain in the city center, the Bombay Municipal Corporation offices, the clock tower at Bombay University, and the jewel in the crown, Victoria Terminus, the colossal central railroad station. It is today a UNESCO World Heritage site. Students and faculty from the Bombay School of Art designed the balustrades of its grand staircases, the ornamental iron and brass railings and grillwork, the wood carvings and the floor tiles. In some ways it is reminiscent of St. Pancras Station in London, but it is even more vast and more lavishly decorated and much more busy. Each morning it welcomes between three and four million commuters. Atop the great building there is a statue of the figure of Progress, which Victoria Terminus itself certainly represented upon its completion in 1888.

Back at the hotel I made an early night of it, for I had to be up at 3:30 to catch my dawn flight to Aurangabad. I was in that city by seven; my car and driver were waiting for me and we were soon on our way to meet my guide at Ellora. I had left all travel arrangements to the Taj Mahal and the hotel managed everything with predictable excellence. The Buddhist monks at Ellora had carved a measure of solitude and they had chosen well, although their settlement was skirted by an ancient trade route. But this part of the Deccan plateau of Maharashtra even today is a relatively unpopulated area. The 34 constructions that comprise Ellora were excavated and carved between the 7th and the 12th centuries. Twelve of them are Buddhist and these are the earliest; the next 17 are Hindu while the last five, which are the most recent, are Jain. They are arranged more or less chronologically along the side of a hill that stretches a mile and a quarter through rather infertile terrain. All of them are entirely man-made, carved with hand-held chisels from solid rock; there were no natural caves here. Some are chaityas, churches or temples or shrines, but the majority are viharas, monasteries or dorms.

My guide and I set off on our walk about 8:00 o'clock and we did not finish until late afternoon, after the temperature had soared to more than 110 degrees. I was told that more than 200,000 tons of stone were removed by hand in the course of this Herculean project. The heroic scale of this stone metropolis set in the middle of nowhere defies description: four hundred million pounds of rock were carried away and all the rest of the hillside was carved as intricately as though it were an ivory miniature. This is what one contemporary guidebook has to say: "If you could imagine an earth-moving feat on the scale of the Pyramids, a flowering of sculpture and painting worthy of the Renaissance and a religious fervor as intense as that of medieval Europe, you might begin to have an idea of the cave temples of Ellora and Ajanta. But it would be only a small beginning.... artists literally carved cathedrals and monasteries out of solid rock, and they worked for hundreds of years. Today, the thirty-four temples of Ellora and the twenty-nine temples of Ajanta are one of the wonders of ancient art and, in themselves, a sufficient reason for visiting India." That is not an idiosyncratic judgment. Today both Ellora and Ajanta are UNESCO World Heritage sites.

At the same time the last Buddhist chaitya was being excavated, an army of Hindu artisans was at work close by. Their creation would come to be called the Kailasa Temple, or Site 16. Many scholars believe Kailasa is incomparably the greatest single achievement in Indian sacred architecture. Its name is derived from the mythical mountain in the Tibetan Himalayas that is Siva's home and which the temple is intended to replicate. This is the world's largest monolith, which is to say, one single mass of rock chiseled out of a hillside and then elaborately carved by the greatest artisans of the day. Like all the Buddhist structures, Kailasa was excavated and decorated from top to bottom--first the roof, then the "supporting" columns and finally the floor from which the columns spring. I believe the total extent of the floor, including the courtyard, is just a little less than 42,000 square feet. The sculptors had to remove by hand three million cubic feet of rock before they could even begin to carve the temple. A Government of India brochure on Ellora says, "The Kailasa Temple has to be seen to be believed. The Kailasa is approximately twice the area of the Parthenon...(and half again as tall.) No nobler monument exists to India's genius, daring and skill." I would be happier to say simply that it is among India's greatest treasures.

The gateway to Kailasa leads to a spacious and busy courtyard where there is a pavilion that is the shrine of Nandi, Siva's mount. It is flanked by twin obelisks that are fifty feet tall and covered with symbols of Siva. Nearby there are two colossal stone elephants. Behind all this there is the three-storeyed temple itself, set on a huge and very high base, soaring ninety feet above it into the air. There is also a large assembly hall or chapter house. The elaborately carved interior walls of the shrine tell stories from the great epics of the Mahabharata and Ramayana. There is an especially fine carving of the demon Ravana shaking Kailasa, which I had also seen just two or three days earlier at Elephanta. Ravana tries to flaunt his power by shaking to its foundations the heavenly home of Siva but the Lord of the Dance, his countenance utterly serene, simply stamps his foot and pins Ravana to the floor of his subterranean lair. After Cave 16 we explored a number of other sites but then exhaustion set in and we turned back toward Aurangabad as the shadows lengthened, although we paid a ten minute visit to the little village of Khuldabad. I wanted to see the burial site there of Aurangzeb, the sixth of the great Mughal emperors. He wanted no great mausoleum for himself and denied the request of his father, Shah Jahan, for a black marble memorial across the Yamuna from the white marble mausoleum of his favorite wife, Mumtaz Mahal. Instead, his memorial lies in the Taj Mahal beside hers. Aurangzeb's tomb, in the compound of a Sufi saint at Khuldabad, is as modest as a tomb can be. I was very thankful when we eventually got back to the hotel and I could have a swim at dusk because the heat at Ellora had been terrible.

We set out for Ajanta at eight in the morning because we had 70 miles of poor road to cover. It was more than 2,000 years ago when Buddhist monks first began a community in this very remote location. Using the same techniques later employed at Ellora they excavated 29 "caves" in a horseshoe shaped cliff, one side of a very steep ravine carved by a fast-flowing river. These creations are all rock-cut; there were no natural caves. Some were completed between 200 B.C. and 200 A.D. and the others in the 6th and 7th centuries. Five are chaityas or churches while the other two dozen are viharas or monasteries. The caves are smaller than those at Ellora because the site is so much more constricted. They are exclusively Buddhist and so their sculptures are much more sedate and restrained than many of those at Ellora. But that is unimportant because one visits Ajanta to view the paintings there, which have been called "one of the glories of Asian art."

The paintings that cover the walls and ceilings of these viharas and chaityas are called frescoes, even though the creative process employed here was very different from the method developed in the early Renaissance in Italy. These are the finest examples of "cave painting" in this part of the world, although some are badly deteriorated. In the words of one recent art historian, "Ajanta is an artistic milestone, not only for India but for the world. Sweeping, accented lines and luminous colors and shading create a subtle and refined world of human and angelic beings and also of tropical flowers, birds, animals, textiles, jewelry and architecture. The themes are presented in continuous narrative around the walls and the language of gesture intensifies their meaning." This is great religious art, but not in any sense immediately recognizable to Western eyes. Our senses are filled with such vitality and motion, such apparent spontaneity and busyness, that we are left searching in vain for the signs of reverence or the aura of serenity that characterizes so much Christian art. The story of the Buddha and the legends that later piety ascribed to Gautama himself and to early Bodhisattvas (near Buddhas) in the Jatakas were told in the often unvarnished imagery of everyday life. As a Government brochure on Ajanta says, "Here ancient Indian art attained the zenith of its development and revealed a dynamic rhythm of life.... Although the dominant theme is religious, the paintings, in their range and treatment, are really an epic of life during a span of almost a thousand years. Here, in vivid color, a whole age comes alive; their artistry is superb." There are many vignettes of domestic life, court and street scenes, and portrayals of animals and birds and celestial beings.

My two favorite sites are Cave 1 and Cave 17. The first is a 5th century vihara where every surface is painted. Here are the "Three Ominous Signs" that inspire Gautama's first reflections: a sick man and an old man and a corpse. There are also two splendid Bodhisattvas, Padmapani and Vajrapani, perhaps the finest portraits at Ajanta. There is also a colossal sculpted stone Buddha. Cave 17 has a wonderful fresco of the king of the gods flying among clouds followed by his retinue of musicians and celestial maidens or apsaras. There is also a line of mithunas or loving couples, all of whom are differently attired. In the portico outside the vihara itself, a prince holds a princess in his arms and the Buddha calms an elephant that has been running amok. On the rear wall there is a superb fresco of a mother and child encountering the Buddha, who has returned to his own ancestral palace as a mendicant. The paintings in these two viharas are certainly among the best preserved anywhere at Ajanta.

The next morning I flew from Aurangabad to Bombay but when the time came for my flight to Bangalore the plane had already departed. Eventually Indian Airlines offered me a flight to Goa where it would provide me with a

HALEBID, Hoysalaswara Temple
At the entrance to the Halebid temple the author stands with Dr. M.S. Nagaraja Rao,
Director of the Archaeological Survey of India. This is one of the greatest treasures of India.
It has more than 20,000 statues and, again, each one is breathtaking.

car and driver for the day and then I would be given a seat on the night flight from Goa to Bangalore. I accepted because I had no other option. Goa was the capital of Portuguese territory in India until it was seized by Indian troops in 1961. I have never seen a more beautiful beach and that is where I stayed for most of the day. My little Aurangabad adventure had been not only wonderful but absolutely exhausting. Eventually I roused myself from my torpor, however, and my driver gave me a brief tour of Goa, which has a considerable number of Christian churches. Portuguese influence is evident everywhere in the old town. Se Cathedral, built in the 16th and early 17th centuries, is stunning and it is the largest Christian church in Asia. The Basilica of Bom Jesus holds relics of St. Francis Xavier. The young Jesuit had been sent from Rome to foster moral and spiritual regeneration among the expatriates who had come from Portugal to the many seductions of the colony of Goa.

When my plane arrived in Bangalore I was met at the airport by Nagaraja Rao. Even though I had heard so much about him from Seshagiri, this was the first time we had actually met. I knew from our first few minutes together that he and I could work with one another very well. Bangalore, which today is the

Belur, Channakeshava Temple
The temple at Belur was built by the Hoysalas in the 12th c.
It has more than 10,000 sculptures and each one is a masterpiece.

happy recipient of a large share of the "outsourcing" of American jobs, is a very large city and the capital of the thriving state of Karnataka. It is a new city and has no ancient monuments. In their place it has parks and flowers and wide tree-lined avenues; I walked through the best of the parks, Lal Bagh, on my way to give a lecture at the Mythic Society of Bangalore and then another one at the university, where my friend V.K. Gokak had once been the vice chancellor. But at seven the next morning it was time to set off for Mysore. Much of the southern part of Karnataka is one great garden; we drove south and west along roads shaded by endless tamarind trees, wonderful banyans, and many pipal and eucalyptus.

Farther off, there were great groves of mango and guava trees, as well as millions of palms, betel and date and coconut and also the quite distinctive toddy palms. The fields were mainly rice paddies, although there were coffee and cardamom plantations too. We had planned to visit along the way two of the three important Hoysala Dynasty temples in Karnataka, both built in the 12th century. One is located in the agricultural hamlet of Belur, dusty and ramshackle, and the other in a similar village, Halebid, once an imperial capital but today showing no trace of that lost eminence. As we approached Belur I felt a sharp pang of disappointment. The place was totally uninteresting. There was not another car within miles. No one had the slightest interest in this temple except us. Belur was not only remote but forgotten, and it was not difficult to think of reasons for that. From a distance it was apparent the temple was really very small, exceedingly small and only a single storey, and very squat because its roof, whether by accident or design, was absolutely flat. I emerged from the car with, to say the least, radically reduced expectations.

Then I was simply struck dumb by what I saw. The proportions were exquisite. Every bit of every wall was filled with carving, innumerable figures whose beauty was truly astonishing. There we were all alone with one of the greatest stone creations that I had ever seen or heard of. The walls seemed to be alive; they appeared to be in motion before my eyes, so sinuous and energetic and vital as everything was--countless figures of mortals and gods, angels and demons, men and women, soldiers and nobles, royals and hunters, dancers and musicians, birds and animals. On the six bands that encircle the base of the temple, the figures are so diminutive they measure less than eight inches tall. The little building is a flamboyant mixture of the sacred and the secular, the heavenly and the earthly; the whole universe is displayed on the walls of this very modest structure sitting in the middle of nowhere. I have never seen nor heard of comparable sculptures anywhere in the West. Nagaraj told me there were approximately ten thousand figures adorning the Belur temple, and the quantity is entirely matched by the quality, for here there is breathtaking beauty everywhere. I was astounded by all of this, and who would not be? But how could cold stone be infused with such warmth and the appearance of so much movement and energy?

Part of the answer, of course, has to do with the virtuosity and genius of the artisans who created Belur. But I also think a large part of it has to do with the creative power of leisure. The craftsmen of Belur never faced a deadline. Whole generations were involved in this construction. Work on it was continuous but it was not completed until a hundred years had gone by. There was always time for reflection and the free play of imagination. A third part of the answer concerns the material the Hoysala artisans used whenever it was available, a stone called chloritic schist. It is very malleable and plastic when it is quarried but after exposure to air and sunlight it becomes as hard as iron. This is why some of the

Halebid, Hoysalaswara Temple, Detail
The bands that surround the base of the temple are only eight inches or so high.

Hoysala temple carvings have not been coarsened and blunted by the passage of time. So Belur has whole throngs of gods and goddesses and their many incarnations, all in pristine condition. They still look as though they had been fashioned only yesterday. There are also many friezes depicting stories from India's great religious epics. One external wall has 80 separate and quite large and beautiful statues of different goddesses. But soon Nagaraj interrupted my musings to say we must hurry away if we were also to do justice to Halebid.

Halebid is Belur doubled and a good deal more. Begun in 1121 by the same king who had completed Belur ten years earlier, it consists of two matching sanctuaries that parallel one another and are connected in their middle by a short corridor. They resemble one another and Belur as well, even though the

Halebid, Hoysalaswara Temple, Detail
The two great Hindu epics are the subjects of many temple friezes but nowhere sculpted with more flair and artistry than at Halebid.

latter is dedicated to Vishnu and these are Siva shrines. All were erected above a star-shaped plinth and have <u>mandapas</u> or pillared halls and dance platforms in front of the sanctum. Nearby there are two beautiful many-columned pavilions sheltering huge Nandis. The more southerly pavilion leads to a small and utterly charming shrine to Surya, the Sun God, which is elegantly decorated.

There is a band of friezes that entirely encircles all of the temple bases and that portrays scenes from classical Hindu mythology, all of which are presented in terms of the profane and ordinary ways of life in the 12th century; the heavenly is well and truly earthed. Perhaps the finest aspect of the Hoysalesvara temples is on the West exterior, where there are 280 separate statues of gods and goddesses and their various incarnations, each about three feet tall, all more elaborate than anything I have ever seen carved in stone elsewhere, most provided with pedestals and ornamental arches or canopies.

These statues are among the best of approximately 20,000 carved figures that adorn the Hoysaleshvara temples and make the shrines a great museum of some of the finest of ancient Indian art. Most scholars regard Halebid as the best of the Hoysala temples and I concur with that judgment, although it is not my personal favorite. One of Nagaraja's predecessors in Mysore wrote that, "none can compare in magnitude, exuberance of carving and artistic majesty with the Hoysaleshvara Temple. On its outer walls are sculptured several thousands of figures and groups.... on a platform which closely follows the contour of the temple rises the basement which is one of the most elaborately carved in the world." Other art historians have made even greater claims for Halebid in their comparisons of it with Gothic cathedrals and with the Parthenon. How to assess these extraordinary claims must be left to that very small band of experts who are not only familiar with the treasures of the West but who have also come to

Somnathpur, Keshava Temple (Hoysala)
This was built a century after Belur and Halebid and did not suffer the depredations of the others by invading Mughal armies. There are three shrines in this Vaishnavite temple.

visit this humble, dusty little village. Soon Nagaraj and I drove on to Mysore and the Lalitha Palace Hotel, for it was very dark now and it had been quite a day.

The Lalitha Palace was a royal guesthouse before its recent conversion into a hotel. It retains some touches of splendor, including a very grand Italian marble staircase and a wonderful baroque ballroom which is now the hotel dining room. During my visit I was the only guest. I spent the next morning with Nagaraj in the Indo-Saracenic City Palace, which is among the largest palaces in India and is probably the best of them all. One guidebook calls it "a sort of gigantic synthesis of Hindu and Muslim styles. Entrance gateways, domes, arches, turrets, colonnades, sculpture--all are here in magnificent profusion." The centerpiece is the Durbar Hall, where the Maharajah had received the nobility and leaders of the state of Mysore. It is absolutely vast, with wonderful colonnades and intricately decorated and gilded chandeliers everywhere.

In the late afternoon we drove to Srirangapatna, once the capital of the Mysore princes, where there is a picturesque and finely carved wooden summer palace that Tipu Sultan built at the end of the 18th century. It has many murals that portray his two great victories over the British army. Then in the late afternoon and early evening we wandered through the fabulous gardens of Krishnarajasagar, where there is a stone dam more than a mile long that was constructed without mortar because the stone had been so meticulously chiseled. Below it are the lovely Brindavan Gardens, which have often been compared with the gardens at Versailles. First we saw them at twilight and then as darkness fell they were illuminated by thousands of tiny lights.

The next day quite early we set off for Somnathpur, the last of the three important Hoysala temples I saw. It is very close to Mysore, only 18 miles away, but the road is worse than terrible and it was more than an hour later before we arrived at this poor and totally unremarkable little village. All that struck my eye were mounds of red chilli peppers drying in the sun in the middle of what may or may not have been the town square; there was no way to be certain. And then we came upon the temple, situated in the midst of a compound framed by a quite beautiful cloister or colonnade. The temple at Belur has one sanctuary, at Halebid there are two, but here in the smallest of the temples there are three.

Instead of the flat roofs of its sisters, the Keshava Temple at Somnathpur has three Shikharas or small towers that rise above the sanctuaries. So many of the gopurams and spires that rear up from the myriad temples of South India are grossly inappropriate for the rather modest structures they are intended to complement. But at Somnathpur the little shikharas are perfectly proportionate and add immeasurably to the beauty of the whole. Even though this is the smallest of the sisters its towers give it a majesty the others cannot match.

Somnathpur was built in the second half of the 13th century, about 150 years after its sisters. Consequently, some writers have found the carving here rather mannered and formalistic, lacking some of the vibrancy and spontaneity

Somnathpur, Keshava Temple (Hoysala), Detail
Because of the properties of the stone used for the friezes the temple shows little weathering.

so clearly evident in the earlier temples. Others have argued that this is the crown jewel of Hoysala architecture, the mature and indeed perfect fruition of a creative impulse that endured from the 11th century to the 14th, when the Hoysalas were overthrown. To some extent I side with these writers, for Somnathpur is probably one of my most favorite temples in India. The interior is carved as exquisitely and elaborately as the outside, which has six narrow bands each no more than eight inches tall that run entirely around the temple. The lowest band consists of war elephants, the next of charging cavalry, then highly decorative scrolls and above them narrative scenes from the religious epics, and then many birds and animals. Above the bands are many much larger figures: deities and their many incarnations, especially avatars of Vishnu to whom the shrine is dedicated, musicians and dancers, hunters and courtesans, apsaras and mithunas, and more scenes from the religious epics.

Somnathpur was undamaged by the Mughal incursions which swept down from the north and which Belur and Halebid did not entirely escape. So it remains today much as it was when it first emerged fresh from its sculptors' hands. Sun and wind and rain have done it little damage over the years because of the extraordinary resilience of chloritic schist. In a letter that I sent from Mysore about the Keshava Temple I wrote, "Nowhere in Europe is there any building that has been so untouched by the passing centuries. Nowhere in the Western world is there stone carving so elaborate, so exquisite, so vibrant and alive, so delicate, so endless with its thousands upon thousands of individuals and groups, so magnificent. It resolutely and absolutely defies any attempt to describe it. I have never seen anything like it and I will never forget it. I hope that some day you and I can be here and see it together."

My last week in Mysore was entirely devoted to business, concluding with a lecture at the university to a large and interested audience. It was followed by a very pleasant bon voyage party. I had come here because I needed formal approvals from the Indian authorities so that our students could receive credit for courses taken at the University of Mysore and, even more important, we needed to find both board and lodging for forty-some American students most of whom had never been out of their own country before and who were really unprepared to live in any other fashion than as they had always done. We had arranged appointments for me with the Vice Chancellor and the Registrar at the university. They were very gracious and welcoming, answered all my questions, acceded to my various requests, and told me how much they looked forward to having University of Virginia students on their campus. Then I met with the Deputy Registrar and with the directors of two institutes as well as various other people just to make certain that all necessary bases had been covered.

Meanwhile, Nagaraj had contacted the Central Food Technology Research Institute and he had made appointments for me there to discuss the possibility of board and lodging in their facilities. Partly supported by the United Nations, CFTRI was the sole institution in India at this time that was devoted exclusively to issues that had to do with food packaging, preservation and distribution. I told their administration that it would be wonderful if some of our students could be exposed to this sort of research into some of the fundamental problems of the developing world. The CFTRI campus was adjacent to the university and it included a brand new dormitory with a large swimming pool where we could have as many as two dozen rooms with private Western-style bathrooms. All rooms were doubles. That pleased us because we did not want any of our students in single accommodations. All meals would be served in the dormitory refectory. We would be granted a special concessionary rate: room and full board would be $40 per person per month. I was absolutely delighted.

It seemed to me that the UVa semester in India program was off to a most auspicious beginning and that the demand for places in it would be very strong. My expectations certainly were not disappointed. The program we nailed together had few real competitors among American colleges and universities. Later I said a most reluctant goodbye to Nagaraj; we had worked very well together and had accomplished some important goals. I thanked him both for his memorable kindnesses to me personally and for his very significant service to the University of Virginia. I told him how pleased I was that he would accept an appointment as a part-time adjunct professor in religious studies and teach a course in our program. Then I went on my way to prepare for the next leg of this remarkable journey.

The flight to Madras consumed less than an hour, so I arrived in good time for breakfast at the Chola Hotel, a fine place that I much enjoyed. I was no sooner in my room than the telephone rang. It was Nagaraj, to ask whether I had enjoyed the flight and to tell me once again that I would now be the guest of the Director of the Archeological Survey of India for Tamil Nadu, Dr. Srinivasan. I had an early celebratory lunch, rejoicing in the prospect of a free afternoon, but it was not to be. The telephone rang again and it was my new host, calling to say that he would meet me at the Chola in fifteen minutes and then we could set off for an afternoon in Mahabalipuram. He thought we would get back to the hotel in about seven hours. He arrived very promptly, along with two of his deputies, three drivers and three landrovers. He was bright, interesting and proved to be a very good companion for the next three days.

Our little caravan set off on a lovely drive of perhaps sixty kilometers along a road that hugged the coast. There were millions of palms, especially toddy palms, and remarkably green and verdant rice paddies. There were also many little fishing villages, their huts roofed entirely with palm fronds. Many of the villagers' beds were outside the openings to the huts, for this far south much of life is an outdoor affair. The Bay of Bengal, a brilliant blue-green, creamed up the vast white sandy beaches, which seemed to stretch on forever. Mahabalipuram was once a busy and thriving town which was the principal seaport for the Pallava Dynasty whose capital was in Kanchipuram during the 7th and 8th centuries. Today, however, the old town is abandoned and all that remains there are the stone relics of another age. What sets Mahabalipuram apart and gives it a particular fascination is the very unusual variety of these monuments that were built so long ago. There are both rock-cut shrines and free-standing temples side by side. The site is a sort of architectural laboratory that displays all the known possibilities in the 7th century for the transition from the one to the other. There are also free-standing sculptures as well as carved bas-reliefs, some of which are among the finest and most dynamic in all of India and one of which is the largest bas-relief in the world.

All of this has been carved from solid granite, and it is an awesome display of great art triumphant over rather recalcitrant material. Perhaps there are

66

four entities or groups of them that are most important. The first are the Five Rathas--the word means a temple chariot--which are actually very small and delicate temples in different styles, all of them exquisitely proportioned monoliths. Their walls have been carved into a wonderful anthology of Hindu myth and symbol. Nearby stand three monolithic lifesize protectors of the Rathas, an elephant and a lion and a bull. Second, there are ten shallow mandapas or pillared halls leading to small sanctuaries, although two of them are unfinished. In the mandapa dedicated to Krishna, there is a beautifully

MAHABALIPURAM, Krishna's Mandapam
*Perhaps there is no other naturalistic carving of agricultural life in India
as tender and well-known as this.*

carved pastoral scene of a cowherd milking a cow that is nuzzling the face of her calf. But perhaps the best of them all is a lavishly decorated shrine devoted to Siva. On its walls we meet the fearsome Durga astride a lion--a goddess who is actually Parvati, the consort of Siva, in her form and role as the destroyer of evil--overcoming the buffalo demon, Mahishasura. These reliefs simply explode with vitality and life and movement.

Third, there is the world's largest stone bas-relief nearby. It is called "Arjuna's Penance" and is approximately 90 feet long by 36 feet wide. Carved on a single rock face, it portrays about 400 figures, animal and human and celestial. The harmony, the balance, the incredible motility and exuberance are superb. Two elephants in the lower right quadrant are said to be the finest carved anywhere in India. I am particularly fond of a little family of mice frolicking in front of them. Finally, there is the Shore Temple, which was built in the 7th or early 8th century and is one of the finest early free-standing shrines in India. It is the prototype of half the Dravidian temples in the South but very unusual because although dedicated to Siva it also contains a sanctuary devoted to Vishnu. It gazes out to sea, stalwart and stately and serene, its two shikharas

MAHABALIPURAM, Arjuna's Penance
This is the world's largest bas-relief, approximately 96 feet by 44 feet, called the
Penance of Arjuna or sometimes, the Descent of the Ganges.
These two elephants have often been described as the finest ever carved by an Indian artist.

immensely picturesque, girdled by a garland of foam as the waves break gently against the stones of its foundation. This is certainly one of the enduring images that any visitor will carry away from Mahabalipuram. I went swimming in the shadow of the temple (this was still possible in 1978) and felt I had received some sort of benefaction.

The caravan returned to the Chola the next morning bright and early, with even more people in the vehicles, and off we went into the interior to Kanchipuram, a bustling town now because of its silk industry and a bustling city long ago as the Pallava royal capital. In the Hindu tradition Kanchipuram is considered one of the seven most holy cities in the land because it is sacred both to Siva and to Vishnu. It was only now that I learned why my host had rolled out for me such a spectacular red carpet; he was Seshagiri Rao's old hostel roommate. They had gone through school together. Two shrines in particular attracted my attention on that morning. The earliest of all the shrines is the Kailasa Temple, dedicated to Siva and built in the 7th or early 8th century. It is decorated with some excellent paintings in the small monastic cells around its courtyards. In the nearly contemporaneous shrine devoted to Vishnu there are many more paintings that are said to be among the finest murals anywhere in India. At least in some small way, or so it seemed to me then, the relation between Kanchipuram and Mahabalipuram is analogous to that between Ajanta and Ellora--the dominance of painting in one and of sculpture in the other. Later temples have gargantuan entryways or gopurams that soar many storeys into the sky and give the city its remarkable skyline. One from the 16th century rises about 190 feet; so it provided me with an introduction to what I would see in Madurai.

We arrived back in Madras for a very late lunch at the Archeological Survey of India offices, located in the Admiralty which once had been the headquarters of the British East India Company and where Robert Clive, the fabled governor of Madras, had lived. Next door, built in 1689, fifty years before the Admiralty, is the oldest Anglican church in India. After a fine meal I had a long walk on the Marina. This vast beach, along which the city sprawls, runs for more than a dozen miles and it is between 200 and 300 yards wide. It is very beautiful, the white sand glinting in the sun, and sometimes very crowded, but with men and boys who gather there for cricket, not with bathers. Not many Indians swim and none enjoy lying on a beach because they do not want their skin darkened by the sun. Madras is the fourth largest city in India, but this fact is well disguised; it has almost no tall buildings and there is no town center at all. It has just laid itself down and stretched out along the beachfront.

Our third and final ASI expedition did not take us very far afield at all, but it was something in which I was particularly interested. Our three vehicles drove a short distance outside the city to a very prosperous farm. We spent some time listening to the farmer discuss his current agricultural practices and then we watched his peons harvest millet and rice for a long time. We stood in the shade and the scene was very picturesque. We were here because this farm had been a pioneer in the Green Revolution that had transformed much of Indian agriculture and had brought a measure of financial security that few farmers had hitherto ever enjoyed. The Green Revolution was the transformation that the introduction of petrochemical fertilizers had effected. New varieties of grains had been developed to take full advantage of petrochemical fertilizers and now where before there had always been only a single crop there could be three bountiful harvests every year. The fertilizer was very expensive by Indian standards but the results far more than justified the cost.

I was puzzled, though, as I watched the peons gather bundles of the rice and millet in their arms and carry them to the highway. Then, when no traffic was coming, they spread their armloads all across the road. They did not seem distressed when lorries and cars and buses ran over their handiwork and scattered it in all directions. So I turned to my ASI host and told him I was quite mystified by whatever it was that was going on. He turned toward me very abruptly and with a fleeting expression of disgust he answered, this is the way they thresh the grain, this is how they separate the rice seeds and the millet grains from their stalks. Then at dusk the peons collect the seeds and the grain from the roadside and carry it all to the village for storage. He was silent for a minute; then, anger choking his voice, he added, "Four times as much rice in the bushes and maybe no more rice in the bellies." I am sure that was a considerable exaggeration born of his deep sense of frustration. But the morning's farm visit taught me a graphic lesson about modernization. An expensive advance here or there will accomplish nothing at all without the syncronization that requires much thought, a careful design, and the coordination of a great many things. In its early days, the Green Revolution was sometimes more hoopla than substance because no one had ever really thought it through. This was precisely the sort of problem that CFTRI, in whose new dormitory our students would soon be living, had been created by the United Nations to undertake.

The next morning I walked to the National Art Gallery and the Government Museum which sit side by side on Pantheon Road. On my first trip to this country I had spent a long day at Sarnath, a few kilometers outside Varanasi. This is a very important Buddhist place of pilgrimage because it was in the deer park here that the Buddha preached his first sermon. Several centuries later the emperor Ashoka raised a commemorative pillar to mark where Gautama had first proclaimed the Four Noble Truths and prescribed the Eightfold Path. Now the Ashoka Pillar is in the Sarnath Museum, which I had visited. This four-headed lion column was adopted by the new Republic of India in 1947 as its national emblem. But there is a second image which is equally well known as a symbol of Indian art and culture and that is the figure of Siva Nataraja, Siva the Lord of the Dance.

There have been hundreds of millions of representations of Siva Nataraja and they have been created for thousands of years. But perhaps the finest of them all is an 11th century bronze created by an unknown artist during the reign of the Chola Dynasty. The opportunity to see this was the reason for my walk on Pantheon Road. I was very surprised to discover that what I had assumed was at least life size was in fact not even three feet tall. But its charisma more than compensated for its proportions. It is breathtaking, unforgettable, a figure of amazing grace with one foot so lightly balanced against the other leg. He and his circle of fire are alive, utterly electric, forever in motion. Now I had seen them close up, the two images incomparably most important to express the greatness and the glory that is India. My travels through the South on this trip had taken me first to the carving of Siva Nataraja on the wall of the rock-cut shrine at Elephanta and now as the end approached I stood in front of the 11th century bronze masterpiece that was perhaps the myth's supreme expression. Some sort of circle was finally complete.

❀ ❀ ❀

CHAPTER FOUR

Virginia Finds an Indian Home

When I left Madras the next day, my flight transported me to a whole new world, one that I was not at all eager to visit. But I recognized with some reluctance that it was an inevitability. I had spent a long time visiting some of the finest sacred art and architecture that had been created between the 2nd century B.C. and the 14th century A.D. in South India. But there was another chapter to this story because creativity in art and architecture did not end in the year 1400. The final chapter could be read in Madurai. So to Madurai I had come, 300 miles south of the state capital of Madras, to see the culmination of the Dravidian temple style in the 16th and 17th centuries. In many ways these two cities stand in stark contrast.

Madras is relatively young and affluent and it has a certain sparkle; many new cars cruise along its wide boulevards. It was the first home of the British East India Company years before there was a Raj. But Madurai is very ancient, encrusted with the grime of centuries, very poor and with roads choked with two-wheeled bullock carts. Madras has one of the world's finest beaches and it is set in the midst of amazingly lush countryside. Madurai is far inland and, once the monsoons have gone, its neighborhood is sere. The land is sandy, flat and featureless, and whispers no promises to humans or animals alike; the rewards for farming are largely confined to rice and cotton. Where the land is not irrigated, nothing much will grow except giant cacti and toddy palms. Madras has no tall buildings blocking the sun from its green and numerous gardens. Madurai seems to have no gardens and its dusty streets are frequently unpaved. But it certainly does have tall buildings, the massive temple entrance towers which are called gopurams, mostly built since the 16th century.

I had come to Madurai simply to see the Minakshi Temple, dedicated to Siva and Parvati in their incarnations as Lord Somasundara and Sri Minakshi. It occupies 15 acres in the middle of the city and is surrounded by a high wall which has four entrances, one on each side. These four massive gopurams are more than 150 feet tall and they are complemented inside the enclosure by eight more, though these are not so high. The entrance towers are each nine storeys while the eight others have only three to seven storeys. The 16th century southern gopuram has more than 1,500 stucco figures of different gods, goddesses, incarnations, angels and demons. All the other gopurams are no less elaborately decorated. Inside the gateways there is pandemonium, or at least a constant swirl of activity that often seems more reminiscent of a marketplace than of a sanctuary. Perhaps the wild exaggerations of the gopurams are a warning that everything inside the temple will be larger than life--and so it is. One example is the Tank of the Golden Lily or Golden Lotus which is so large that it resembles a lake more than it does the usual temple tank. It is surrounded by cloisters decorated with paintings and more stucco figures.

In the Minakshi Temple there are more than 2,000 intricately but not expertly carved pillars, half of which can be found in the "Thousand Pillar Hall." The figures carved on the pillars seem to express the whole range of possible human emotions on the faces of soldiers, dancing girls, musicians and various divinities and demons. The hall was built in the 16th century and is dedicated to Siva Nataraja. All of the statues in the chamber are more than life-size; from whatever angle one views them, the 985 pillars are arranged so that they fall in a straight line from the point where the viewer stands. The creators of the Minakshi Temple must have believed that if they built something so overwhelming, people would come. And they did come and they do come today, hordes and hordes of them. This is the most famous and popular of all the later temples in South India. But the thousands of sculptures are crude and coarse and, at least to my Western eyes, entirely unpleasing. The focus is everywhere on quantity, not quality, and the implicit expectation that somehow the first would metamorphose into the second is, of course, unfulfilled. Indian sacred art has a wonderful accessibility because of the way the divine is humanized. At Madurai I felt the human was demonized. Here it was, the culmination and degeneration of a tradition that spanned two and a half millennia. The Hoysala temples of Karnataka and the Minakshi Temple built by the Nayak rulers of Tamil Nadu: both are in India, neither is more Indian than the other, and yet they are worlds apart.

The Minakshi Temple was my sole reason for coming to Madurai, where there is not much else to see. Now that I was done with it I was eager to return to Madras and the comfortable embrace of the Chola Hotel. Someone had told me the hotel had an ice-skating rink; I went in search of it and, yes, there it was. I spent a lovely and relaxed last day in Madras and then flew to Hyderabad and on to Delhi, where a room awaited me at the India International Center in Lodi Gardens. After only a day or two, however, I was back at the airport, this time to catch a plane to Chandigarh, where I hired a taxi for the hour-long drive to my old home, Punjabi University in Patiala. I had a joyous reunion with Harbans Singh and his wife, with my former colleague, Lal Mani Joshi, and with our old cook, Parakram, who was still the chef at the university guest house where I was staying once again. When I had finished dinner the first evening I asked Parakram to come and sit beside me for a minute. I pulled three photographs from my pocket and handed them to him, one of Kit and one of Tim and one of the two of them together. Parakram looked at each one for a long time, smiled and said, the boys looked very strong; maybe they will join the army and be generals, he added. Then he looked at each photograph again and reluctantly handed them back to me. I told him that I had not brought them for him to look at but to keep. His eyes filled with tears and he lowered his head for a moment before saying that they would always be among his most prized belongings. I knew that he meant every word. Parakram was a prince among men; I was devoted to him.

The next two weeks were extremely busy. Early Monday morning I went to the Bhavan, first to spend several hours with Dr. Bhatt, our new lecturer in Jainism, then much of the day with Harbans Singh, and finally I spent three hours with Joshi, who had become greatly more mature and self-confident. It was a delight to be with him again. Of course I did not know that he was soon to be taken from us; so I am all the more grateful for the time we had together in 1978. The next day was the 509th birthday of Guru Nanak, so I went with some friends to the local gurdwara for a special celebration. Soon after I returned there was a knock on my door and there was the university's new vice chancellor, Dr. Amrik Singh. We had a long and interesting chat before I went back to work in the Bhavan until it was time for Parakram's dinner. I was the only resident in the guesthouse and so he was trying to prepare what he remembered as my favorite dishes. Amrik telephoned to propose a seven o'clock breakfast. We talked for more than two hours. I certainly found him a thoughtful and quite remarkable man. Amrik asked me to accompany him that afternoon to Chandigarh. So I hastened to the Bhavan to make my excuses there.

For several hours after we arrived we had an interesting private discussion with the political analyst for the <u>Chandigarh Tribune.</u> He was also a confidential advisor to the Chief Minister of the Punjab. Then Amrik and I had a long walk all around the university campus, which may well be the handsomest in India. We had dinner with this same political analyst. Later, from my bed in the university's guesthouse, I watched the gorgeous full moon and the foothills of the Himalayas looming above me. The lights of a hill station twinkled in the distance a thousand meters above my head. Early the next morning I toured Chandigarh, its lakes and markets and residential areas and its imposing public buildings. This is an entirely new community. It did not exist until some years after Partition in 1947 when it was built to be the new capital of the Punjab and, later, of the state of Haryana. So it is one of India's very few wholly planned communities; Le Corbusier was the architect of all of it.

Amrik had to stay in Chandigarh for another meeting but I had a class to teach and so I could not remain with him. I returned his car and driver and took a public bus back to Patiala. Intercity travel by local bus in rural India is not for everyone, or perhaps the trouble is that it is, including sheep and goats, but only if they each paid the same fare their owners did. Our bus was so crowded that for long periods we literally could not keep our feet on the floor. Other people clung to every protrusion outside the vehicle. Yet everyone was in a remarkably good if not festive mood, eager to assist one another. Never having experienced this sort of Indian idyll before, I thoroughly enjoyed it, but I would not like ever to do it again. I arrived back with only minutes to spare before teaching a M. Lit. class. Then Bhatt, Joshi, Harbans Singh and I read <u>Encyclopedia of Hinduism</u> entries until dinner. The days that ensued went the same way and I did not return to Delhi until the last possible moment.

I went from Delhi to Agra aboard the Taj Express, which is the most luxurious train I have ever ridden. There are usually said to be three reasons for visiting Agra: the Taj Mahal, the Agra Fort, and Fatehpur Sikri, 25 miles to the West, and all of them are essentials. I went first to the Taj, which is incredibly more beautiful than pictures of it, all of which seem to have been taken on a cloudless and broiling midsummer noon. I was fortunate to see it first in the gentle afternoon sunlight of an early winter day, and then to visit it again at dusk amid the mists that rise from the Yamuna River at this time of year. The mists are kind to it, lending it a softness and agelessness, an apparent fragility and mysteriousness, as it floats above the bank of the Yamuna. Is this one of the most beautiful buildings the world has ever seen? To me, the answer is simple: Yes, it is. Certainly it is one of the most extraordinary edifices I have ever seen. Shah Jahan was an architectural genius and this memorial for Mumtaz Mahal, the love of his life, is his supreme achievement.

Inside the tall and imposing gate to the Taj there is a simple walled garden with a large rectangular reflecting pool, so the visitor sees two Taj Mahals, one facing him and the other a perfect similitude beneath his feet. The utterly perfect proportions of the Taj rise above two bases, the first of rusty red sandstone and above that a checkerboard platform in black and white. On each corner of this platform is a slender minaret that reaches 130 feet into the air. As you walk through the entrance to the Taj itself, you see close at hand the lavish inlay which is all over the building. It is exquisite and of almost unparalleled intricacy. Many varieties of semi-precious stones are set into the walls of the memorial and into the incredibly delicate marble screens and, supremely, into the bier of Mumtaz Mahal. When the sun strikes them, the interior is a blaze of colored lights. Perhaps the greatest of all the inlaid designs are the many flowers, each only one or two square inches, which contain many different pieces. The matches are everywhere perfect, so that it is impossible to see any seams or breaks between these nearly infinitesimal pieces of stone. The perfectly hemispherical dome arching overhead is the distinctive contribution that the Mughals made to Indian architecture. Within the building there are four dome rooms, one at each corner, which filter light toward the biers. Far above them floats the marble dome that guards this whole magnificence, which itself seems to float high above the bank of the Yamuna. Everything is ethereal, heavenly, seemingly made from nothing except light and air. There is nothing earthly here.

But the earthliness is certainly not far away. The Agra Fort that Akbar built when the city was the capital of the Mughal empire bears a striking resemblance to the Red Fort in Delhi, at least from the outside. Even though it is earlier it is better preserved than its sister. There is a 70 foot high outer perimeter wall built of rusty red sandstone, then a wide moat and another equally tall and forbidding defensive wall. Within all this, however, the buildings were mostly designed by Akbar's grandson, Shah Jahan. His spectacular brilliance is evident wherever one turns. Akbar, Jahangir and Shah Jahan together reigned for only one century, from the 1560s to the 1660s, but during that brief time a very major chapter was written in the world's history of art and architecture. After you enter the fort through the Amar Singh gate, you are facing the Pearl Mosque, built of white marble; it is so gracefully proportioned you know it must have been the work of Shah Jahan. It embraces a marble courtyard surrounded by delicately carved cloisters. Three handsome domes cover the whole mosque. The most massive building inside the fort is the Hall of Public Audience, set on a platform four feet tall from which a raft of slender marble columns sprout. The throne room, which is just an alcove in the great hall, bears the unmistakable stamp of Shah Jahan because of all the incredibly intricate mosaic inlay which invites comparison only with the memorials to Mumtaz Mahal and Itmad-ud-Daulah.

Nearby is the Hall of Private Audience, outside which is the Throne Terrace supporting two thrones, one black and one white. The first was built for Akbar's son Jahangir and the white for Jahangir's son, Shah Jahan. Next the visitor comes to my favorite building in the fort, the Musamman Burj, an octagonal tower that Shah Jahan built for Mumtaz Mahal but within which he was imprisoned by his son Aurangzeb for the last years of his life. The first floor is a courtyard with exquisitely carved screens through which the ladies of the court could watch the activities in the fort. In the center of this is a magnificently carved fountain. The palaces of Jahangir and Shah Jahan also deserve extended examination, especially the baths built by the latter. Cleanliness and personal hygiene mattered far more to the Mughals than to their 17th century European counterparts. But now dusk was near and so I headed back to the Taj Mahal.

The next morning I hired a taxi to take me to and from Fatehpur Sikri, less than an hour away across the quite sere and barren landscape. Akbar moved the Mughal capital from Agra to this magnificent new city in 1571, only to abandon it fourteen years later in 1585. Why the abandonment? The traditional answer is that the always erratic water supply dwindled until it could no longer support life in the city. But it is much more reasonable to assume that the endemic conflict in the Punjab compelled Akbar to move the capital to Lahore, from which he could more easily monitor the unrest. There is no evidence of which I am aware that he ever intended his absence from Fatehpur Sikri to be anything more than temporary. But death had other plans and so there was no return.

It is a strange sensation to approach a truly awesome city that looks as though it could have been built yesterday and then to find within its formidable walls that extend for seven miles not a single resident, no one at all except a few guides and the visitors who clamber down from their tourist buses. As we approached Fatehpur Sikri we could see from miles away the Gateway of Victory, the Buland Darwaza, the entrance to the great mosque. The gateway was built by Akbar to commemorate his conquest of Gujarat in 1573. It soars nearly 170 feet into the air and is crowned by graceful chhatris. These are delicate and very decorative pillared and domed kiosks. Even today the Buland Darwaza is the largest gateway in all of Asia. It is decorated with many carved Koranic inscriptions. Today Fatehpur Sikri is a city that has two parts, one religious and one secular. The religious area consists of the Buland Darwaza, the great mosque and its enormous courtyard, and the Dargah of Sheikh Salim Chishti. A dargah is a shrine dedicated to a Sufi saint. By extension, the whole religious complex here is called the Dargah of Sheikh Salim Chishti. The great mosque or Jami Masjid was finished in 1571 before the work on the palaces was even begun. The front is an arcade of pointed arches divided by the monumental central gate. The roof is capped by a row of pleasing chhatris. This mosque was intended to be the largest shrine in Akbar's empire. It can accommodate more than 10,000 worshippers and is still in use today. Everything is red sandstone. The huge area for congregational prayer is surrounded by cells for priests or monks. Above the

78

FATEHPUR SIKRI
The centerpiece of the Diwan-I-Kas or the Hall of Private Audience
is a magnificent and elaborately carved red sandstone column.

congregation there are three great domes. In each of the numerous bays there are mihrabs, niches pointing toward Mecca, to which all Muslims turn during their devotions.

The mausoleum of Sheikh Salim Chishti has been called "One of the finest and most famous examples of marble work anywhere in the world." The entrance has four slender columns of white marble with simply fabulous serpentine supports that link the columns to the eaves. They are the most stunning element in this whole exquisitely decorated marble exterior. The jalis, wonderfully carved thin sheets of marble perforated with floral and geometrical patterns, enclose the verandah and serve as windows, admitting lovely dappled light but excluding the fierce rays of the midday sun. Even the tomb chamber has an inlaid white marble floor. The memorial above the tomb is crowned by a spectacularly fine mother-of-pearl canopy. These jalis are among the finest that can be found anywhere. But why is there even today such veneration of an obscure and indigent 16th century holy man who lived in the middle of nowhere? By the time he was 25 Akbar had reigned for more than a dozen years. His empire stretched from one coast of North India to the other; its borders were secure and its people more or less prosperous and at peace. But Akbar's life was shadowed by one great sadness. None of his male offspring had survived infancy; he had no heir. Some of his advisors suggested that he consult a Sufi saint who lived in the village of Sikri about fifty kilometers away from Agra. So the emperor went to this forlorn little hamlet and prostrated himself in prayer before Sheikh Salim Chishti, who told him that he would have three sons, all of whom would grow to manhood. The prophecy was fulfilled and a jubilant Akbar decided to construct the great mosque that we know as the Jami Masjid outside the village of Sikri, and it became the centerpiece of what would be a new imperial capital.

Unlike the Dargah of Sheikh Salim Chishti, the secular side of Fatehpur Sikri consists of many buildings, some for public use and others for the harem and for various royal residences. Many grand open spaces include the Pachisi Courtyard, where the emperor allegedly played pachisi using slave girls as the playing pieces. The most arresting exterior is that of the five-storey

FATEHPUR SIKRI
In the courtyard of the Jami Masjid is Salim Chishti's tomb, begun in 1571.
The breathtaking marblework, as this detail testifies, is some of the finest in India.

Panch Mahal, a pyramidal structure which has 84 columns on its first floor but only four on the top to support the elegant small dome of a kiosk. Probably this was used by the ladies of the court to watch the passing scene. The cloisters and the courtyard of the Hall of Public Audience are most impressive, although the Hall of Private Audience or Diwan-i-Khas is even more so. In the middle of this small building there is a massive and ornately carved pillar which is crowned by a great stone balustraded flower. This is connected by four bridges to a gallery midway up the walls that surround the stone flower, which serves as a platform for the emperor's throne. Perhaps this also served as a Disputation Hall, where Akbar could question theologians from a variety of different traditions. This most tolerant of all the Mughal emperors was intensely interested in religion and even devised a new syncretistic faith for his people and himself. Whatever the original uses of the building may have been, the placement of the throne assured that Akbar could be present but still distanced from his guests or disputants or supplicants. There are many other truly splendid buildings at Fatehpur Sikri and all of them together, in their virtually pristine beauty, constitute perhaps an unparalleled monument to the grandeur and folly of human vanity.

We had set off for Fatehpur Sikri at dawn; now it was noon and the sun beat down relentlessly. I looked for my driver and told him I was ready to return to Agra, where I had two places I wanted to visit before returning to the station to catch a night express for the trip back to Delhi. First, I wanted to visit the Taj Mahal one more time, for I had not yet seen it in full noonday sun. Then I wanted to go to a place about which I knew nothing at all, the Tomb of Itmad-ud-Daulah. He was the father of Empress Noor Jahan, the favorite wife of the fourth of the great Mughal emperors, Jahangir. Her father had been Jahangir's chief minister and a very powerful confidant. Noor Jahan hired artisans from her father's Persian homeland to build his mausoleum on the bank of the Yamuna River, three miles from where Shah Jahan would later construct the Taj Mahal. I was told that I must not miss it, not for its own sake but because it was the direct antecedent of the Taj Mahal. I had no idea what to expect but I climbed into my taxi again and off we went. The three mile trip required an hour; we were caught in the worst traffic congestion that I had ever seen, in the middle of the very extended Agra city bazaar.

Itmad's tomb is only one storey and in a way it is very modest, built of white marble that is softened by a hint of beige, so that it is not at all as blinding as the Taj had been in the noonday sun an hour earlier. Its four minarets, one at each corner of the roof, do not soar far into the sky. They do something better. Their relative modesty is perfectly proportioned to the building they crown. The Tomb is situated in the middle of a large enclosure bordered on one side by the river and planted with flowering bushes. There was no one else there; I was all alone. The silence was electrifying; no human voice penetrated the serenity of this astonishing place. I examined with much care all the pietra dura work that

AGRA, Tomb of Itmad-ud-Daulah
The direct precursor of the Taj Mahal it testifies to the profound influence of Persian artistry and has a calm and serenity the Taj Mahal cannot match.

adorned every external wall. It is exquisite, even more brilliantly and intricately done than some of the similar work at the Taj Mahal. Inside, the inlay and the paintings, especially the flower paintings, match the virtuosity exhibited on the exterior. I had come here to see something that allegedly had inspired aspects of the Taj. I stayed to marvel at it for its own sake. I lingered for hours, simply overwhelmed. The virtuosity so proudly on display at the Taj Mahal, the Agra Fort and Fatehpur Sikri is, if not excelled, certainly matched. But here it is married to restraint and modesty that give to the whole creation the human proportions so evidently lacking at the other three sites. And that is why I walked away believing that my last visit had been in many ways my best and most memorable.

I decided I would spend my last several days in Delhi, revisiting places seen too briefly or too hurriedly before, until my last academic appearance at the University of Delhi. I wanted to spend some time at Qutb Minar again and at Humayun's Tomb and its charbagh gardens, and a dozen other sites where I wanted more time. Most of my last day was spent in Old Delhi in the neighborhood of the Jama Masjid, which looms over the whole town. It is by far the largest mosque in India, more than twice the size of the mosque that Akbar built at Fatehpur Sikri, and the last of the creations of Shah Jahan. Soon it was time to go to the University of Delhi, which was not far away. There I was warmly welcomed by Professors Pandeya and Chatterjee and their colleagues. Their plan was that I should lecture to the Philosophy Faculty and to a horde of graduate students from various disciplines for an hour and a half and then answer questions for as long as I was able. The audience was large and most appreciative; the questions were very interesting and virtually endless. But I had to halt the proceedings after three hours because I had completely lost my voice. Clutching a garland of blossoms I emerged from the university into the midst of early rush hour traffic when there was not a single free taxi to be found. Eventually in Chandni Chowk, I found a free motorized rickshaw with a Sikh driver. Such rickshaws were as common as cows on the streets of Delhi in 1978. Chandni Chowk is a legendary thoroughfare; Shah Jahan led majestic processions along it to the gateway of the Jama Masjid. Today it is always a hive of activity. a frenzy that is in strange contrast to the pace of the traffic that perpetually jams the street, where the Mercedes cars can move only at the plod of the overburdened donkeys that are invariably right in front of them.

The trip from the far side of Old Delhi to the Lodi Gardens on the far side of New Delhi in a three-wheeled motor rickshaw can take an hour and a half and more. So I had much time to reflect on my city tourism and its great oddity. As I have said, India describes itself as a secular state, although its people are overwhelmingly Hindu by a margin of about four to one. But in my travels around

Delhi I had visited or revisited a dozen and a half major monuments and all but three or four were Muslim sites--this was the oddity. My Sikh driver seemed to take me through every narrow street and winding alley and crowded bazaar in the old city and I loved every minute of it. I had seen such magnificence in stone during these happy months. But there is another sort of magnificence, equally mesmerizing in its own way, to be found in the bustle of the teeming bazaars, in the crowds of people so colorfully clad, so various, so strange and different from me. But I knew them now as my own kin, members of the same family, bound together in hopes of the promise that dawn would bring, no matter how variously the promise might be fulfilled in our different lives, theirs and mine.

So the rickshaw ride across the entirety of Delhi, old and new, was the most fitting conclusion I could have imagined to this long but deeply satisfying journey through environs that had increasingly become in some sense a second home. Then, just as we entered New Delhi, we were struck without warning by a violent sandstorm. These are not fun. Within a minute or two every inch of exposed skin begins to sting very painfully and one must keep eyes averted or shut tight, for the blowing sand can cause blindness. Then suddenly it was over, just as suddenly as it had begun. My driver charged me ten rupees for our very long trip and I added an extravagant five rupee tip--about two dollars, all told. So it turned out to be a good day for both of us. I was deeply thankful for my most important trip to India yet. But I was also very sad to leave behind in a few hours so many things I cherished so much.

The trip from Palam Airport to Dulles at night is very long and tedious, almost twenty hours in 1978, with only a single brief stop to refuel in Tehran. On my return flights from India I have never tried to read anything but only to sort out my memories of the trip. I do not know why, but in this particular night my thoughts kept returning to the alarming problems that India faced in 1978--or, more accurately, continued to refuse to face. There were many of them and they were all interrelated. Perhaps they can be catalogued under the twin rubrics, Socialism and Caste. Socialism does not like the first person singular. It means the centralization of civil authority that sooner or later strangles private enterprise and initiative. It has no tolerance for what is individual and particular, no patience with entrepreneurs, and so it does not understand what is most creative and critical for every developing society. In 1978, India was wedded to an economic model that had long since been abandoned almost everywhere except within the Soviet bloc. If the emphasis lies ultimately upon feeding the center, then one day all else will starve. So it is no wonder that one-third of the people in India were living below the poverty level in 1978. Nor should it be cause for surprise that at least one quarter of India's population is illiterate. The government pays far too little attention to public schooling, and education is certainly not a high priority for the rural poor. Illiteracy and poverty always go hand in hand and in India this is especially obvious because perhaps as many as ten percent of the populace are children who have either chosen or been forced to join the workforce. There is a direct link between Socialism, its excessive and onerous over-regulation of the economy, and poverty and illiteracy. India has not yet recognized that yesterday's answers will never resolve today's problems. Who or what will liberate this land? Is there anything that can release this giant from its chains?

On the other hand, perhaps no less insidious and destructive is the focus upon caste and status symbolism, matters of supreme importance to the society of the subcontinent. I want to link the thirst for status first of all to the uncontrolled population growth that is another massive problem for India today. This may seem to be an odd pairing but it is not. Most Indians live in rural areas and own or labor on very tiny farms. Indian peons have little reason to pay attention to conventional gauges of affluence but there is one standard that is everywhere acknowledged in rural India, the number of male children born to a man and his wife. The more there are, the more laborers there will be to work in the fields. Boys mean prosperity; their absence signifies deprivation. Girls mean hard times ahead, for someday each must be provided with a dowry. So there will not be many years of schooling for little boys; they are too valuable a commodity to be squandered so frivolously. Illiteracy is inevitably the companion of uncontrolled population growth, illiteracy and even greater poverty, because all the economic growth is being outstripped by population growth.

Of course there is no more profound and enduring affirmation of the importance of status than the caste system, which has survived for three millennia. There are four great Varnas or caste pools, although there are literally thousands of subcastes as well. At the top are the Brahmins who are priests and teachers; then come the Kshatriyas who comprise the warrior class; third are the Vaishyas, various sorts of shopkeepers and business people; below them are the Shudras, the laboring classes, and finally there are the Dalits, once called the Untouchables or, in the compassionate language of Gandhi, the Harijans. These unfortunates are the uncasted or outcasts. Certainly there have been great strides toward breaking down these thousands of caste distinctions in the years since Independence, but 3,000 years of a caste system cannot be expected to vanish without a trace so quickly. Membership in the third varna means that entrepreneurs and other would-be capitalists struggling against the reigning economic model are not much honored for their contributions to societal change. Now many places have been reserved in universities and in the civil service for Dalits, but still the completion of such reforms may require generations. Meanwhile it seems that all is static, resistant to significant change.

How is it possible to move from one varna to another? The only answer is Samsara, rebirth for a better life if one has lived well, rebirth perhaps as an animal if one has lived wickedly. But even if a Shudra somehow earns millions of rupees in this life he remains a Shudra still. There is a profound streak of fatalism in the Indian psyche which both reflects and reinforces the paralyzing social structure. Because history seems to be a cyclic affair, there is no reason to expect there will ever be anything new under the sun. So is it not rash even to dream of private initiatives and social mobility? Why should there not be a constant "Brain Drain" as people avail themselves of every opportunity to begin new careers in the West? The status gap between the varnas is large and important, but fades into relative insignificance beside the gender gap. The servitude and subjugation of women in traditional households can be, at least to Western eyes like mine, not much less than a crime. Of course women no longer need to immolate themselves on their husbands' funeral pyres, but they remain no more than second class citizens who often seem more their husband's property than his partner. Someday this too will change, but like all things Indian the pace of change may not be rapid. Illiteracy is half again as common among women as it is among men.

In a way, concern about status is at least one cause of what seems to me a profoundly misguided educational orientation. When I visited Udaipur in 1969 I discovered to my astonishment that every bellboy I met in the Lake Palace Hotel had a master's degree in English literature from the University of Udaipur. This seemed incredible to me but it is certainly what I was told. Whether this was a requirement stipulated by the hotel or simply a reflection of the fact that there were no other jobs available for young men with master's degrees in English literature and literary theory, at least not in Udaipur, I simply do not know. I do know their degrees were not guaranties of fluency in spoken English. What India needs, I thought then and now, are more people who can speak good and fluent English. What it does not need are more people versed in literary theory. We need simple interpreters and not arcane scholars, no matter how much more prestige the specialization affords. We need less theory, more application, less philosophy and religion, more science and mathematics.

Finally, I must mention the Indian Civil Service, a gift from the days of the Raj but with its own peculiarly Indian character because it is so incompetent. And it is incompetent because so many people have sought employment for the sake of the prestige and security of working for the government in posts where they are virtually guaranteed life tenure. So the emphasis is not on solving problems, devising innovations and developing skills but on getting the respect that is one's due, on the static and not the dynamic, on rewards and not achievements. There are other problems too and they are numerous--air pollution in all the big cities, corruption everywhere and in everything and, at least in my judgment, a profoundly inhibiting lack of pride. But I have focussed upon these because each of them is so integrally related to all the others: socialism, poverty, and illiteracy; security, the caste system, and population growth; gender inequality, the Civil Service, and educational theory. So what string does one pull to begin to unknot this tangled skein of problems so longstanding and so severe? I sat in the darkness as the plane flew over Afghanistan and thought about the notes I had made but I could find no solutions. After a while I put down my pen and then like everyone else I went quietly to sleep.

When I returned to Charlottesville I could scarcely have imagined that my next trip to India was less than 18 months away. `That bit of travel would be very brief, no more than six weeks of so, and it would take me to no new places but only to some I already knew rather well: Delhi, Bangalore, Patiala and Mysore. The reason for the 1980 trip was that I had decided to leave the University of Virginia after 13 years, almost all of them at the helm of the department of which I was founding chairman. Now I wanted to try my hand at something new. But our semester-in-India program in Mysore, to which I was very much committed, would be in some jeopardy if I did not pay it another visit, or so I was told. Why this was true I never really understood, but if Seshagiri and Nagaraja both told me that was the situation then it was indisputable. And so I went.

There was a full moon in a cloudless sky when the plane first touched down in Delhi and then in Bombay, bathing each city in its white radiance. As I have written before, there is much that dazzles and amazes the eyes in India, but it is really your nose that tells you where you are. Always the smells are what I have remembered, and they are what first has always welcomed me back again. My connecting flight to Bangalore was delayed until late the next morning, so Air India generously gave me a free room at the Centaur, a new five-star hotel on the airport grounds. When I finally arrived in Bangalore I was met by Nagaraja Rao; we were delighted to see one another again. We had to rush back to the city immediately, however, or we would have been late for the first of several meetings with the Karnataka Secretary of Education, a particularly important member of the Cabinet. We would have much to do with one another during these weeks.

Dr. Ashwathnarayan and I spent several hours together and I was much impressed by this genial and unpretentious man. It was still light when Nagaraj and I set off for Mysore and I marveled anew at what a garden city Bangalore is; there are millions of blue acacia and jacaranda trees and, best of all, millions of orange and red gulmahur trees, covered with so many blooms it is difficult to see any leaves. It was late spring and the fragrance of the blossoms was quite overwhelming. Nagaraj briefed me as we drove about all the people I needed to see; we arrived in Mysore about ten and soon found my suite at the Central Food Technology Research Institute, in the new dormitory where our Virginia semester-in-India students were quartered during their time in Mysore. The accommodations were not exotic but they were clean, comfortable and spacious. The next day I had appointments with Dr. Natarajan, the director of CFTRI, and with Dr. Hegde, Vice Chancellor of the University of Mysore. Both meetings turned out to be long but very pleasant and productive.

The morning after that was spent entirely with Drs. Nair and Manjrekar, the two senior professors at CFTRI under whose direction some of our students could participate in some food preservation research that CFTRI was engaged upon. I had a very interesting time with them both. The day was a major government holiday commemorating the Enlightenment of the Buddha; so I had a few free hours to wander around the city. It is surely no less one great garden than Bangalore. Everywhere I looked there were huge piles of fruit that all looked delectable--bananas, lemons, oranges, apples, mangos, papayas, coconuts, pineapples, grapes, dates, and much else that I could not identify. Then I went off to dinner with Dr. Hegde and another vice chancellor from Mangalore as well as various others. All of us sat talking and drinking Chivas Regal until well after one in the morning. By then Nagaraj and I were desperate to get away because we had to be awake by five in order to drive three hours to Bangalore for my very crowded day of critical meetings. The two most important were with the Chief Minister of Karnataka and the Minister of Education. I placed garlands of sandalwood blossoms, and quite beautiful I thought they were, around each of their necks. These two conversations were much more ceremonial than substantive but pleasant enough, nonetheless.

After that I met with the Chief Secretary and the Secretary to the Chief Minister; all I remember of these meetings is that the Chief Secretary and the Secretary to the Chief turned out to be two people and not one. Then I spent several hours once again with my friend the Secretary of Education, who impressed me much more than his Minister had. There were some briefer meetings with various other people before the day was done. On balance I was pleased. So, at the end of a 21-hour day after three hours of sleep, I was more than ready to fall into bed. I remember smiling to myself as I did so. As these busy but pleasant days became busy but pleasant weeks, who would ever have believed how many appointments seemed necessary just to keep my little program afloat? The morning after my meeting with the Chief Minister, my picture stared at me from the front page of nearly every newspaper in Karnataka, both those written in Kannada and those in English. This whole day was a reward for me; it was wonderful because I did not have a single meeting until late in the afternoon. I could just be a tourist again.

Nagaraj and I began it by returning to Srirangapatna, to see more of the island from which the rulers of Mysore had exercised their power for two centuries until the death in battle against the British of Tipu Sultan in 1799. My first visit to this place had been in early winter; now it was late spring and the seasonal change had really worked miracles in the gorgeous gardens. At my request, Nagaraj then drove us on to Somnathpur, for the Keshava Temple there was not only a favorite Hoysala site but a personal choice among all the shrines I had seen thus far in India. Once again we were the only visitors; nor were there many signs of any life at all in this impoverished village. On second acquaintance, Somnathpur did not disappoint. It dazzled me just as much as it had the first time I saw it and I counted myself blessed to stand again on this holy ground. But after two hours we had to return to Mysore because I had another long session scheduled with Dr. Ashwathnarayan, which was not an imposition at all because I much appreciated his company. We had a quite interesting conversation as usual and I asked him to join me for dinner the next evening. I had few nights in Mysore remaining that were free; Dr. Manjrekar had invited me to his home for one of them and Nagaraj and his family were expecting me for dinner and farewells on my last night in the city.

I felt very fortunate that we had our tourist day when we did, because there was a European Economic Community delegation, headed by Britain's Roy Jenkins, poised to descend on Mysore. Jenkins had written to Nagaraj to ask if he personally could offer the EEC contingent two brief tours, one of

Somnathpur and the other of the City Palace. Fine, I thought, but I did not want to share "my" temple with the EEC, whose presence there would probably double the number of Western visitors for the year. The next evening Nagaraj and I drove to the top of Chamundi Hill outside the city to watch the lights of Mysore and its surrounding plain wink on at dusk so far below us. We briefly visited a 2,000 year old temple there and paid our respects to a very famous Nandi nearby, 16 feet high and carved from a single rock. Then we drove back to Mysore to the City Palace because one night each week it is illuminated by 50,000 tiny lights and tonight was the night. This is a most beautiful scene which surely no visitor will ever be able to forget. It was Nagaraj who first created this display during his time as the curator of the palace. Mysore is the inhabited palace that I found more pleasing than any of the others I ever visited elsewhere in India. Its Indo-Saracenic architecture is simply matchless, even though it was not built until the last years of the 19th century.

My last four or five days in Mysore were rather a blur, although I did find three hours or more one afternoon to wander through the City Palace again. The architectural grandeur of its interior provides a home for such diverse and numerous treasures that the effect is finally quite overpowering. I also had several important meetings, one with Dr. Hegde at the university, another with Dr. Natarajan at CFTRI, as well as conferences with various lesser lights who might someday be useful to assure the welfare of my students. But soon it came time to leave. Nagaraj was able to drive me to Bangalore to catch a night flight to Bombay, where I could connect with a plane to Delhi that would arrive in the capital a few minutes after midnight. Nagaraj accompanied me to the gate, and I thanked him profusely for his many kindnesses to me and for all his efforts to insure that our semester-in-India program would continue to be a great success. Once again he had orchestrated all my appointments for me just as he had done in 1978 and I could never even have begun to do this for myself. He was an indispensable companion.

When I left him I felt confident that what had been so well begun was now in no jeopardy and would continue to thrive. I had to acknowledge, though, that my presence in Mysore again had proven quite essential. I had certainly made some new friends. We would have more American students in India and we would have more Indians visiting America. Finally I reached the India International Center in New Delhi a bit after one o'clock but I was received as graciously as ever despite the late hour. It was pleasant to be back in surroundings I knew rather well and where I had spent so many happy times. I fell into bed and when I awoke a whole day stretched out before me, all mine for rest and recreation after a few chores. The first pleasure was a long and leisurely walk in the Lodi Gardens, where our boys had spent so many days playing together while we lived in the Punjab. I spent all the next morning at our Embassy in a fascinating conversation with Bob Goheen, the former president of Princeton who had become one of the most popular ambassadors we ever sent to India. Bob had himself been born in Asia of missionary parents, and he was superbly conversant with India's problems and possibilities. We had a long and pleasant lunch together, just the two of us, and then I spent the afternoon with his second-in-command, the United States Minister, Archer K. Blood. When Bob was first offered the ambassadorship, he said he would accept on the condition that Arch could accompany him. Once that request would have been a huge problem, but the problem vanished when Mr. Carter entered the White House. As our senior diplomat in what was then East Pakistan and as a former chief of the Foreign Service, Arch had written what came to be known as "The Blood Cable" to the White House. It was signed by 40 career Foreign Service officers, asking the President to protest vigorously against Pakistan's slaughter of defenseless Bengali civilians, for if our nation kept silent it would be complicit in this genocide that eventually embraced perhaps as many as a million people. But Richard Nixon and Henry Kissinger did not protest because they did not want anything at all to jeopardize their planned China initiative.

Instead, Arch, probably no more than a year away from some important ambassadorship, was instantly recalled from East Pakistan and banished to the Army War College in Carlisle, Pennsylvania, where he remained until rescued by Bob Goheen. Arch told me years later, "I had to do it. I could not have lived with my conscience if I had not." In his quiet and humorous fashion, he was one of the most principled men I have ever known. He was a University of Virginia alumnus and was so greatly interested in our semester-in-India program that he came all the way to Mysore to make a site visit. Before I left the Embassy in the late afternoon Arch invited me to come to the Bloods' bungalow the next day for a swim and a late lunch. I accepted with much pleasure. The bungalow where Arch and Meg lived had once been the residence of Chester Bowles, who was perhaps the most beloved ambassador America ever sent to India--and it had a large and most welcoming swimming pool.

We drank Indian beer before our lunch while doing lazy laps; two servants scurried back and forth, up and down the pool, carrying our drinks, each glass in the custody of its own servant, so that at each end we could have a swallow of beer. This was a standard of service that I had never seen before and would never experience again. I stayed until almost dark and had a wonderful time. With so few days remaining before my return to America, I had less time than usual for Patiala, although I did have some obligations to fulfill there as well as in Delhi. But Patiala now had for me a bittersweet taste because so many of the people I had cherished there were now gone and the Bhavan where our department was quartered was now populated by a good many ghosts.

Bob Goheen suffered a serious coronary not long after I left Delhi and he was invalided home. He recovered well and later headed a prestigious national fellowship program from an office in Princeton. Archer Blood took his place in India for more than a year, which delighted Bob, whom I visited for a happy reunion in his new office. After the election of Mr. Reagan in 1984, Arch retired from the Foreign Service and settled in Virginia. I telephoned him soon after his return and invited him to come to Allegheny College as Diplomat in Residence and Professor of Political Science. Arch and Meg agreed. They made masses of friends at Allegheny, contributed enormously to the quality of life in the college, stayed for many years and certainly became two of our closest friends.

For twelve years my life had been bound up with the life of India. This was nothing I had sought or planned; it simply happened. It was unexpected and certainly undeserved. In all of this I was a patient, not an agent. Christians have a special word for a gift that comes from somewhere and someone else, entirely unexpected and entirely undeserved. The word is <u>grace.</u> Can grace be mediated to a Christian through Sikhs and Hindus? That is perhaps one of the few big questions in this world that I can answer without a doubt or a moment's hesitation. As the Air India jet flew through the night sky over Afghanistan, I saw in my mind's eye Seshagiri Rao as I had first encountered him so long ago. I am who I am in some part because of India and Seshagiri Rao, although I had not the faintest premonition of this on that August day in 1967 when we first met. He began it all for me when I surely would never have begun it for myself. As my old University of Edinburgh roommate titled his autobiography, <u>I Was Invited</u>. This is the strange stuff from which little miracles are made, like the one I met, now so many years ago, in the darkness of early evening in the crowded bazaar in Varanasi, the holy city of the Hindus.

CHAPTER FIVE

The Subcontinent 25 Years Later

A few days before Christmas in 2004, Christopher telephoned and in the course of our conversation told me not to expect a holiday package this year, although one had already arrived for Elaine. Instead, I should look for a Christmas morning e-mail. I was a bit disappointed because I always enjoyed packages from Kit, but then I forgot about it and even forgot to check for e-mail on Christmas morning until Elaine brought me a rather long letter at noon. These are the first and last paragraphs:

Dear Dad,

For this Christmas we are giving you and Mom a trip to India. Many years ago you gave me this present and it has been one of the most elemental building blocks of who I am and how I think about mankind, interpersonal relationships, a willingness to embrace others and my place in the world. I am forever grateful to you for that gift and so many others. I want to try and give a little bit back. You are a wonderful Dad, and I tell you that far too infrequently .... I love you. Your son, Kit .... and his lovely wife Elizabeth and beautiful daughters Ellie and Kit. Merry Christmas!!!!

The body of the letter was devoted to details. Kit ended with the stern admonition: "No corners can be cut."

I was astonished. Neither one of us had even mentioned India to the other for years. Nothing could have surprised me more. We telephoned and I thanked him most profusely for this extraordinary gift. But the truth is that I was also very shaken and ambivalent about all of this; in simpler words, I was more than a little scared. It had been 25 years since I had last set foot in India. I would soon be 73 years old. Three weeks unconscious in intensive care in a London hospital after an abdominal aortic aneurysm had schooled me thoroughly in the frailty that age can bring. So I had more or less pushed to the corner of my mind my passion to show Elaine in central and South India so many things that I had come to love so much. We had lived for a year in North India, of course, but I had never been able to take her to South India, where so much magic is. Elaine was utterly thrilled at the prospect of the trip, so I really had no option except to plunge into it. On March first, we left from Dulles for New Delhi.

We arrived at Indira Gandhi Airport on a Thursday mid-morning, more or less rested and fit after our very pleasant Virgin Atlantic upper-class flight. We were garlanded by the man who met us with marigolds and white zinnias, our two modest suitcases were stowed in the car, and off we went to The Imperial, the hotel where I had spent my first nights in India 36 years ago and to which I had first brought my family a year later. Suddenly my eye was caught by a balloon seller pedalling his bicycle on the other side of the road, several dozen helium-filled spheres bobbing behind him. The sight was gay and festive yet also a bit forlorn. His wares were so fragile, so ephemeral, and yet who knew how many elderly people and little children depended for their evening meal on what he could gain for his brightly colored toys? I wanted to run after him and buy all his balloons, give him a holiday; instead I thought, he is too far away, I am too late, and this is a very silly notion anyway.

There are now two hundred million more people in India than the last time I was in Delhi. The traffic testified to this; our driver, Ranouq, played bumper tag adroitly all the way to the hotel. Very soon everything was familiar to me again: Shantipath and Rajpath Roads, India Gate, the colossal Secretariat buildings, the great expanse of parkland, and Rashtrapati Bhavan, built for the British Raj but now home for the president of the world's largest democracy. This is Lutyens' India, designed by Sir Edwin Lutyens to display the matchless power of the Raj and to dwarf and humble the natives. Today it is a symbol of the strength of a great people to throw off the yoke of oppression and become masters of their own destiny. Soon the car turned down Janpath, and we passed countless millions of blossoms, yellow and red and purple and blue, before we arrived at the hotel. But something was missing: Delhi did not smell right. The magical elixir of fruits and spices and flowers and diesel fumes was gone. What had happened? Delhi had been one of the more polluted cities in the world, although its pollution was more automotive than industrial. Now all city buses and taxis and a good many lorries and other vehicles are fueled by compressed natural gas, a non-pollutant, and the problem has been dramatically reduced. How is it that, in comparison with Delhi, the United States has done so very little?

The improvement in air quality has done much to restore Delhi's reputation as a verdant garden city and "the greenest capital in the world." I am told the city can boast of approximately 4,000 gardens and parks accessible to the public. Some of them are huge and provide homes for 300 kinds of trees. Our second morning, quite early, we went to one of these, the thirty-acre Mughal garden surrounding Rashtrapati Bhavan, one of the finest Mughal gardens in India and open to the public annually for only a single month. No one has ever made more imaginative and beautiful use of water in gardens than the Mughals. More resplendent than the flowers, however, were the gorgeous and obviously expensive outfits worn by throngs of Indian ladies, many in their twenties and thirties. This was our first contact with the huge new Indian middle class; today it is the largest middle income group in the world. India has always been wealthy, but now there is a far more equitable distribution of wealth than had ever been true hitherto. All this has happened since the 1991 financial crisis when Manmohan Singh, who is now the Prime Minister, first became Minister of Finance and began to transform the Indian economy. All these women had come to the gardens in smart new cars, some of them driving themselves; that would have been unimaginable, even in 1980, when there was not a woman driver to be seen in all of New Delhi.

There is another dimension to this social change which is also noteworthy. Sunday morning we were in the crowded Red Fort, seeing once again the exquisite detail and wonderful proportions of Shah Jahan's architecture. His personal quarters, the public and private audience halls and the lawn near the Pearl Mosque were all very crowded with the same people we had seen at the Rashtrapati gardens, now accompanied by husbands as well as children. We did not see a single Western face and Gauri, our guide, told us the Indians were all local, not sightseers from other places. This new and rapidly expanding middle class is proud of its inheritance and thirsts for closer acquaintance with its heritage. These are not people in search of greener pastures; they are wealthy enough to travel wherever they want but they certainly have no intention of ever leaving home permanently. Pastures here have become as green as anyone could wish. In what new and different ways will the future be shaped by this well educated, staunchly nationalistic, very affluent and modern middle class with its constantly rising expectations? I think we are in for some real surprises.

We made several trips to Old Delhi or Shahjahanabad; the first was to revisit Shah Jahan's final creation, the Great Mosque or Jama Masjid, with its alternating stripes of white marble and red sandstone. One of the three largest mosques in the world, it is a vast building but not at all overwhelming. Its

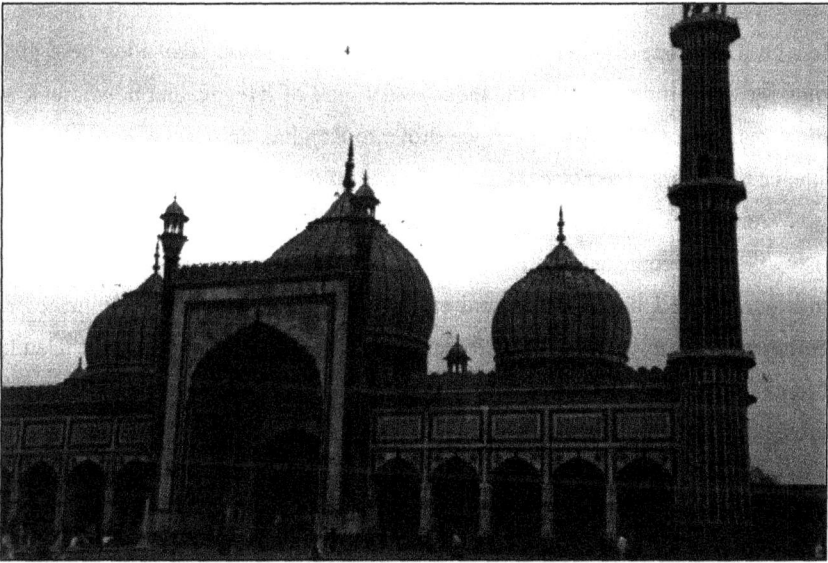

DELHI, Jama Masjid
Begun in 1656 this is the last structure designed by Shah Jahan. It is widely regarded as one of the most supremely beautiful houses of worship in the world.

perfectly proportioned domes and minarets rise gracefully into the sky and whisper a benediction upon all the children playing tag in the forecourt of the building they ornament. The mosque is approached by more than forty steep and treacherous steps and there are no railings. There is no way I could have climbed them if Ranouq had not held my hand very firmly in his. There is nothing remarkable about men holding hands in India; it is a token of friendship that is a daily commonplace. Here and again and again at other sites it gave me access to what otherwise I could never have seen. His hand made everything easy; without it much would have been impossible. As Ranouq and I left the mosque, I thought of my old friend and mentor at Edinburgh, John MacMurray, and his marvelous Gifford Lectures. The fundamental unit of human existence, John wrote, is not the individual but persons in relation, and the paradigm of this is a mother and child. A relational notion of selfhood has always been at the center of my thought and one of the chief sources of inspiration for me: always you and I together, never the self alone.

Coming and going to and from the Jama Masjid we had lingered in Chandni Chowk, once Shah Jahan's highway to prayer and now the bazaar that is the choked main artery of Old Delhi, where nearly four million people live more or less on top of one another. It is a fascinating locale. There is an alley here that runs for three miles, lined with shops every inch of its way, and nowhere is it more than three feet wide. Then we drove to Rajghat, an oasis of serenity and silence that marks the place where the Father of the Nation, Mohandas Gandhi, was cremated after his assassination in 1948. It is still visited every day by many devout people and there are always many fresh flowers placed there in his memory. Then I had a lovely and entirely unexpected surprise. We turned a corner and came upon the superb sculpture which commemorates the Dandi March, when Mahatma Gandhi led a great march from Ahmedabad to the sea in protest against the British imposition of a tax on salt produced in India. It was a memorable instance of the exercise of Gandhi's ultimate weapon, Satyagraha, non-violent resistance. The sculpture includes eleven figures, the first being Gandhi himself, and a picture of it graces the reverse of the 500 rupee banknote. This splendid work of art has always been a great favorite of mine. Seeing it so unexpectedly was a fine climax to a memorable day.

Much of the next day was free, so I asked Ranouq to drive us to the site of what was chronologically the first of Delhi's seven cities, the Qutb Minar complex that lies some miles south of the capital. I had never been there until now. Its highlight is a massive stone tower, once the tallest in the world, that rises some 234 feet in the air. The construction was begun in 1193, but it looks so freshly chiseled it could have been built only yesterday. The calligraphy that decorates it consists of Arabic verses from the Koran. It seems strange to speak of anything so huge as at the same time ineffably delicate and ethereal, yet that is the impression it had on me. The vast tower seems to float in space, but it is so firmly anchored to the earth that after eight centuries its 376 steps are still perfectly safe to climb. At its base there are the remnants of the first mosque built in India as well as some wonderful colonnades with a great variety of pillars. There is also a mysterious iron column from the fifth century that is 24 feet tall, entirely exposed to the elements, and yet after fifteen hundred years it has not a single trace of rust. The Qutb Minar complex is a remarkably serene and quiet place and very much deserves its status as a UNESCO World Heritage site.

We drove back to the city by way of Humayun's Tomb. Four storeys tall and set in a charbagh garden, it is constructed of red sandstone and black, white and yellow marble, each color complementing the others in a most harmonious way. Humayun was the second of the great Mughal emperors, and the father of Akbar. His memorial is one of two direct inspirations for the Taj Mahal. We also looked at the Bangla Sahib Gurdwara, a wonderfully beautiful building and perhaps the second most important Sikh shrine after the Golden Temple in Amritsar.

NEW DELHI, Humayun's Tomb
Built by the widow of the second great Mughal emperor. This testament of love
is the precursor of the Taj Mahal built by Humayun's great grandson.
Note especially the typical Mughal Charbagh garden.

But then it was time to hasten back to The Imperial again because Elaine had an appointment with the curator of the hotel's art. The Imperial has the largest collection in the world of paintings and prints and drawings produced in India during the days of the British Raj. There were a dozen handsome prints in our suite.

There was a small and unobtrusive sign in our bathroom saying that The Imperial provided bottled water as a courtesy to its clients, but that the tap water was eminently potable and refreshing. A quarter of a century earlier there was only one hotel in all of India that could make that claim, and it was in Bombay, not Delhi. This was another miracle, like the clean air we breathed in the city. At least wherever the tourism industry was active, water filtration and purification had greatly reduced health risks. Water had been the most virulent killer in the developing world for millennia; now, in a remarkably short span of time, the danger to visitors, at least, was much diminished. There have also been great efforts of one sort or another to acquaint the people with the dangers of impure water.

So there have been enormous strides in the battle against water and air pollution, much technological innovation, the achievement of a new level of affluence of which earlier generations could only dream, and a redistribution of income that begins to correct the injustices of days gone by. But modernization, like all things human, is filled with ambiguities. One example is marriage, which has always been a remarkably stable institution in India. Today these bonds are beginning to fray; perhaps as many as one in six is in some disarray. The new affluence is a major contributing factor, for it means that many people now have the economic freedom to extricate themselves from marital situations that they have come to find intolerable. There are many other ways too in which affluence seems to dissolve old ties and family bonds and erode traditional assumptions about right conduct. As hundreds of thousands of new cars pour from India's factories into the hands of the insatiable middle class, the highways and byways become ever more choked. Consumption far exceeds what the infrastructure will bear. As people in ever greater numbers purchase inexpensive bottled water, the nation is threatened with burial beneath a sea of plastic bottles, few of which are biodegradable. When I first knew India it was the cleanest country I had ever seen. Not only were standards of personal hygiene higher than at home, there was no litter anywhere because everything had some value for someone. It is different today. Affluence has deposited litter everywhere.

On our trip to Agra Ranouq stopped a few miles short of our destination so we could visit Akbar's tomb at Sikhandra. I was very interested but surprised to find it as charmless as I did. In Agra itself we encountered the worst traffic jam I have ever seen. The cacophony was deafening as every driver leaned on his or her horn. But no one seemed at all unhappy--no imprecations, rude gestures,

AGRA, Taj Mahal
As seen across a sea of green, the Taj Mahal at dawn from a room in the Oberoi Amarvilas, 600 yards away.

raised fists or rage. Eventually we reached the Oberoi Amarvilas, a dream of sandstone arches and wide reflecting pools and carved elephants all cradled in glorious gardens. Every room has a view of the Taj Mahal, which is less than half a mile away across a little sea of green treetops. I met our Agra host, Ankush Sharma, and each of us knew he had found a new friend. Ankush told me we had the best room in the hotel, number 425, because we were exactly facing the Taj, not at an angle to it.

Later we went to the Taj in a chauffeured golf cart, because cars were allowed no closer than the Amarvilas. Then Elaine and I went separate ways. Because I had been there a number of times, I wanted to sit in a deserted part of the garden and watch the play of light on its marble façade as the sun set and darkness fell. I had a marvelous time. Then we found our golf cart in the dark and went back to the Amarvilas, where we sat on our balcony and watched a troupe of acrobatic Rajasthani dancers perform by the pool below us. The next morning Ranouq met us after breakfast and we had an hour's drive through the countryside. This was the first time we had been able to see agricultural villages. We were astonished at how prosperous many of them seemed. There is certainly still great poverty in India, but it is not entirely a rural phenomenon. Even in 1980, the pace of traffic was set by the two-wheeled bullock cart; now it is established by thousands upon thousands of large new John Deere tractors. In the fields there were women at work, harvesting potatoes and millet.

Our destination was a favorite place of mine, Fatehpur Sikri, the imperial capital that Akbar built. Its red sandstone architecture is very well preserved. We had it much to ourselves; there were fewer tourists than I had expected and no Westerners at all. European visitors during its brief life as the Mughal capital wrote that its population and its grandeur were both far greater than could be found in London. We spent several splendid hours walking around the remnants of the city, and then made our way back to Agra in the early afternoon. Our progress was a bit slow because this was Lord Siva's birthday. The streets outside temples were thronged and there were little processions of holy water bearers ("Ganges water") trudging along the highway with amazing frequency.

It is important to see the Taj Mahal at different times of day as well as in the moonlight, because the white marble changes its hues from one hour to the next. This morning we had been awakened by hundreds of small songbirds nesting in the luxuriant bougainvillaea beneath our balcony. We sat in bed for several hours as the Taj began to emerge from the pre-dawn mists and then swan into the light of day, changing from grey to white and then to pink and many other pastel shades as well as molten gold. It was a fascinating time that was repeated every morning and yet each day was different. But we also needed to be there not long after noon, because you really need full sun to appreciate the intricacy of the inlay of semi-precious stones. This is the greatest glory of the Taj, apart from its perfect proportions: the little flowers and leaves and vines that are set into the white marble, so exquisitely and delicately crafted.

The next day, after we watched from our bed while the morning sun roused the Taj Mahal from the mists it wore at night and painted it with a dozen lovely and subtle shades, we met Ranouq and set off for what I hoped would be one of the great surprises of the whole trip for Elaine. Our destination was only three or four miles from the Amarvilas, but we had to negotiate an extremely narrow and very long bridge that was never intended for two lanes of traffic, and then we had to proceed the length of Old Agra and its bazaar. But our reward was huge: the tomb of Itmad-ud-Daulah. The monument is set in a beautiful garden, where a class from a neighboring school came to play. But we had the memorial to ourselves.

The artisans who created the memorial brought with them much yellow and brown Persian marble and their use of intricate marble inlay in the Persian style is the first instance of this in India. Its prominence at the Taj Mahal suggests that Itmad-ud-Daulah served as a model and inspiration for the later work. The marble screens, as intricate as lace, rival those at Fatehpur Sikri and the floral inlay that graces the exterior is in no way inferior to that

AGRA, Tomb of Itmad-ud-Daulah
The wonderful complexity of the exterior is captured in a photograph of the entrance to the tomb.

AGRA, Taj Mahal
This memorial is not dazzling white marble although it is sometimes described that way. The exterior is inlaid with black marble Qu'ranic calligraphy of wondrous delicacy and beauty.

of the Taj. The beauty of the calligraphy on the monument is wonderful. I have seen no other tourists to speak of at this uniquely enchanting place, so serene and meticulously kept. Obviously it is not well known and it is a bit inconvenient to visit, but it is one of my half dozen favorite places in all of India. It appeals all the more because it never hosts a crowd.

When we left the tomb we drove to the Agra Fort, where Elaine had planned an extended visit. Eventually, however, the heat of the afternoon sun led us to retreat to the Amarvilas. Later our chauffeured golf cart reappeared so that we could revisit the Taj Mahal and examine more extensively some of the best of its inlay. Although it was very crowded we stayed for a long time and found several corners of the garden where we could sit undisturbed. As the sun set, our little vehicle returned us to the hotel, satisfied and thankful. The birds below our balcony awakened us as usual so that we could watch the Taj emerge from its slumber and dress itself from its limitless wardrobe of pastels. But then we had to hasten to the railroad station to meet the Shatabdi Express, which would carry us to Jhansi. There were only two or three other passengers in the entire carriage and they disembarked in Gwalior. We were the only people bound for Jhansi. A car and driver were waiting for us there and we set off for the town of Khajuraho, five hours away.

The views from both train and car were of sere and cheerless land where nothing grew, treeless and unpopulated. This terrain bore not a trace of a print of a human hand or foot; it seemed to be just as it must have been on the first day of creation, indifferent and inhospitable. Khajuraho is a rather small and charmless place in the middle of nowhere. There is no access to it by rail, air transport seems to be canceled as often as not, there is no attractive city anywhere nearby, and the main road approaching the town is the worst I have ever been forced to travel. In the town itself--inhabited by some 20,000 souls, which is rather minuscule by Indian standards--there is no industry; everything depends upon the annual deluge of tourists who come, like the yearly monsoon, with wonderful regularity. Khajuraho has twenty-six or so Jain and Hindu temples, mainly from the tenth century, which are weathered almost not at all and which constitute the greatest architectural legacy in all of central and northern India before the advent of the Mughals. The entire temple area has been declared a UNESCO World Heritage site.

Khajuraho is known in some circles as the world's premier garden of sculptured pornography. Erotic yes, pornographic no. What is the difference? I suppose I would be the last person to know, but I will hazard at least a few comments, for I have had high regard for this place since I first saw it thirty-six years ago. First, I think of pornography as joyless; these temple reliefs brim with joy, joy because people are freely being together with one another. Second, I think of pornography as filled with awkwardness, while everything here is of arresting beauty and sinuousness and spontaneity. Third, I think of pornography as rather clinical; in other words, every last thing is on display and nothing is left unstated. In contrast, everything at Khajuraho suggests there are mysteries yet to be unravelled and dimensions still unseen. Pornography is created by crude people; Khajuraho was made by some of the greatest sculptors the world has ever seen. Perhaps this can all be summed up by saying that the key is simply harmony and unity: everything fits with everything else in testimony to the beneficence of the Creator. Everything says with disciplined exuberance, life is very good. The temples have countless portrayals of ordinary life and certainly sexuality is a part of it. All together this is a fabulous record of what Indian life was like in the tenth century.

Our driver and guide appeared the next morning shortly before ten and we set off for the Western Group of the temples. These are the most impressive and I have already described the three most important of them, Lakshmana and Vishvanath and Kandariya Mahadev, which is reputed to be one of the supreme examples of sacred architecture to be found anywhere in India. They and numerous others are all clustered close together in a beautiful and immaculate park. Even though they were built by the Chandela Dynasty, they look as though they were newly carved, for the granite and extremely durable sandstone show only very moderate weathering. The plinths on which they stand are very high and the steps are numerous, steep and uneven. Both of us needed a helping hand at every shrine. The Devi Jagdamba Temple has a roof which internally resembles the amazing one at Kandariya Mahadev. Originally dedicated to Vishnu it is now Shaivite and it has an extremely fine three-faced statue of Siva. The Chitragupta Temple is devoted to the sun god and contains a large and splendid carving of Surya with his chariot and horses ready to mount the heavens. On the exterior walls there are lovely reliefs of musicians and dancers, artisans at work, royal processions and animals locked in combat. But the one Khajuraho image that has always remained most memorable for me is at Lakshmana Temple, the carving of a young maiden gently pulling a thorn from the foot of her lover. All of this can be seen comfortably in three hours, and so we went on to visit briefly the Eastern Temple Group.

When we returned to the Taj Chandela we were quite tired and so we decided to spend the remaining hours of daylight at the pool. The hotel was modest compared with where we had been, but it could not be faulted for failing to try very hard. We had dinner in the handsome gardens in the midst of a grove of neem trees from which hung thousands of fairy lights that softly illuminated the night. After the meal we visited the hotel shops and Elaine found much clothing she wanted to buy. Everything had to be custom-tailored for her, of course, but the shopkeeper said all would be ready early in the morning. He did not disappoint us; everything fit perfectly. A few hours later we left our beautifully manicured patch of tenth century temples and then traveled to Varanasi in a Boeing 737 so new and burnished this could have been its maiden flight. Such was our introduction to Jet Airways, which we have come to believe is the finest domestic airline anywhere. It is said that if you live in Varanasi and are cremated on the river bank and your ashes are spread on the Ganges, you will be liberated from the otherwise endless cycle of death and rebirth. Mother Ganga is life-bringing but the force of her water

KHAJURAHO, Western Group of Temples
Perhaps nothing in India rivals the two dozen temples that comprise the Western Group of sacred architecture in this village. Pay special attention to the shikharas and especially to Kandariya Mahadev. The temples are adorned with thousands of apsaras and mithunas like these.

is such that she would also be life-destroying, were its fall from the heavens not modulated by the intervention of Lord Siva, whose city this is.

Just as dusk began to soften the edges of the shops and houses of the town, we set off for the holy river, no great distance away but the drive required more than an hour because it was through the city bazaar. Possibly there is no other quite like it. What is disorienting is the simple mass of it, the unbelievable density of the crowd. It is oceanic, countless irresistible waves overwhelming everyone.

Eventually we arrived at the bathing ghats, to which we had come to watch the evening Aarti worship, the Hindu puja asking Mother Ganga to relieve the sufferings of the world and of one's own self. We found the little boat we had hired and set out on the breast of the holy river, our guide and our oarsman and the two of us. We were rowed all the way to the cremation ghat, where there can be as many as a hundred cremations in a few hours. We bumped against the ghat and from there we watched six or eight of the fires. There were quite a few other bodies on the steps awaiting their turns. As we drifted back downstream we saw a brilliant sliver in the dark sky; it was the second night of the new moon and there was not a single cloud overhead.

We made our offerings to Mother Ganga, which were intricately crafted little flower boats, each with a lighted candle in it, and set them adrift. Then we moored amidst a great tangle of small boats filled with townspeople waiting for the aarti ceremony. There were half a dozen priests chanting and solemnly dancing on the ghat. Finally they brought out great trees of lights to hold at bay the surrounding dark. Somehow I managed to stumble up the steps from the ghat in the darkness and we found our car. This was March twelfth, the 75th anniversary of the Dandi March, when Gandhi led his great non-violent civil disobedience in protest against the tax the British were trying to levy on Indian salt. Where better to spend such a memorable anniversary than on a Ganges ghat? Where better than in very close proximity to where I had stood, so bewildered, so alone, when I was a young man visiting the land for the first time?

It had been thirty-six years ago when I had first found myself or more accurately lost myself in the Varanasi city bazaar near the bathing ghats on the Ganges. I had felt then overwhelmed by this maelstrom of humanness, this endless cataract of bodies that fused into an organism with a heartbeat of its own, pulsating at a tempo no individual could hasten or slow. Robbed of my personal space, I was simply a moment, a spasm, a tic within a larger whole that dwarfed and then devoured me, a scrap of flotsam on a flood tide that overpowered everything in its path and dictated the speed and direction in which all else moved. But I was a part of what had engulfed me; it was not hostile but a guide and a guardian.

My memories of that night have always been elusive; I remember best just the sobbing that shook my body until I could not walk any longer in a normal way. Part of whatever it was that happened to me was simply the physical contact, something from which I had shrunk all my life long. I liked people to keep their distance; I was always uncomfortable with violations of my personal space. Now I was constantly being touched, shoved, pushed and jostled, stumbled against and thrown off balance, touched by the inquisitive fingers of curious people in response to my obvious foreignness. Except that I was not a foreigner, at least not any longer. I was fully a part of this river of bodies that flowed ineluctably down to the river of life swirling ahead of us, the Mother of rivers. There was nothing at all impolite or rude or impatient about this physical contact. It was simply enforced on everyone as all these separate bodies seemed to coalesce into a greater reality with its own rhythms and independent life.

I think it is fitting to speak of that night in terms of revelation, by which I mean that I was given a new place, a new angle of vision, from which I could see things that I had never noticed before, a new perspective on what was old and familiar until it divulged new secrets I never knew it held. Revelation means a gift of sight, something we cannot give or will to ourselves. It is conferred on us from we know not where. Revelation means an expansion and enhancement of our vision so that we can capture and learn to love aspects of reality that have long been present with us but which have been unrecognized or dismissed or thought of little value. There is a circularity in this: revelation affords us a store of new imagery and the new imagery further sharpens our vision and perhaps inspires a new love. Seeing is the prius and foundation of moral life, the indispensable prelude to action, as I have written so often. Everything depends upon the health and acuity of our sight and imagination, both literally and figuratively understood.

What happened to me that night in the darkness on the bank of the Ganges? After months of travel the carapace of my Westernness was somehow shattered, my preoccupations and usual concerns left behind; a veil was lifted, light struck down into the dusk where I had been living, and I saw--saw in its alienness, its mystery, its incomprehensibility, its squalor, its endless variety, its overwhelming beauty--India. And my life would never be the same again. All these preoccupied bodies that brushed against me were so different from me and yet no different from me at all. All of us were kin. I had come home in a foreign land and the land would draw me back again and again. This was a different homecoming because it was a home I did not know. So this homecoming was at once joyful and solemn, a gift and a challenge. I have written some pages in Christian ethics about the importance of placement and of all the satisfaction that we gain from being in the right place. I think all of it goes back to the Varanasi bazaar and its overwhelming crowd.

Early the next morning we drove three or four miles from the hotel to Sarnath, a place that figures as prominently in the Buddhist tradition as Varanasi does in the Hindu. It is a holy place because it was in the Deer Park here that the Buddha preached his first sermon after his enlightenment under the Bodhi tree, the tree of wisdom. Sarnath was destroyed by Mughal invaders centuries ago; what remains is the great stupa erected by Emperor Ashoka in the third century before Christ to commemorate the exact place where the Buddha proclaimed the Four Noble Truths and the Eightfold Path of the Middle Way. There is a contemporary shrine nearby where most visitors pause for at least a few minutes. There one can read the text of the Buddha's first sermon in many languages, including English. The shrine is shaded by a great and ancient bodhi tree which is reputed to be the "grandchild" of the one under which Siddharta Gautama sat and meditated. We picked up three perfect bodhi leaves that had fallen from the tree and brought them back to Charlottesville. The Sarnath Museum is small but choice. In the foyer there is the capital of the great pillar that Ashoka raised beside the stupa; they are contemporaneous. The capital is crowned by four magnificent standing lions. Beneath their feet is the Wheel of the Law, Dharma or right conduct, of which they are the guardians. Inscribed on the wheel are the four strongest beasts in the animal kingdom, a bull, an elephant, a horse and a lion. The capital is seven feet tall; it is sandstone but has been polished until it gleams like marble.

In the mid-afternoon we began a city tour that was quite interesting because the surfeit of temples was broken by a long and tranquil time at Benares Hindu University, where I remember having once given a talk. It is a strikingly beautiful and green campus where there are accommodations for 20,000 students. This is the largest residential university in all of Asia and its academic standards are first-rate. When we left Varanasi the next day I hoped we would be at the Taj Mahal Hotel in Mumbai by six. It was not to be. We arrived well after midnight because of a long delay in New Delhi that was caused by air traffic control problems. But Jet Airways did its best to make our time as pleasant as possible and plied us with excellent food and drink. We never got to bed until four o'clock and so we used the next day for rest and relaxation. We needed it; we had been traveling hard. We were in a Taj Club room, which meant that we had our own lounge where we could have breakfast or tea or enjoy cocktails and canapes in the evening, all this at no charge.

Our Mumbai guide was waiting for us at 8:30 the next morning and we walked across the road and past the Gateway of India to the ferry pier. Our destination was Elephanta Island, where I had first been introduced to great Indian sacred art more than two dozen years earlier. But I was eager for Elaine to see this 7th century rock-cut shrine dedicated to Siva and which is another World Heritage site. Our ferry took an hour to cross the nine nautical miles between the mainland and the island; it was a fascinating trip across one of the world's busiest harbors, skirting a huge double pipeline that carries crude oil from tankers to a refinery. After slipping and sliding and sloshing ashore, we clambered aboard a pleasant little toy train that carried us a mile or two to the foot of the basalt hillside which is crowned by Elephanta's temple. We were surprised to find there were two sedan chairs waiting for us, with five peons lounging by each of them--four to handle the stout poles to which each chair was affixed and the fifth to be a spare tire. The climb was quite long and involved 120 steps, sometimes very steep and often uneven. Two or three times the bearers had to stop and rest.

Then we had a wonderful visit to Lord Siva's domain until it was time to begin the whole journey again to return to the Taj Mahal--the sedan chair, the toy train, the ferry and a short walk. The whole adventure took between six and seven hours but it was thoroughly worthwhile. We came down from the temple just as we had ascended, passengers facing the mountain rather than the sea. This contributed to better balance and it was less intimidating for the passenger. We were both grateful for the sedan chairs, although no one could ever claim that is a comfortable way to travel. A columned verandah with three bays welcomes the visitor to the temple, which has a forest of fluted columns which divide into bays the nearly 17,000 square feet the shrine occupies in the flank of the mountain. In the central recess facing the entrance there is the unforgettable 18 foot high Mahesamurti, a Lord Siva with three faces; on the left he appears as the destroyer, on the right as the creator, and in the center as the world's preserver. The sculptors have awarded to Siva the roles of Brahma and Vishnu as well. The companion carved panels that decorate all the walls tell stories of Siva's life and I have discussed each of them earlier. We reached the hotel in time for afternoon tea and looked down at the Gateway of India from our window in the lounge, watching some ferries come and go in its shadow. We were amazed by how many scores of little boats there were clustered together asleep on the motionless sea.

The next day began with a brief visit to the handsome University of Mumbai. Because the city is one of the great financial capitals of the world, many of its buildings are nothing short of majestic. When one thinks of Victorian Gothic architecture, one tends to think of London and Glasgow because, after all, these were cities in Queen Victoria's own land. In fact, however, a large share of perhaps the greatest Victorian Gothic architecture is on this side of the Arabian Sea in Calcutta and Mumbai. We stopped briefly beside the central railway station, Victoria Terminus, which stretches for more than a third of a mile and welcomes something like three and a half million commuters every day. It is an architectural marvel with lavish Victorian embellishments and ornamentation. Then we went to Crawford Market, the great fruit and vegetable establishment whose legions of merchants serve some fifteen million people. It would be very difficult to exaggerate the color and variety and frenzy of activity always on display at this Victorian Gothic landmark. I was very pleased to be here again.

Then we needed a respite, which we found in the charming Hanging Gardens atop Malabar Hill. It was great fun to see all the fascinating animal topiary. Our next stop was at the most important Jain temple in Mumbai. The reverence for all life which characterizes this community marks it as a particularly estimable religious tradition. I was impressed by the extraordinary amount of activity within the temple precincts. There were many worshippers and many white-clad priests and nuns, many bells and chimes and voices raised in prayer, and yet the scene was quite tranquil in comparison with the extraordinary bustle in a typical Hindu temple. We went on from there to the Parsi Towers of Silence on the summit of Malabar Hill. Mumbai holds much of the wealth of India and the Parsis hold much of the wealth of Mumbai. They are the last remnants of the ancient Zoroastrian religious tradition, people who were forced to flee Muslim persecution in Iran more than a thousand years ago. Mumbai welcomed them, albeit reluctantly, and under the British Raj and Independence they have played a crucial and beneficial role that has served all of India very well, even though most of them choose not to venture far from Mumbai. Parsis undertake no missionary activity at all, although their charitable works are wonderfully generous. Visitors are not permitted inside their fire temples or near the Towers of Silence, and they do not marry outside their own religious tradition.

Our next visit was to Mumbai's busiest dhobi ghat. Today there are more than 5,000 families involved in the laundry business in the city and they all work together at several locations. Clothes are beaten clean against large stones. We are visiting the only country on earth where hundreds of thousands of people spend their lives breaking boulders by beating them with cotton and silk. This same day service provides immaculately cleaned and pressed clothes but sometimes their life span is shorter than one might have hoped. A dhobi ghat is a marvelously colorful place. An added bonus for us was a passing local train with many hundreds of people on the roofs of the carriages and hundreds more hanging out of windows and doors. We paused for a few minutes on Laburnam Street at the Gujarati bungalow where Mahatma Gandhi had resided during the 1920s and 1930s. It was quite an elegant place, much more so than I would have expected. Our final visit was to the Prince of Wales Museum, one of the finest in all of India. My eyesight did not permit me to enjoy the miniature paintings that are among its finest treasures, but I was fascinated by the small but fine collection of Indus Valley artifacts fashioned more than 3,500 years ago.

During our last cocktail hour in the Taj Club we feasted on some superb cheeses and biscuits and decided to let that serve as our dinner because of our pre-dawn departure for Aurangabad. Even at five in the morning there were many people on the streets, some of them jogging, others still asleep on the sidewalks; many taxis were already preparing for the morning rush hours. Most taxis today are fueled by compressed natural gas like the buses in New Delhi. This is terribly important for pollution control because the city has 75,000 taxis. We were in Aurangabad before 8:30 and our guide and car and driver were awaiting us. This is said to be India's fastest growing city. When I was here in 1978 I believe the population was in the neighborhood of 55,000. Today there are wildly differing estimates, ranging from ten to 25 times that number. But whatever an accurate count might prove, this is exponential growth with which no infrastructure could possibly keep pace.

Our destination today was another UNESCO World Heritage location, Ellora, where there are 34 temples and monks' dormitories carved out of a basalt mountainside in the course of the six centuries between 300 and 900 A.D. Many centuries ago Ellora was a rest stop on the great spice route that traders frequented every year. What makes this site especially interesting is the variety of traditions that flourished here. Sites one through twelve are Buddhist, one a shrine and all the others monastic dormitories. The most impressive is number ten, which is brilliantly and intricately carved and houses a massive statue of the Buddha teaching his disciples. The cave also has a superb ribbed ceiling. Then the visitor moves from the serenity of the Buddhist creations to the exuberance and tremendous vitality of the Hindu shrines, of which there are eighteen. The final four temples are Jain. We began our survey at site 32, a splendid Jain shrine with an arresting sculpture of Mahavira, the last of the twenty-four great Jain sages. Our guide for this tour was excellent, thoughtful and immensely learned about Ellora. He took us next to site twenty-nine, which is the second largest of all the shrines, because it is a direct precursor of Elephanta, which he knew we had seen only a day or two earlier. I was astonished by its proportions; even though I had been to Ellora once before, I had forgotten how vast this temple is. Its many pillars are strikingly reminiscent of Elephanta. It is also a Shaivite shrine, created about the year 550, perhaps a century or less before Elephanta was completed. The friezes of Siva as cosmic dancer, of the wedding of Siva and Parvati, of Siva's victory over Ravana when the demon was trying to shake Kailasa, and Siva throwing dice with Parvati were all reminiscent of what we had seen at Elephanta but in a considerably better state of preservation.

Finally we came to site sixteen, Kailash, named for Siva's mythical home on Mount Kailasa in the Tibetan Himalayas, which I mentioned at some length earlier. This temple by itself captures UNESCO World Heritage status for Ellora. It is one of the most magnificent creations ever devised by the human mind and heart. Kailasa is the largest monolithic sculpture in the world, several times as large as the Parthenon and far larger than Abu Simbal. The army of inspired artisans who created this matchless masterpiece had to excavate more than three million cubic feet of solid rock with only the simplest tools. Virtually every scrap of the surface of the temple has been carved with great delicacy and intricacy. Thousands of divinities and other celestial beings, as well as humans and especially mithunas or amorous couples, and birds and animals both real and imagined, and everything else in all creation appear on the walls of Kailasa. The base of the sanctuary is covered with stories from the Mahabharata and the Ramayana. The lowest band of carvings consists of wonderful elephants that are obviously straining to support the great weight of grandeur they are carrying on their backs. Kailasa is a superb encyclopedia of Hinduism and probably this structure deserves to be called the greatest expression of Hindu faith in the world. It was difficult to tear ourselves away from such a feast for the eyes as this, but the heat in this part of the great Deccan plateau is very intense. We stopped across a small valley to look back at the panorama Ellora offered: the thirty-four ornate entrances stretched in a single line along the mountainside for three and a half kilometers. What must it have been like in the days when camel caravans on the spice route stopped here to rest and refresh themselves? And how did they mix, the merchants and the monks?

The next morning when we set out for Ajanta I was delighted to find that the very uneven old road has been replaced by a splendid new toll highway. This area has been in the grip of a serious drought for four years but the fields at the roadside were all bursting with nature's bounty because the land management and water management offices in Aurangabad are operating very effectively and their supervisory efforts are a sign of considerable progress. Cotton gins had huge piles of snowy cotton waiting to be processed, the seeds to be used for linseed oil. The fields were planted with sunflowers, wheat, millet, onions, sugar cane, maize, chickpeas, chilis, lentils, perhaps as many as twenty varieties of mango and other crops. There are many signs of prosperity in the villages in this part of the Deccan. New brick homes are replacing dilapidated old mud and dung structures. Telecom towers are sprouting everywhere as village women earn a good living by charging others who would like to borrow their cell phones. Our highway seems canopied because it is lined with so many leafy trees. Indian forest management seems exemplary to me; the trees have painted stripes as a warning they must not be vandalized in any way. When we get to Ajanta we must leave our car and board an eco-friendly bus to travel the last few miles.

There are twenty-nine shrines and monasteries at Ajanta, all of them Buddhist and built between 250 B.C. and 600 A.D, when the site was abandoned for mysterious reasons and the monks moved to Ellora. The existence of Ellora was always known, but Ajanta was forgotten entirely for a dozen centuries until it was accidentally rediscovered by a British soldier in 1819. The caves were hollowed from the side of a very steep ravine through which a small river rampages during the monsoon months. Walking is very treacherous, often on the edge of deep chasms, and really more demanding than old frames like ours can comfortably manage. So we once again had recourse to bearers and sedan chairs which ferried us up and down and back and forth over hundreds of sometimes difficult steps. The pathways at Ajanta are narrow and twisting; there is something quite claustrophobic about Ajanta in comparison with the spaciousness of Ellora. Nevertheless, this is the great statement of Buddhism in the subcontinent and among the greatest in all of Asia. I must confess that I was appalled at the degeneration of the frescoes since I first saw them in 1978. There are rumors that the caves will be closed to tourists within the next ten years and visitors will have to make do with replicas erected in the valley below. That may seem unthinkable now but it may prove a necessity, for tourist breath is one of the most corrosive and toxic agents we know. Ajanta has no single stellar attraction the way Ellora does in Kailasa; all of the shrines are fascinating in their different ways.

Site one is among the very best of them, with cells for as many as two dozen monks. There is a huge seated Buddha in the cave but what is most memorable is a superb fresco of Padmapani, a bodhisattva who is holding a lotus in his hand. This may be the finest of all the images at Ajanta because, apart from its great beauty, this monastery never had any residents, and so no smoke from cooking fires ever damaged the Padmapani fresco. The second shrine has some excellent sculptures on its facade; equally notable are some reasonably well preserved frescoes that portray the birth of the Buddha. There is also a very splendid ceiling here. The ninth and tenth sites are probably the oldest. The tenth is dominated by a huge and impressive stupa in the prayer hall; it also has some lovely frescoes. Site sixteen continues the story of the Buddha's birth that begins in site two, but its most memorable fresco depicts a princess swooning when she learns that Nanda, her husband, is leaving her to become a monk. The next cave is really the Ajanta art gallery, with many frescoes in fair condition. We see the Buddha taming a rampaging elephant, a prince and a princess making love, charming scenes of women grooming themselves, and an encounter with the man-eating ogresses of Ceylon. Meanwhile, heavenly maidens fly effortlessly above our heads. Cave nineteen has some very fine sculpture and lovely frescoes as well. We stayed a long time at Ajanta and it was good to return to our air-conditioned car, for the temperature had hovered between 106 and 108. What should be stressed is not only that these rock-cut shrines are beautiful, although they certainly are that, but simply that they are here at all, still preserved more or less well in the midst of this wild and remote ravine, an inhospitable and virtually inaccessible ravine in semi-desert where no one lives. The miracle, if it can be described as such, is that these ornate and intricately decorated shrines were constructed two millennia ago in solid stone by people who had no tools except hammers and the crudest chisels.

On Sunday morning we had another very early flight. This was no World Heritage day; but one of the hazards of travel is that sometimes one must actually travel. We arrived in Mumbai seven hours before our connecting flight left for Bangalore. Jet Airways had announced schedule changes for the summer more than a month before our trip, but our American travel agent in New York never notified us. That bungle left us spending hours in airports we would have preferred to spend elsewhere. The representative who met us in Mumbai said we had fifteen minutes to catch the morning flight to Bangalore if he could arrange new tickets for us. He did but then we had security problems that would have delayed us for a long time if the security people themselves had not closed down their own operation and pitched in to help us because they knew we had only a few minutes before boarding would be closed. Meanwhile, our luggage was transferred to the earlier plane and the Bangalore Oberoi was notified that we would arrive seven hours early. Both the travel representative and the driver in Bangalore had to be routed from their beds, for they had been up most of the night waiting for delayed arrivals on some international flight.

There is a moral in this story, although I must be careful not to romanticize it. The travel person who met us in the Mumbai airport, the several security officers who went far out of their way to help us, the Jet Airways personnel and the people from the Bangalore hotel who got out of their beds several hours early to meet us are quite typical. The ordinary Indian really will go out of his or her way to make your life more pleasant. Obviously this is not always the case but it is certainly true more often than not. If you are in need an Indian will not cross the street to pass you by; more often than not he will come to your assistance and share whatever meagre resources are his. You must be careful not to admire anything in his or her home, for if you do you will find to your embarrassment that it is now yours. I have never seen worse traffic jams than in India, notably in Agra and Varanasi. But they are sorted out and almost never does anyone display the slightest trace of anger or even of impatience.

There really is a pervasive sense of decency here, a politeness and graciousness that Westerners find it difficult to understand and certainly not easy to emulate. There is a negative aspect to this: sometimes Indians are uncomfortable with change because it threatens to be disruptive; sometimes they tell us whatever they know we want to hear because they want to shelter us from unpleasantness. By and large Indians cut in the traditional mold are not as aggressive, not as sometimes ruthless and self-centered, and therefore not always as successful in business or finance as their Western counterparts. But who would not prefer to live in such an environment? Time and again I am humbled by virtues that I cannot even pretend to share. Sometimes I hear this described by Westerners as Indian "spirituality." I am skeptical of such language, for what impresses me is not the expression of any form of religious faith but simply a cultural phenomenon that appears here and there throughout a whole civilization. But whatever you want to call it, this is something very special.

❋ ❋ ❋

CHAPTER SIX

Highways to Treasures

The Bangalore Oberoi is a superb hotel and its service is impeccable. Our balcony was unusually attractive. In the evening we ate a fine Thai dinner in the garden under the stars. Rightly called "The Garden City," Bangalore is the Silicon Valley of India with a modernity and affluence and cleanliness and level of education that are not matched elsewhere. Our driver, Krishna, gave us a brief tour of the city on our way west to Mysore, three or four hours away. The public buildings are outstanding; when we passed the colonnaded Mythic Society I remembered that I had lectured there years ago. We stopped at Srirangapatna as we approached Mysore to visit the summer palace of Tipu Sultan; it is filled with wonderful frescoes of his military exploits against the British.

Eventually we arrived at our hotel, the Lalitha Mahal Palace, which until the early 1970s had been the guest palace of the Maharajah. It was originally built for a state visit by the British Raj. The hotel had only one or two other guests, so we were given our choice of any room in the palace. We chose one on the wide gallery that overlooks the city and that is framed by eighteen massive Corinthian columns. The room was approximately 900 square feet and had an eighteen foot ceiling. We had wonderfully decorated mosquito netting that was draped all around the bed. We were urged to be careful not to leave our door open, for if we did we would soon be dispossessed by the monkeys that passed by on the gallery. Our old friend Nagaraja Rao joined us for cocktails at the hotel and we had a joyous reunion. He and I had done so many things together that it was great fun to reminisce about some of our adventures. Nagaraj had been Director of Art and Archeology for eighteen years and curator of the Mysore city palace, which he had first opened to the public in the 1970s. Then he finished his government career by serving a three-year term in New Delhi as the Director General of the Archeological Survey of India. This is a Cabinet-level post, for the ASI is responsible for some agricultural affairs as well as the conservation and maintenance of all India's antiquities.

On our drive from Bangalore we had seen much of the luxuriant bounty of the farms in Karnataka--endless rice paddies wearing their distinctive shade of green, oceans of sugar cane, many banana and pineapple plantations, millet and other grains, an incredible variety of vegetables, mulberry bushes to feed the silkworms, jacaranda trees and endless blooms the names of which I did not know. All that drive-by window shopping had given us healthy appetites. When we went to the dining room we were the only guests. They turned on the lights for us and then two musicians began to play in honor of our arrival, one on the tabla or drums and the other on the sitar. The Mangalore fish curry was magnificent. The dining room had once been the ballroom of the palace and I have seen very few rooms of any sort as ornate as this rococo chamber. We certainly felt that we had been transported to some other era.

If I were asked why I thought someone should come to India, I suspect that I might answer, Somnathpur. This is no World Heritage site and I think there is not one chance in a million that it will ever be so designated. The little temple lies no more than eighteen miles from the Lalitha Mahal. It was one of the three or four sites I had most wanted Elaine to see; it is my favorite temple. This is not a trip for the faint-hearted, for the road really is one of the worst I have ever seen in my whole life. Once or twice our car briefly managed a brisk trot but most of the time our progress was only marginally faster than walking. Almost all vehicles we saw were double-yoked bullock carts. No tourist bus could ever negotiate this road. I have never been in more seemingly rural India. The tiny villages are clearly very prosperous today, however; everyone has electricity and the paint on the sunbaked brick homes was usually fresh and clean. What an amazing difference since I last traveled this road in 1980, when deprivation was everywhere to be seen. Now everything is quite idyllic except for the sensation of traveling inside a cement mixer at full throttle.

No sign announces Somnathpur; it is simply a crossroads with perhaps two dozen tidy little mud brick dwellings with thatched palm roofs. There is a gate to the temple precincts to deter all motor traffic but we were VIPs and so the gates were opened for us. There is a beautifully manicured lawn of eight or ten acres with flowering bushes and fine trees. The temple is surrounded by a lovely cloister where one is always sheltered from the harsh South Indian sun. Most of the cloister pillars are thirteenth century, very polished and exquisite, although some toward the rear are sixteenth century and not nearly so good. The cloister itself is framed by a gorgeous stand of palms which do much to enhance the whole prospect. Somnathpur was built in the mid-thirteenth century at the behest of one of the senior ministers of the Hoysala court. It is the only Hoysala temple extant that was ever fully completed and even though it suffered a bit of damage at Muslim hands over the centuries it was never badly defaced or vandalized.

The Keshava Temple at Somnathpur is a small and modest affair. It has five little towers crowning its single storey and from a distance they seem diminutive and even pedestrian in comparison with the high arching shikharas of Khajuraho and the far taller gopurams of Kanchipuram and most notably of all at the truly horrible Minakshi Temple in Madurai. But beauty need not be grand. The temple sits on a high star-shaped plinth and the angles of this base are reproduced all the way up the external walls of the temple. I know of no place where greater attention has been given to proportion than here in the Hoysala temples, except perhaps at Agra. The external surfaces are alive with carvings that are truly exquisite and everything has weathered the centuries so well that it might have been made only a few years ago. The reason for its astonishing condition, as I have said earlier, is the stone used in the construction. This is a shrine dedicated to Vishnu; he and his consort Lakshmi and all his ten avatars can be found in different poses and in many places.

Six bands of decoration, each eight inches high, run entirely around the temple just above its base. Above these and below the fabulously carved shikharas there is a great variety of much larger statuary, crafted with much delicacy and attention to detail. Maidens human and celestial have dozens of different hair styles. The points of spears are still sharp, the filigree crisp, the shields elaborately detailed. On a sculpture of Lakshmi one can actually feel the fingernails of the goddess and the wrinkles in the flesh of her hand. Each of the Hoysala temples is a differently edited encyclopedia of Hinduism. Somnathpur is the only one of them to have three sanctuaries, although they are very small and the whole temple could not contain comfortably more than 25 or 30 people. The ceilings of these sanctuaries are absolutely breathtaking and each is different.

My first two visits to Somnathpur were with Nagaraja Rao and on neither occasion did we see another soul in or near the temple precincts. Today there were perhaps a dozen people who appeared in the course of two hours but they were quiet and appreciative and, of course, all Indians. I have never been anywhere more serene and I never have seen anything in this world that has filled me with greater awe. At the Lalitha Mahal last night Nagaraj told me that he had been waiting for 15 years for me to write a grand coffee table book about Hoysala temple architecture or at the very least a long article for National Geographic. I told him I had been waiting all these years for him to do it and that I knew next to nothing compared to him; after all, he had been Director General of everything ancient or important or beautiful in the whole subcontinent. But there was still no book or even a lengthy article in a major magazine and few people have ever been privileged to see all of this, and fewer still who were from some other country.

Krishna told me that we should leave no later than seven the next morning if we were to accomplish comfortably all that I wanted to do. Driving on a great many Indian roads is punishment and sometimes the punishment is extreme. Today was certainly a time of such extreme and protracted punishment. But this was a trip to which I was absolutely committed, a visit to the two other major Hoysala temples, one at Belur and the other at Halebid, both of which are 12th century and therefore antedate Somnathpur by a hundred years. Krishna drove us to Belur in not much more than three hours, which was quite a feat. The temple is flat-roofed--although I am not sure it began its life that way--and this has always detracted a bit from its beauty in my eyes. There are many subordinate buildings close by, including a marriage hall and a wonderfully elaborate great stone Garuda, a mythical bird which is Vishnu's mount and an important Vaishnavite symbol. The whole complex is surrounded by a cloister or colonnade but it lacks the beauty of Somnathpur because it is at such a remove from the main temple that it seems unrelated. The temple rests on the usual star-shaped plinth and the external walls of the shrine conform to this design.

The lowest decorative band encircling the temple consists of 650 elephants found in different positions and with different expressions. But they all seem to bear the weight of the shrine on their backs. Above them there are bands of lions and then horses, then geometrical and floral patterns and, at eye-level and in a pre-eminent position, pictures from the narrative of the Ramayana. Above the epic there are larger carved bracket figures that are the particular glory of Belur. The star-shape of everything means that the external walls offer far more space for carving than any other shape would provide, and the artisans of Belur have used it consummately well. There are more than ten thousand magnificent sculptures decorating this temple. Inside the building the ceilings are simply wonderful and there are more of the splendid bracket figures of celestial maidens. The interior columns are all different and, like those at Somnathpur, look hand-lathed and are highly polished; columns are a very important component of Hoysala architecture and they are usually elaborately carved. By the entrance to the temple there is the emblem of the Hoysala kings, a stalwart boy killing a lion. Outside the temple there is a footprint that is thought to belong to Vishnu, and here the devout can gather for worship whenever the sanctuary is closed. Belur is a very busy temple. We watched a large party assemble in the wedding pavilion, the women resplendent in their brightest colors and most lavishly gold-threaded saris.

Halebid lies only a half an hour away; it supplanted Belur as the capital of the Hoysala kingdom in the 12th century. The Muslim invaders who spared Belur showed no such mercy at Halebid. The temple was never completed, construction having been interrupted by the fortunes of war. There is no colonnade at all, simply a beautifully maintained park in the midst of what is now a very small village. Halebid is much the largest of the Hoysala temples; actually it is two almost identical temples side by side, one for the devotions of the king and the other for his consort. The temples are yoked but distinct, and yet all of it coalesces in a unity of overwhelming beauty and harmony. Halebid is a shrine dedicated to Siva and therefore behind the temples there are linked pavilions for two Nandis. It is said that the highly decorated Nandi behind the temple for the king's worship is the finest image of the sacred bull anywhere in India. Behind this pavilion there is another one, a small subordinate shrine dedicated to Surya, the Sun God. As one might expect of a double Hoysala temple with two sanctuaries, there are more than twice as many sculptures at Halebid than there are at Belur, more than 20,000 and each one seems to be a masterpiece. The composition of the bands that decorate the base of the shrine is no different than at Belur, but somehow everything seems fresher, more alive and majestic and breathtaking. So it is important to see Belur first and then come along to Halebid. There is no comparable artistry done in stone in the 12th century anywhere else in the world that I know of. This is it. This is the best.

Part of the secret of the Hoysala temples, of course, was the use of chloritic schist, but more important were the eyes and hands of the artisans and the unlimited time at their disposal, the leisure that is the matrix of creativity. I will not repeat what I have already written about Belur and Somnathpur; it is all here again at Halebid, except that now it is writ large--109 most ornately carved columns rather than half as many, two platforms for sacred dances instead of one. Even though I have seen many Hindu temples I have never seen another double shrine like the one at Halebid; its sculptures deserve many days of study. From all this fabulous exuberance we drove for an hour or so to one of the most tranquil and simple religious sites in all of India, the tenth century statue of a Jain Tirthankara near Sravanabelagola. This is one of the most important Jain pilgrimage destinations anywhere in India.

Begun in the year 981 the enormous statue of Bahubali or Gomateswara is one of the tallest carved monoliths in the world, reaching 58 feet into the sky. It is simply a representation of a naked man who is a symbol of worldly renunciation. Bahubali stood motionless for a year contemplating the meaning of life after renouncing his kingdom. His lower limbs are covered with ivy and creepers to reflect this discipline. Bahubali stands unclothed and unadorned, freed by his act of renunciation and finally at peace. We looked at him from afar, for the only access to the statue is by more than 640 very treacherous and uneven steps carved in a steep hillside, although throngs of people young and old manage the climb every year. From there we went back to the Lalitha Mahal for some well deserved rest. Dinner in our magnificent ballroom was excellent as usual and there were only two or three other guests.

As we drove to Belur Elaine noticed large patches of the road were covered by stalks of millet and rice. She asked Krishna for the reason and he told her it was for threshing, to separate the grain from the chaff. All day cars and lorries and bullock carts rumble over the harvest amd then as evening approaches the grain on the road is carefully collected and taken back to the village. I had asked the same question nearly thirty years ago in Tamil Nadu on an Archeological Survey expedition, part of the reason for which was to introduce me to the Green Revolution, the amazing impact of petrochemical fertilizers on agricultural productivity in India. The farming we have seen in Karnataka reaps bountiful rewards and creates much affluence but still huge problems persist, and winnowing grain by allowing lorries to dribble oil on it is no improvement on the situation that existed half a century ago. As the old axiom has it, the more things change the more they remain the same.

The next day belonged entirely to Nagaraja Rao. We set out with three objectives: to visit his favorite charity, a school for little deaf children; to visit the institute he has just created for American and Canadian university students who want to spend a semester studying in India; and to explore the Mysore City Palace. The school for deaf children was for both of us a wonderful and unforgettable experience. There are currently 86 children, some as young as eighteen months and a few as old as fourteen years. Each child is there with his or her mother. There are no barriers to admission; every race, color, creed, caste or clan is welcome without any regard for how much someone can pay or whether he or she can pay anything at all. There is only one requirement: no child is admitted without his or her mother in residence. There is a hostel that can accommodate 26 mothers with their children, and others can find good quarters close by. We encountered a very happy scene. Every mother and child sit near others in a spacious room or well-lit corridor busy at work learning in all sorts of ways. Because mothers do become impatient with their offspring, they change places during the day, and this enables the children to learn to read the lips of different people. All wear hearing aids to maximize whatever hearing they may have. The whole course of instruction usually requires three or four years, after which the children are able to be integrated into ordinary classrooms. When the children enter normal schools their mothers are expected to tutor other deaf children and their mothers. So all the mothers and all the children become seed corn, so to speak, from which in future generations a truly glorious harvest may be made.

As we made <u>namaste</u> gestures to the children they smiled and made namaste signs to us. Then we took their little hands in ours, careful that we held every one. The head counselor and principal is a handsome woman in her early forties who came here simply as the mother of a deaf child and then chose to remain as the superintendent. She spent more than an hour very graciously explaining the curriculum and Elaine was delighted to recognize so many similarities with her own teaching of dyslexic children. The principal's son is now a university graduate who holds a fine position with IBM. The school has just launched a capital campaign for a new building that will house several laboratories. The building and the equipment for it will cost forty lakhs of rupees or one hundred thousand American dollars. It is hard to believe that so much good can be achieved with such a modest amount of money. The school is supported by the West Mysore Rotary Club and Nagaraj is its president this year. My time there was an experience I will always treasure. After the visit Nagaraj told me that Seshagiri had especially wanted me to see it.

Nagaraj's own new institute is literally just around the corner from the school for deaf children. It has beautiful old trees set in very pleasant grounds. The modern building has a fine reception area and lounge, a kitchen and attractive dining hall, an auditorium and lecture hall and classroom, a library and a computer room and some offices. The dormitory has twenty single rooms and four doubles, each with a small balcony and excellent western-style bathroom with shower. All the rooms are large, light, airy and immaculate. There is good transportation from this suburban area to the center of the city and the handsome University of Mysore is only a stone's throw away. I would have loved for my University of Virginia program to have been quartered here, but we would have required twice as many rooms. I explored with Nagaraj the possibility that the facility could be used by American seniors who might come for two or three week short courses and then tour Indian art and architecture for two weeks with Nagaraj. The facility is most attractive but simple and it would not be appropriate for people who insisted on five-star luxury. The furniture is Scandinavian.

After our host gave me my first ever glass of watermelon juice, we set off for the palace. This is one palace that really brings one to one's knees; it is awesome, stupendous, unbelievable. We had to see it with Nagaraj because there is no one else who has his total access to everything. We were met at the doors by some ASI personnel and palace officials who accompanied us on our long and exhausting but quite wonderful tour. It was made somewhat easier because we used corridors from which the public was excluded and we rested for some time on elephant footstools in the trophy room, where we sat among a very adversarial collection of animals from here, there and everywhere. It adjoined the armory, which had a magnificent hoard of weapons as well as a beautifully carved Burmese teak ceiling and floor.

The most important and unique rooms in the palace are the Durbar Hall and the magnificent pillared corridor that borders it, the Marriage Hall and the exquisite private Durbar Hall. Perhaps the most remarkable single item in all this Indo-Saracenic splendor is the Maharajah's golden howdah, the elephant seat on which he and his predecessors sat during the annual ceremonial processions. The howdah is fashioned from exactly 176 pounds of pure 22 carat gold. But its opulence is almost rivaled by the wonderfully hammered silver doors rescued from the old palace and several fabulous ivory inlaid doors as well. The fly whisks used by His Highness in his howdah were also ivory, two tusks incredibly carved for half their length into the thinnest of ribbons. A great mural of the annual Durbar parade covers the walls of the Marriage Hall. The stained glass ceiling crafted in Glasgow has a peacock design which is replicated in the floor. The turquoise blue and gold and white pillars that border the Durbar Hall are one of the most amazing architectural decorations that I have ever seen. There are more such pillars in the private audience chamber, which is where the antique silver doors are hung. In this room and some other places there is splendid inlay done with semi-precious gems. The Maharajah's family, the Wodeyars, was long regarded as not only one of the wealthiest but one of the most enlightened of the world's ruling families. After Independence the Maharajah of Mysore was chosen by acclamation to be the first governor of the state of Karnataka.

Nagaraj joined us for dinner at the hotel; we thanked him and said our farewells and he promised to visit us in Charlottesville in the late autumn. The next morning Krishna drove us to the airport outside Bangalore. In the car there were fresh flowers; Krishna never traveled without them, usually jasmine or bougainvillaea. Our time at the Lalitha Mahal had been important for us because this "Heritage" establishment had been our only truly Indian hotel on the trip. It was difficult to say goodbye to Krishna; he had become a real friend. Today is Good Friday, surely the strangest one I have ever spent, driving for four hours to Bangalore and then flying to Madras or Chennai as it is called now.

Our car and driver were waiting for us in Chennai and drove us to the Hotel Chola, where I had first stayed 27 years ago. It is much different now and we had a large and elegant suite. Everything was very lovely except that the passenger lifts do not work and so we must use the freight elevators. So we ride up and down with the hotel sweepers and other odd bodies in what is truly a classless society. This is one way to overcome social inequality but I doubt it will ever become wildly popular. When I first stayed at the Chola I was a guest of the ASI. The three senior officers came to the hotel to collect me and I invited them to my room for morning tea before we embarked on our first expedition. We had a fine time and then went to the elevator still chatting. We stood in the lift and chatted some more until it finally dawned on me that I was the only one who knew how to make the elevator work. So I crossed the lift and pressed the button marked Down.

Here is a parable about modernization and we must make of it whatever we will. Modernity had certainly come to Madras 27 years ago and more, for there were many lifts functioning in the city then, some of them already ancient. But my three senior architects of the petrochemical revolution in Indian agriculture in Tamil Nadu did not know how to make one of them work. Today everyone in Chennai knows how lifts function, except that these in the Chola do not actually move. Then we had the hardware without the knowledge. Today we have the knowledge but the hardware is kaput. This seems a fair summary of much of our ordinary experience. We had a leisurely first morning in Chennai, for which we were grateful. In the afternoon we were scheduled for a city tour and even though the temperature will be about 106 the car will be well air-conditioned.

As you fly into the city you are very conscious that you are in the south of India; the predominant colors are green and white, white painted walls on all the buildings and green palms everywhere and of every description. But the coconut palm takes pride of place because every scrap of it has some significant use until nothing at all remains. Coconut water is the most hygienic drink available in the country. Madras was built by the British for the East India Company which began here, but to tell the truth, there is very little to see. We have come here like most tourists in order to visit what lies elsewhere. Even so, the first stop on our tour brought us to something enormously important that I was especially eager for Elaine to see. We went to the Bronze Gallery in what is now named the Chennai Museum; when I first visited, it was the National Museum of Madras. The Bronze Gallery is a single balconied room with no more than one or two hundred artifacts but it is still one of India's finest small museums, in part because of its superb eleventh century Chola Dynasty bronzes. One is an astonishingly beautiful figure of Siva as Androgyne, half man and half woman. The femininity of the left side is exquisitely delicate and the musculature of the right is utterly remarkable.

But at the end of the hall was what I had really come to see again and show Elaine for the first time: the bronze of Siva Nataraja, Siva the Lord of the Dance, posing within the circlet of fire that is our universe. There are millions of statues and carvings on the same subject fashioned in the course of thousands of years, albeit often smaller and cruder, but this is the one, the peerless and classic work of utter genius by someone whose name has long since been lost. The sculpture is quite small; its diameter is probably little more than two feet. Even so, the figure is electrifying. Siva in the Hindu trinity is the Destroyer, but unless there is destruction there can be no new creation, just as there would be no oak trees if acorns did not die away from their parents and fall into the soil. Stasis is death; life is motility, motion, movement. As Lord of the Dance it is Siva who brings life and dynamics to the world. The Mahesamurti at Elephanta Island has good reason to portray Siva performing the roles of Brahma and Vishnu as well as his own. Creativity must destroy whatever is opposed to creation or else nothing can be protected and preserved. So the world when it is truly seen discloses itself as a great cosmic dance; it is the play of the gods and all of us who dwell within it are players too.

What made this such an important occasion for me is that there are two images of India that are of unsurpassable importance. The first is the four-headed lion pillar of Ashoka in the museum at Sarnath, which is the symbol of Indian nationhood. The other is the eleventh century Chola bronze of Siva Nataraja in the Chennai Museum which is the symbol of Indian civilization. Perhaps the latter is the more widely known of the two. Now, toward the beginning and toward the end of this extraordinary trip, I have had the opportunity to revisit them both and to show them to Elaine. They capture not only the heart and soul of India but so much of what I believe. Ashoka and Siva Nataraja, the lawgiver and the cosmic dancer—law and liberty, form and vitality, order and dynamism, the two of them together and never either one alone, for without them both no one could be a player or a dancer. There can be no game without rules and no dancer can disregard his partner. Is not saying this what my whole career has been about, the inseparability of Ashoka and Siva Nataraja? Has not my topic always been, in one way or another, relationality? Humanness means two persons together and not one alone. We can try to play and dance alone, of course, but these are always best done together, and for that we need rules, norms and shared expectations.

When we left the Chennai Museum we drove through the central markets of the old city, an area called George Town, on our way to Fort St. George, which was the original redoubt of the British East India Company. Today the fort is very much in use by a host of government agencies and it is the seat of the Tamil Nadu state administration. We stopped to visit St. Mary's Church, the oldest Anglican church in India and the first Anglican church to be built outside Europe. It opened in 1680. The British governor of Madras who brought the East India Company to dominate so much of India, Robert Clive, resided at Fort St. George and worshipped in St. Mary's. So did another early governor, Elihu Yale, who sent from here the gift that enabled colonists in Connecticut to establish a little college they named in his honor, my own alma mater.

Next we drove along the Marina, the astonishing beach that is the eastern border of Chennai. The white sand is between 200 and 300 yards wide and stretches for more than ten miles. There are few beaches that can rival it. Nevertheless, virtually no one swims here, not so much because of pollution or fear of sharks but simply because very few Indians swim at all and women in

Western-style swimsuits would be very much at risk. The Bay of Bengal seemed very beautiful, just as had the Arabian Sea ten days earlier as we looked down upon it from the Taj Club above the Gateway of India. Several hundred miles south of us the sea and the bay touch each other and marry and that is the Indian Ocean. There is a splendid statue of Gandhi on the Marina. When we left there we did several less interesting things. We visited the Basilica of St. Thomas where some people believe the doubting disciple of Jesus is interred. Then we explored the largest Hindu temple in Chennai but it held no more allure than the basilica. The nearby shops selling offerings were more interesting. Our city tour left me with a question for which I have no answer. The greatest Victorian Gothic architecture in the world is in Glasgow and London and Calcutta and Mumbai. It has always struck me as odd that in Madras, the home of the East India Company where the British imprint is so strong, there should be no Victorian architecture at all. But there is none. The greatest public buildings are the High Court and the University, both of which are quite remarkable complexes in Indo-Saracenic style rather like the city palace in Mysore, but lacking its delicacy and airiness. The Hindu temple concluded our Holy Saturday. We retired to the Chola and its residents' lounge for canapes and drinks.

Since I just used the words "Holy Saturday" I should probably add a footnote about India as a secular state. If it really is, then why is the whole nation now celebrating a four day Easter holiday weekend with all government offices tightly closed? The answer, as set out in India's Constitution, is that the word "secular" does not mean here what it does in the West. In Indian usage, secularity means tolerance, openness, willingness to embrace diversity. It is the opposite of dogmatism and ideology and it is always the foe of partiality, preference and favoritism. India is a Hindu nation, but Hinduism is not necessarily a religion as that word is understood in the West. It has little of the exclusivist emphasis that characterizes Islam, Judaism and Christianity. Hinduism sometimes means little more than that you or your parents were born within the confines of the subcontinent. You can be a polytheist, a theist, a pantheist, an agnostic or an atheist; pick yet a different option and you will still be welcomed within the broad embrace of Hinduism. When you are told that Pakistan or Iran is an Islamic republic, that is a very different kettle of fish. It can seem to legitimate much repression because of an exclusivism which most Hindus simply do not share. Needless to say, one should be wary of people who want to talk about a Christian nation, for such talk can also bring serious repression in its wake. In any event, secularism in India does not mean anything a religious or anti-religious; on the contrary, it says to religions, the more the merrier.

Easter morning was quite fine in its way. We decided we wanted to worship at St. Mary's and set off at 8:30 through utterly deserted streets. But life was abroad; as we drove north along the Marina we passed hundreds upon hundreds of men and boys playing cricket on the sand. The congregation numbered about 140 people; I think we were the only Westerners. I liked the preacher very much; he was not particularly charismatic but I thought he was quite sensible and solid. I felt there was a genuinely deep rapport between the man and his congregation and I was very glad that we were there. Then we drove south for an hour and a half to the small town of Mahabalipuram, on the coast south of Chennai. I was a bit apprehensive about the trip because the Boxing Day tsunami did strike here although it wrought even greater havoc much farther south. So I was completely surprised to find no wreckage of any sort anywhere. This great cruel mouth of water, that swallowed so many and so much, digested all it destroyed so that when the waters receded they carried with them everything they had splintered and smashed. The shore now had very few trees and no villages at all, but it looked as though it had not changed in a hundred years. In fact, there had been dozens of small fishing villages and groves of toddy palms all along the shore. One of my favorite photographs was of life in such a community. Now the village has been erased and its only memorial is ten or a dozen refugee camps for tsunami survivors along the beach.

The first of the major seventh-century monuments at Mahabalipuram is Arjuna's Penance, the enormous bas-relief that is my favorite antiquity in the town. Just to the left of it there is another bas-relief, smaller but still gargantuan. This is the Krishna Mandapam. It portrays Krishna raising a mountain in order to use it to shelter mankind from destructive floods. At some distance from these two reliefs there are the Five Rathas, which are named for five princely Pandava brothers who figure prominently in the Mahabharata. Ratha means chariot but I fail to see any relationship whatsoever between these five small temples and chariots of any description. What the Five Rathas do give us, however, is the best short course there is on the evolution of South Indian sacred architecture around the 7th century.

Finally we visited the Shore Temple. Now it is sadly eroded by wind and waves, but it was a hugely influential prototype for the later development of temple architecture in South India. Unfortunately but perhaps inevitably it is now guarded by a retaining wall that keeps the Bay of Bengal at a distance. Although the tsunami dislodged a few large stones, it did no more extensive damage because of this new wall. When I first came to the Shore Temple I was able to swim right up to its foundation. There is one other phenomenon at Mahabalipuram that attracts the attention of many visitors even though humans had nothing to do with it. This is a gigantic boulder perched on a very steep incline where it has rested since time immemorial. No one understands why it does not roll on down the hill and crush scores of people passing by. It is called Krishna's Butterball because according to legend Krishna was extremely fond of butter and on occasion could not resist stealing balls of it from other people. All in all, the Mahabalipuram antiquities are an indispensable textbook for the study of South Indian temples and their differences from those in the North like Khajuraho. Later, back at the Chola, we had cocktails and canapes in the residents' lounge and ate omelettes for our Easter dinner.

The next morning was reserved for Kanchipuram, one of the seven holy cities of Hinduism, which lies several hours southwest of Madras. This is farming country but it was sere and brown during these months before the monsoons. Our trip solved the mystery of why I remembered so little from my earlier visit: there really is not very much that is memorable in Kanchipuram and what there is I did not see. When it was the capital of the Pallava Empire from the 7th to the 10th centuries, it was known as the city of a thousand temples. Our first destination was the Ekambaranathar Temple which was constructed in the early 9th century. It is dedicated to Siva and is absolutely huge. It has a fine large tank or pool for the ablutions of worshippers where a number of Brahmin priests were bathing. But what is most remarkable are the 9th century columns, about 600 of them, which are richly and strikingly carved in most attractive ways. This is a very busy temple and a popular center of pilgrimage because of a mango tree within its precincts which is said to be more than 3,000 years old and beneath which, or so the legends have it, Siva and Parvati were married. We were told that it bears four quite different varieties of mango at the same time. Hindus around the world decorate their wedding sites with mango leaves in homage to the tree at Ekambaranathar.

Why had I not visited here in 1978? I have no idea but it seems a very strange omission, all the more so because of its fame and the fact that my guides were Hindus. In front of the temple is a gopuram or gate that is ten storeys tall. I am not fond of such things, although they are ubiquitous at South Indian shrines. They represent to me the degeneration of Hindu spirituality, especially when these often garishly painted edifices tower over the far more ancient temples to which they lead. Our second destination, Kailasanatha, is a tiny shrine I had visited in 1978; it was commissioned in the 8th century by the same Pallava king who had built the Shore Temple. Kailasanatha represents an evolutionary step, because it has a granite foundation beneath a sort of sandstone that was more amenable to the sculptor's craft. Unfortunately, however, this sandstone has weathered very badly. The Nandi at this shrine is especially charming.

But part of our reason for coming to Kanchipuram was that we had squandered a good many hours trying to find some presents to bring back to America and we had found nothing at all. There really is very little that would be appropriate because one of the impacts of modernization is the decline of old handicrafts which are no longer practiced either as widely or as well. Many toys are still beguiling, but often they are decorated with lead-based paints. Kanchipuram promised a possible remedy because it has been known for many generations as the place where the finest silks in the whole subcontinent can be found. The silk industry here gives a good living for more than half the population. The city is extremely picturesque because everywhere there are skeins of brilliantly colored silk thread drying in the sun. In any event we spent a very long and pleasant time in the best of the silk and sari stores. We both were delighted by two heavy silk saris, one a rich and lustrous burgundy and the other a dazzling apple green. What splendid gifts for our daughters-in-law, or so we thought, for they could have the silk tailored to make lovely suits. So, flushed with triumph, we made our way back to Chennai. Our plane leaves early tomorrow morning for Bhubaneswar, our last destination before returning to Delhi for our flight to London. Unfortunately, Jet Airways does not fly to Bhubaneswar at the moment, and so we have no option but to travel on my old nemesis, Indian Airlines.

Since I mentioned the decline of handicrafts as technological advance creates countless new employment opportunities, let me add another word about modernization. If I no longer wish to practice the craft that my ancestors have mastered for a dozen generations, then does not my relationship with my family change profoundly? If I no longer admire the skills of my grandfather's craft, then will I not also think less of him? If there is no longer a family vocation to which I am apprenticed, then am I not subject to a new sort of loneliness and uncertainty that earlier generations have never known? Does not modernization mean that all the bonds that constrained us but also brought us such comfort and nourishment have been loosened and so the extended households of earlier generations are fracturing beyond repair? Everywhere we turn there is a loosening. Modernity means that so often we meet in ever more tangential and fragmentary ways, for it makes nomads of so many of us. So does it really matter where I throw my plastic water bottles that are not biodegradable if, though here today, I will be gone tomorrow? No wonder the litter continues to accumulate so quickly. So perhaps it is not altogether surprising that, if modernization is cleaning up the potable water supply and expanding it, progress is also responsible for a massive pollution problem that never existed hitherto.

Our flight from Chennai to Bhubaneswar was delayed for an hour because the Indian Airlines people could not figure out how to close the door to the plane. Very soon after our arrival we set out on a tour of some of the 500 surviving temples in Bhubaneswar which--or so I was told by our guide--could boast of ten times that number in the 13th century. Our first destination was the lovely Rajarani temple, built in the 11th century and in remarkably fine condition today. Many of the sculptures seem not to have weathered at all, which reminded us of the Hoysala shrines. This small temple is set within a beautiful garden that obviously receives constant and meticulous care. Two large snakes with human heads welcome visitors at the temple entrance; they are companioned by a host of other creatures, all beautifully carved. From there we went to Brahmeswar, a larger and earlier shrine which has four subordinate temples at its corners. Here the sculptures are especially numerous and elaborately wrought. Our next visit was to the Parasurameswara temple, the oldest in the city and built by the middle of the 7th century. It has a high spire over the sanctuary and the carvings here are even more intricate than elsewhere. This is, at least to my eyes, a prototype of an Orissan temple, shaped not unlike a Buddhist stupa; the proportions of the whole shrine struck me as superb.

Next came the Mukteswara temple, erected in the 10th century. It is quite small but most delicately and lavishly carved. It is devoted to Siva, as are most of the city's temples. There is a most distinctive stone arch over its entrance and many people regard this as the finest shrine in Bhubaneswar. There is a marvelous great stone cobra over the lingam in the sanctuary. Adjacent to the Mukteswara is the Sidheswara temple, beautifully proportioned but less interesting because its walls are unadorned. We saw a good many other shrines as well, simply because you cannot turn around in this city without encountering more of them. Very late in the afternoon we drove to the lovely little lake around which many medieval temples are clustered. In the middle of the lake there is a small island on which a shrine was erected long ago. I watched the tranquil scene as the sun fell below the building's dome and darkness came. Across the lake was the Lingaraj temple, perhaps the most famous in the city, but it is not accessible to non-Hindus. We circled its high walls and then, more than content, made our way back to our suite at the Trident Hotel.

I was awakened at 6:00 by a little concert outside our windows, unseen birds singing wonderfully. The air was filled with little yellow butterflies and great whirring dragonflies and there was a scattering of egrets on the ground. The hotel has fifteen acres of immaculate gardens with many old trees, including a mango orchard that offers its own contributions to the hotel's breakfast menu. I have been thinking today as I have thought almost every day recently about motion, the whole cosmic dance that Siva began so long ago. All these people: where have they come from, where are they going, whom have they left behind, why are they doing this, what chores do they have or errands to run, and do they have loved ones and confidantes or are we all strangers and alone? From our rooms in Chennai I had watched the street below me, not a great thoroughfare at all, just a city street. In exactly two minutes more than 320 vehicles passed by: tricycle rickshaws, motor rickshaws, motor scooters, motor bikes, cars and vans and buses and lorries. Why? What could Siva ever have had in mind? Are there no limits on this dance, no boundaries? Can we build enduring bridges between us, real bridges, in such a world of ceaseless motion?

I confess that for the moment I have had my fill of Hindu temples; the last few in Bhubaneswar yesterday were more than I could relish very much. But I did have one surprise remaining in my bag of tricks, the Sun Temple at Konarak, which is one of the very few things on this trip that I had never seen before. I wanted it to be a sort of grand finale, a consummation, a bit of punctuation at the end of this tour. And the Sun Temple did not disappoint me. It is most deservedly a World Heritage site. India has about two dozen UNESCO World Heritage sites, and this will be the 14th we have visited on this single trip without having worked at it at all. It was a two hour drive to Konarak over the usual wretched roads and there was much construction. The workers were mainly women and children who labored much harder than the few men. The women were usually clad in wonderfully colorful and bright saris with interesting tribal designs. Not far from Bhubaneswar was the hill at Dhauli where in 272 B.C. Emperor Ashoka laid down his sword forever. When he surveyed all the corpses strewn over the countryside after his victory over the Kalinga, he converted to Buddhism. On this hilltop are the Ashokan Edicts proclaiming that all men are his children and therefore brothers to one another. The site is marked by the Shanti Stupa, built thirty years ago as a symbol of peace.

Suddenly the majestic bulk of the Sun Temple appeared above the trees ahead of us. It was constructed in the middle of the 13th century but it was long forgotten because it was buried beneath the sands of the nearby shore until the water receded and the British could excavate it in the 19th century. It boasts some of the finest and most fabulous sculpture in all of India and much of it is in superb condition because of its long burial. This is one of the largest temples in India, about 225 feet tall even though its gigantic tower partially collapsed a century and a half ago. It is actually two massive structures, one behind the other, intended together to portray the chariot of Surya, the Sun God, rising from beneath the sea to take its place in the high heavens. The chariot is drawn by seven divine stallions and it has 24 gargantuan wheels, 12 pairs of them. My best guess is that the diameter of all the wheels is about 12 feet. The eight spokes of each wheel are carved lavishly and with absolutely dazzling intricacy--and nowhere more so than in the miniatures of the erotic pairings that decorate the exterior walls of the temple. The narrow bands of carvings that adorn them are really marvelous and seemed to us very reminiscent of Hoysala workmanship. There are three commanding statues of Surya fashioned from chloritic schist, each with its own niche high on the temple wall; they are ten feet tall and portray him in the morning, at dusk and at his zenith.

The bottom decorative band consists of elephants, of course, for they must bear on their backs the weight of the whole massive structure. Other bands include lions and mythical beasts, flowers and geometrical figures, and stories from the Mahabharata and the Ramayana. Elaine even spotted a giraffe and proudly showed it to me! There are scenes of sports and war and commerce and concerts, but the most affecting are those of daily life in the 13th century household--women admiring themselves in mirrors, combing their hair, cuddling their babies, bathing or working in the kitchen. Nothing in the world is remote from these walls. There are large and especially splendid sculptures of life-sized apsaras or dancing girls. There is the usual complement of deities both male and female and other celestial beings, but everything here is carved with unusual skill. This is one of the great temples not only of India but of the world. I cannot imagine a more fitting conclusion to our little odyssey. That evening, our last in Bhubaneswar, we sat under the stars by the pool and listened to a concert by some Indian musicians. It was a good way to end the visit.

Travel can consume a great deal of time in India even if you are not using a bullock cart. Our next day was lost to it, although we had a lovely time at the Trident listening to the songbirds, watching the egrets and talking with the many people who had tried so hard to care for us. By the servants' entrance to the hotel on the wall is painted, "Welcome to your hotel." So it is, and that is why we enjoyed ourselves so much. We were made to feel so thoroughly at home because every employee was a host. I thought about that painted sign again the next day as our plane flew along the Himalayas carrying us back to London. I have been a tourist in a great many countries. But in India I have always been a guest. I know the difference. I treasure it.

Finally, what of the "secularism" written into the Constitution of India and on which I have commented. Has it succeeded? In other words, has it brought reconciliation and healing to this land of radical differences and longstanding suspicions? Despite isolated Muslim-Hindu riots that occasionally occur, the promise of tolerance and the acceptance of diversity has been truly realized. A billion people live in amity and concord, Hindus and Muslims, Buddhists and Parsis, Sikhs and Jains, Christians and Jews, the devout and the unbelieving. All of them have full citizenship and free speech in the world's largest democracy. This is perhaps another instance of the courtesy, the consideration and politeness that have always seemed to me to be a part of the Indian character. I came away from this country that I had long since grown to love humbled and exalted by all that has been achieved in not much more than a dozen years, so much indeed that even though the future is unknown one can face it unafraid.

❀ ❀ ❀

CHAPTER SEVEN

Byways to Lesser Known Gems

I hoped that I knew what Christopher and Elizabeth were planning to give us for Christmas in 2005 but of course I could not be certain, even though Kit had asked me several times if I was thinking about another trip to India. Then on Christmas Day an e-mail arrived and it was just what I had hoped it would be. Kit wrote,

Dear Mom and Dad:

As this is a second anniversary type of Christmas gift to you, we apologize for being boring and repetitive! It was so wonderful to hear and see how much you both enjoyed your last trip to India. There's nothing better than giving a gift that is enjoyed from the heart .... which is why it is so important to us to be able to offer the gift of a trip to India once again .... All our love and thanks for everything!!!.

The lion's share of the expenses of another trip to India for more than a month, another visit to the place I love best after my own land--yes, "a boring and repetitive Christmas present" indeed. This year there was no hesitation because of my age and health.

In 2005, my ambition had been simply to show Elaine sites she had never seen and that I thought she would greatly appreciate: Khajuraho, Agra, Sarnath, Varanasi, Elephanta, Ellora and Ajanta, Belur and Halebid, Mahabalipuram and Kanchipuram, Konarak and Bhubaneswar. I had not been very much concerned with how they were related to one another. This time we would have only a few targets and much more cohesive and coherent itineraries. We would rely less on planes and more on automobiles. We would spend less time in cities and much more in rural areas. I had been told many times and for many years that the sacred architecture of the Jains was "matchless" or "peerless." The best of it is at two remote sites in Rajasthan, Ranakpur and especially Mt. Abu. So of course we had to see them for ourselves. I decided that we would use Udaipur as our base for a full week; that was the easiest way to see the Jain shrines.

The second focus would be a trip first proposed to me in 1978 by my friend Nagaraja Rao when he was Director of Archeology and Museums for the state of Karnataka. He gave me then three sets of ASI postcards that pictured sacred sites in the remote villages of Pattadakal and Aihole and Badami which were in his custody. These are among the earliest and most important "cave" and free-standing temples in all of India. The trip Nagaraj proposed would begin at Hubli in the northwest and then visit these three hamlets and end in the northeast of Karnataka at Hampi, now largely a ruin but for 200 years from the 14th to the 16th centuries the fabulous capital of the Vijayanagar Empire. Nagaraj's enthusiasm was certainly shared by UNESCO, which declared Pattadakal and Hampi to be two of India's two dozen World Heritage sites. I have always cherished those ASI postcards. Nagaraj offered again to make all arrangements so that we would be met everywhere by the senior ASI officer, who would escort us and make certain that we did not miss anything we should see. The northern Karnataka expedition, which I was already calling "Hidden India," would probably require seven to ten days. So these twin objectives, together with a tour of some of Kerala and lower Tamil Nadu, would occupy most of our weeks exploring some parts of India we had never seen.

We decided to leave from New York rather than Washington because we wanted to spend four days or so with Kit and Elizabeth and our two little granddaughters. They had just bought a house in Tuxedo Park which they were eager for us to see. The community is called Tuxedo Park because that item of apparel was first worn here, despite the disapproval of some who thought the "short" jacket displayed an informality that a proper gentleman would not wish to show at the dinner table. But times change and that was long ago. Once again we went to India the easy way, an overnight flight of six and a half hours to Heathrow, much of a day walking in the airport and relaxing in the rather splendid Virgin Atlantic lounge, and then another overnight flight, this one of nine hours, and a midmorning arrival at Indira Gandhi airport in New Delhi. We felt rested and fit; the trip had been very easy. When we boarded our flight at Heathrow the first person we saw was a friend from a year earlier, Rahul, our flight attendant. What a good omen the encounter seemed to be for the next six weeks. Elaine thanked Rahul profusely for his gift of Virgin Atlantic chocolates a year ago; since we do not stop for lunch while touring, they were a real blessing. At daybreak as we flew over the foothills of the Himalayas Rahul appeared with a huge bag of chocolates, more than twice as many as last year. Handsome, personable, bright and articulate, for us he is a symbol of the new India.

Two tourism representatives were waiting for us with garlands as soon as we cleared customs and off we set for The Imperial once again. There was an incredible amount of new construction along the road everywhere. Much of it is part of the new superhighway that will link Delhi, Calcutta, Chennai and Mumbai, the four largest cities in the subcontinent. This superhighway is the first such road in all of India, but by the time of its completion it will not be adequate to handle the more than a million new cars that pour off the Indian assembly lines every year. India is hurtling forward, virtually month by month, and that will always mean problems and anomalies as well as blessings. We very much liked our driver, Vinod, and our large air-conditioned car. He seemed young but was obviously very experienced and competent. So I was pleased to learn that he would be with us for nine days and we would cover a lot of miles together.

We drove as usual through the Diplomatic Enclave, past the Gate of India and the empty marble pavilion which had sheltered a statue of the king until Independence, past Rashtrapati Bhavan which was built to house the Raj but now is the home of the President, through one of the great parks in this greenest of the world's capitals, then along Shantipath and Janpath, marveling as always at the millions of blossoms that lined both sides of the road. Finally we glimpsed the tops of the royal palms that welcome every new arrival to The Imperial. This drive was somewhat different, however, because New Delhi had just been bushwhacked. Our arrival coincided with that of the American president, although mercifully he was staying in a different hotel. New Delhi was immaculate. Not even a shred of litter could be found within miles. Everywhere Indian and American flags flew next to one another, many thousands of them.

Where there were no flags there were silk banners dyed in arresting and vivid colors or else in all sorts of exquisite pastels, every color under heaven. And there were soldiers everywhere. It was all very gay, very festive, and all the traffic was slowed, succumbing to total paralysis.

Our hotel is not called the Hotel Imperial or the Imperial Hotel but simply The Imperial, for the words describe first of all not a building but an aura, a nostalgia for a time long gone and for a different world, for once upon a time when there was a place for everything and everything was in its place, people not least of all. The servants wear garb that is intended to be reminiscent of the uniforms of the troops of the Raj. Guests approach The Imperial beneath royal palms that were mature when the Raj still reigned and New Delhi was nothing more than an architect's dream. Yes, this is the old Imperial, in some ways little changed, but the <u>Imperium</u> has been turned upside down and in some strange and ironic sense the biblical prophecy has been fulfilled: the first shall be last and the last shall be first. In India today this is everyone's inheritance, whether they like it or not, for the better and also for the worse. The legacy is inescapable.

On the asset side of the ledger there is the gift of a "national language" which, even though hundreds of millions do not speak it well or do not even speak it at all, has nonetheless brought a new measure of unity to the country that Hindi never could have nurtured. This has been of critical importance for the building of the nation. There is also an entrenched civil service that is now and then more or less competent and meritocratic. Certainly most important after the gift of language there is the idea of democracy and, though the practice of it may sometimes be messy, the ideal is written into the Indian soul and passionately espoused. The longstanding Indian concern with ethics has also been reinforced and broadened, not least by the Mahatma's adaptation of some Judeo-Christian motifs. The British Raj encouraged in other ways Indian respect for education and broadened it to include an increased emphasis on science and technology that today finds most brilliant expression in the various Indian Institutes of Technology. The list goes on and on. The Raj is dead; long live the Raj!

There is an augury for the future in the lobby of The Imperial, where each day so many Indians now mix so comfortably with foreign nationals from dozens of other lands. As India takes its place among the dominant nations of the world one can see a new measure of confidence emboldening its people: India has a great heritage, it has had a good tutor for a long time, it has been well nurtured, it is ready for the future of a world that it intends in many ways to shape. Perhaps this is why I always return to this most Indian of hotels despite all its transparent flummery, because of the mixing that occurs each day. Even though the name looks backward the mixing points us forward to tomorrow. So come where so many things have been turned upside down, relish the irony, laugh at the joke, savor the joining of yesterday and tomorrow.

We slept and breakfasted very well; the madeleines were as delicious as ever. Then we were ready for our first full day in Delhi with Vinod and Avi, our jovial and knowledgeable guide. Avi suggested that we begin the day in Shahjahanabad, Old Delhi, because there we might have six hours or so before Mr. Bush appeared. I agreed because this time we were to be in Delhi for only two full days and so I had no particular schedule in mind. The Red Fort and the Purana Qila or Old Fort were already closed for security reasons but the Jama Masjid was open as usual. This was Shah Jahan's final creation and it is my favorite site in the old town. As we drove north, I noticed an extraordinary number of buses parked on the roadside, first dozens and scores, then hundreds, finally thousands. There were also hundreds of trucks. They had all brought Muslim men wearing their signature white caps to protest the visit of Mr. Bush. It seemed all of them were heading for some rendezvous close to the Jama Masjid. By the time we reached Chandni Chowk, the central thoroughfare that leads to the mosque, the roads were impassable.

We were surrounded by hundreds of thousands of Muslims marching in quasi-military formation, all of them closely supervised by marshalls. The noise was indescribable. No one could doubt the depth of their indignation or the fervor of their passion. Yet there was also discipline and control within the tumult. Many of the marchers peered through the car windows at us and we were not difficult to identify as Americans but there was never a single threatening gesture or even a discourteous word. Elaine was fascinated by the drive and so was I, even though she admitted she had found it unsettling, menacing and finally a bit alarming. It was entirely peaceful but I knew how small a spark could have turned the crowds very ugly, indeed. So I told Vinod to get us away and he managed to do that but it required an hour to edge our way to the side of the marching masses. Newspaper accounts the next morning estimated there were many more than half a million and perhaps more than a million men there.

Exhilarated to be once again on the broad avenues of New Delhi, we drove straight to Humayun's Tomb, one of the two UNESCO World Heritage sites in the city. It was built in the mid-16th century by the widow of this second of the great Mughal emperors. Ten thousand artisans labored for nine years to create it from red sandstone and black and white marble. The stone was brought from quarries between Agra and Jaipur which have been in continuous operation for more than 900 years. I was surprised to discover that we were entirely alone; everyone else seemed to be protesting Mr. Bush's advent. Avi helped me up the steps, which are as numerous as they are uneven. There are approximately at least 155 members of noble and royal families buried here as well as the emperor and the barber with whom he spent two hours every day. Humayun's Tomb is revolutionary for at least two reasons.

First, the Persian influence here is novel and very striking, most of all in the splendid dome, and this has important consequences for the future. Both the Tomb of Itmad-ud-Daulah and the Taj Mahal found some of their inspiration in the monument to Humayun. It is built on a huge two-storey arcaded platform and crowned by a very bulbous double dome that has no direct antecedent in India. Second, the edifice is surrounded by a charbagh garden, one of the first in India. Perhaps the earliest was created by Humayun's father, Babur, in Agra. This geometrical design uses watercourses and fountains to separate the quadrants that comprise the whole. I had visited Humayun's Tomb a number of times but it was only on this day that I was absolutely captured and mesmerized by it. Elaine felt the same way. This is a place filled with mystery and meaning. It is superb.

We continued south away from Shahjahanabad to the second of Delhi's UNESCO World Heritage sites, the Qutb Minar, an immense stone column that rises more than 225 feet into the sky and was built in the 13th century. It too was entirely deserted and serene. Presumably those who might otherwise have been here were in the environs of the Jama Masjid or else safely at home. The great tower rises above the first mosque that was built in India. It was erected in the 12th century from the ruins of 27 Hindu and Jain shrines despoiled by the Muslim invaders. So the wonderful columns that ornament the arcades of the mosque are covered with carvings that are Hindu and Jain. The Qutb Minar was created to celebrate the victory of Islam over indigenous Hinduism but its mosque, ironically, bears witness to the creativity and vitality of the very different ninth century Hindu shrines that preceded it. The Qutb Minar complex gains much of its charm from all of the old neem trees that offer welcome shade and provide the quinine that the world requires to combat the scourge of malaria.

I told Avi and Vinod that we could not finish our day until we had revisited one of our favorite sculptures in India, the Gandhi Memorial that portrays the Mahatma leading ten of his followers on the Dandi March in 1930. This is a sort of carved charter for non-violent civil disobedience. Thanks to Mr. Bush there were soldiers and police at the site directing traffic and they stopped our car squarely in front of the sculpture and held us there for a full five minutes, long enough so that Elaine could even get out of the car for her photographs. What serendipity! The visit of the president had not been a complete waste for us after all.

The next morning Vinod and Avi appeared as scheduled and we drove toward the Lodi Gardens, only to find they were closed for security reasons. So we decided we would drive for an hour around this part of New Delhi, with its broad avenues shaded by leafy canopies, and leading to many fountains and beds of flowers. We saw many stately mansions with gardens and lawns that were beautifully kept. This part of the city would be a lovely place to live. I wondered whether I was exaggerating when I told people this was the greenest and most interesting national capital I had ever seen. I decided that I had not and was simply stating my own view. Suddenly we were halted by a police barrier just in time to watch the Bush motorcade of armored cars sweep down the otherwise deserted boulevard at high speed as if they were in flight from the solitude of their self-imposed quarantine.

The drive back to The Imperial was difficult because police and soldiers blocked every road that Vinod tried. We had to stop several times while he explained to the military that his passengers were American guests at The Imperial and therefore we had to be allowed on Janpath. The police were adamant: Janpath was to be yielded to the demonstrators to get them on their way out of central Delhi. Eventually Vinod won the argument and we returned to the hotel, but Vinod himself was forced to remain there in the parking lot for four hours until the soldiers and police deemed the crowd of demonstrators sufficiently dispersed so that he could drive safely to his home. Elaine watched the crowds on Janpath from a window and then we went down to the pool and the gardens because it was obviously impossible to leave The Imperial. Elaine wrote postcards and I watched earthworms until the cocktail hour.

The next morning we set off on the long drive to Agra at 10:30, leaving behind a city of fifteen million, more than four million automobiles and one American president in a heavily armored car. As usual it took most of an hour to drive from central Delhi to the city limits and I was very impressed by all the stately tombs and elegant gurdwaras we passed, although I knew how large the Sikh population of the city had become. Once again we saw new construction everywhere, much of it related to the metro that was begun in 1995 and is scheduled for completion in 2010 in time for the Commonwealth Games. It is providing fifteen years of good employment for a very large number of people. Much of it is already operational and I have been told it is quiet, air-conditioned and costs no more than standing room in a crowded bus. No wonder city dwellers have adopted it quickly and in large numbers. Apparently wherever it is functioning automobile traffic has fallen by about forty percent. Even if the truth lies somewhere short of that, it still seems to me to be a triumph of urban planning.

Alas, all was not well at the Amarvilas, this flagship of the Oberoi Group. I had spent an inordinate amount of time requesting a superior deluxe room, preferably number 425 where we had stayed for three or four nights last year. The Amarvilas demonstrated to me beyond any doubt that it had never received any request for a specific room and had in fact been asked to provide the least expensive room available. We had no balcony at all and only an awkward and most unsatisfactory view of the Taj Mahal. I was filled with vexation because this was one treat on this trip I had especially wanted Elaine to have. I made my irritation clear to the travel agency employees, the hotel management and everybody else within hailing distance, blameworthy or not. It was clear, however, that the fault lay with the travel agent in New York, who did not do what I had asked and then told me that he had.

But Oberoi has quite a special reputation unlike that of anyone else. They assured me that they would arrange something I would find completely satisfactory by the next day at noon. When we returned from our day's exertions about 3:30 the next afternoon, they had moved our belongings into the Lord Curzon Suite, one of the two or three finest accommodations at the Amarvilas and one with an absolutely unrivalled view of the Taj. I think this over-the-top response to me is not untypical of the Oberoi Group. They knew I was gravely disappointed and so they were determined to make things more than right. This is why we had already arranged to stay with them on three further occasions in the course of this trip. I confess to a bit of embarrassment that I had caused such a fuss, but I shall recover from that as I relax in this truly beautiful suite.

We had only two destinations for our first full day in Agra, the UNESCO World Heritage sites that lie within the city itself, Agra Fort and the Taj Mahal. "Fort" is very much of a misnomer because this great walled complex with its two moats (one for water and the other for carnivorous beasts) is more a small city than simply a stronghold. It was originally constructed by Akbar, considerably enlarged by his son Jahangir and then radically redesigned by his grandson Shah Jahan. It contains several palaces, a magnificent mosque, a variety of civic buildings, recreational areas and numerous other structures. We sat for a long time in the Diwan-i-Khas, the hall of public audience, admiring its 64, columns and watching the passing parade. But my favorite place in the whole complex is the Pearl Mosque, a building that was created by Shah Jahan from his favorite white marble; I cannot imagine any detail of this elegant structure as other than it is. We spent the whole morning at the Fort, longer than we had intended because there were so few other people there. Then I decided it was time to visit the Taj Mahal and so we returned to the Amarvilas for the golf cart that would take us the 300 yards or so to its entrance.

There were perhaps no more than 200 people in the Taj and its gardens because we had come at noon, which is often the best time to avoid the crowds. Anil, our guide, took my hand and hauled me up and down the very uneven steps at the Taj and up and down others elsewhere as though we were two commandoes on a training mission. I was very grateful because I wanted to examine closely again the magnificent but nonetheless ever so delicate inlay above the crypt. More evidence of the old axiom, if we do not hang together we shall all hang separately. We sat for a long time under a great tree in the garden, enjoying the shade and the serenity, for this was the quietest time I had ever spent at the Taj. But eventually it was time to find our golf cart again, regretful to leave but thankful for yet another opportunity to be in this extraordinary place.

At sunset we sat on our lovely balcony and watched a company of Rajasthani dancers perform below us by the pool. Then we watched as Agra prepared for sleep. So many of the houses are painted a beautiful soft shade of blue that continues to glow in the dusk until darkness is fully fallen. Then we listened as the muezzin at a nearby mosque called the faithful to prayer. In the morning we lingered in bed to watch the Taj dress herself in a sample of her pastels. Then Vinod and Anil appeared and we set off for another full day in Agra, much of this one to be spent in what I had decided really is my favorite spot in the entire subcontinent. The Tomb of Itmad-ud-Daulah lies only three kilometers from the Taj Mahal and also borders the Yamuna River, but it is a rather long and difficult drive because the streets form one unbroken bazaar. Everything is incredibly congested. But I love this place nonetheless. It is small and relatively modest, quiet and largely unvisited, but to me the workmanship seems no less delicate and exquisite than the Taj Mahal.

I was delighted when Elaine told me that if she could visit only one site in Agra it would not be the Taj or the Fort but Itmad-ud-Daulah. If I were told that I could visit only two sites in the Agra region, they would be this place and Fatehpur Sikri. We made several other stops on our way back to the Amarvilas, the first at the Chini Tomb where a finance minister of Shah Jahan's is buried. What made this visit memorable was that there suddenly sprouted around us a whole scrum of grinning children who wanted to hold our hands and walk with us. They also wanted to be photographed with us. Anil took three or four pictures of all of us and then they walked with us

JAIPUR, Amber
In the old palace at Amber glass is used in several startling and innovative ways including walls such as this ornamented with small pieces of convex glass.

along the lovely path that led from the tomb back to the car. They gave us huge grins and waved as we left and I waved until I could see them no more.

Monday morning we set off for Fatehpur Sikri with Vinod and Anil. This was the last World Heritage site we would see for several weeks and it is one that I especially cherish. Usually I have been more or less alone here, just me and the myriad memories locked within the red sandstone walls of the deserted city. It was rather crowded today with many Indian tourists and some long crocodiles of school children. Anil showed us many exquisite details carved in the sandstone walls that I had never noticed until he pointed them out and once again he helped me up and down many difficult steps that I could never have negotiated by myself. Then we bade him a rueful farewell as he returned to Agra; Anil is the best guide we have ever had in India. Vinod is a very careful driver but he is also very fast. He had us at the Rambagh Palace less than four hours after we had left Fatehpur Sikri. Much of the road had been utterly wretched, not because of neglect but because it was being expanded. I was saddened to see tens of thousands of stumps by the side of the road and masses of gnarled tree roots, all that remains of enormous and majestic specimens which provided shade and shelter for dozens of generations and on which the Indian forestry service had lavished such unremitting care. At the Rambagh Palace our room was well appointed and very large, as was our terrace. It gave me great pleasure many years ago to bring Elaine and the boys here for a holiday. Now I must admit nothing much remains to remind me of days gone by.

We are awakened very early by hundreds of birds. They are nesting in some handsome ashoka trees just beyond our terrace. Later some peacocks march across the lawn, looking very imperturbable and imperious. At ten o'clock Vinod and our new guide who is named Sharma appear and so we set out for Amber Fort. The original structure was built in the 16th century and it was the capital of this region until the Maharajah of Jaipur built a new palace for himself and a new city for his people in 1727. Originally planned for 50,000 residents, Jaipur now has a population of about two and a half million. But there remain many testimonies to the elegance of the original conception. The avenues are 110 feet wide and the old city exudes a sense of spaciousness. We drove by the fabled "Wind Palace" which is many storeys tall but only twenty or so feet deep. It was built on the main thoroughfare so that the Maharani and ladies of the court could watch processions and festivals in the street without themselves being seen.

Amber lies only a few minutes outside Jaipur. On the way Elaine told our new guide that she had discovered a new fruit at breakfast called a rambutan, but she was a bit perplexed about how much of it to eat. For a minute or two Sharma pondered the question and then he said, "If you like, eat some more; if you do not like, put it down." But then we arrived at Amber, a fortress that is not attractive and even less inviting. It is an exercise in brutalism, a massive sandstone fist emerging from a great granitic mountain sleeve that ascends to sufficient height to seem impregnable. It served its purpose well and kept the Mughal marauders at bay. So when one enters Amber its impact on the visitor is staggering, because inside these forbidding ramparts there is enormous beauty and delicacy and variety and magic, a whole wonderland of artistry. This is a creation of Hindu culture, perhaps the first of their works that a great many visitors to India encounter. The greatest works of art and architecture in Delhi are Mughal and British. In Agra they are all Mughal. Here we see what the hearts and minds of the Hindu people can produce.

Amber is wonderful. It is a joy to be there. I had been there twice before now. Why did I not remember much about it at all? After a while the true answer came to me. I did not remember because then my heart was not engaged. Jaipur was only the second stop on my first trip to India and I had not been very much attracted to what I had seen in Delhi. I was quite indifferent and uncaring when I arrived in Jaipur and so the eyes of my mind were closed. Thank God, my memory is still excellent, but no one's memory retains for very long what his or her heart has not embraced. That is why I did not remember Amber or, to phrase it differently, that is why today I saw Amber for the first time. And I loved it.

The most dazzling part of the palace is the hall of private audience, used by the maharajahs only to meet their familiars and favorites. Its walls are inset with countless tiny mirrors of convex glass facing at different angles so that the whole effect is rather like a shimmering sheet of falling water, an illusion reinforced by the music of the water conduits that furnish the rooms with their 16th century version of air-conditioning. Below the mirrors are white marble panels with exquisitely sculpted flowers which offer their nectar to butterflies hovering in the stone above them. My own favorite place, however, is the hall of private prayer, where only the sovereign and his family offered their prayers. Everything about the chamber is light and airy; the entrancing decorations are done in the most subtle of pastel shades on white walls. Windows of 18th century stained glass are also in pastel hues that render the room even brighter. This same decor is also used in some other rooms that are important for channeling the water that cools the palace. The jalis everywhere at Amber are stunning. On our return from Amber we stopped to explore some 18th century cenotaphs that are memorials of female members of the royal family. A number of the carved ceilings here are extraordinary and the whole complex is certainly worth a visit. But I was searching for some special cenotaphs that had held great significance for me 36 years ago. I remembered them vividly and these were not them. So Sharma and Vinod promised to drive us to some others the next day.

Our first destination in the morning proved more of a challenge than I had anticipated. The Jaipur City Palace is a vast complex painted an enchanting shade of yellow; the effect is one of airiness and calm. Half of the palace is still the residence of the Maharajah of Jaipur, whose personal flag overhead indicated he was at home when we visited. He is one of India's richest billionaires and a noted philanthropist. Much of the mid-18th century palace was converted in 1959 into a series of museums for His Highness' collections. The Maharani is very interested in education and so she has established her own school in another part of the palace. The first museum we entered housed costumes and textiles. Then we went to the hall of private audience, which today is reserved for ceremonial occasions. There are two sterling silver water pots in the chamber that are unique. The maharajah of the day had them filled with water from the Ganges and took them with him when he went to London to attend the coronation of Edward VII. When he was asked why he required his own Ganges water, he replied, "At least in India no elder brother would impose upon his little sister to furnish food or drink." Britain and Jaipur might both be sovereign states but the maharajah was in no doubt about which was the more ancient and legitimate. The water pots are extraordinarily beautiful. Each weighs 375 pounds and stands 5'3" tall. They are the largest sterling silver objects in the world.

The hall of public audience is today the palace's art museum. Here is a truly fabulous collection of Rajput miniature paintings and many stunning examples of early Hindu calligraphy, some of it inscribed on palm leaves. On a large plinth there are six or eight elephant howdahs, gold and ivory and silver and gem encrusted. But the focus of the collection at least for me lay on half a dozen magnificent oriental carpets brought from Amber. The last exhibition hall

I found entirely fascinating. It was a workplace where perhaps two dozen Rajasthani craftsmen were absorbed in their different endeavors. They had been awarded space in the palace as part of the Maharajah's commitment to the welfare of arts and crafts in Rajasthan. Elaine and I could have watched them all day. We were especially interested in one artisan who was creating small teak boxes inlaid with brass wire in delicate and richly complex patterns. I surprised Elaine by buying one for her; she was very pleased. The young artisan said he spent a week and, needless to say, intense concentration on each little box that he made. We returned to the car and began the rather long and tedious journey to the cenotaphs of Gaitore, built in the 18th century for the men and male children of the royal family. The site is on the very edge of the city beneath a forbidding mountain that is topped by a defensive fortified wall. Today Sharma and Vinod delivered us to the memorials that had told me so long ago that India and I had many miles to travel together.

The most beautiful of the cenotaphs is perhaps that of Jai Singh II, the architect and creator of the city of Jaipur. It consists of a raised plinth from which two dozen white marble columns spring gracefully upward to an elaborately domed roof. The sculptures that adorn plinth and pillars are of charging horsemen and war elephants but also vases of flowers and wonderful troupes of dancing girls. The carving is exquisite, some of the best I have ever seen. Nearby is a particularly poignant cenotaph, for it is dedicated entirely to the young male children whom death has prematurely carried away. There are many aged trees in the area and therefore many monkeys, descendants of those I had shooed away 36 years ago. I had promised myself that I would not leave Jaipur in 2006 without seeing these cenotaphs once more; after all, I think I owed it to them.

These memorials are one of the glories of Rajasthan; no visitor should ever miss them. I asked Sharma how many tourists came to this place and he answered me, "Not one in a thousand." I asked why and he responded that it was primarily a matter of time. Amber Fort and Jaipur City Palace are the primary attractions; there is little time for anything else except cocktails and anyway how many tourists really know what is worth seeing? This visit through the white marble forest of exquisite columns and superb domed roofs was for me an absolute joy and one of the greatest visits of my last several trips to India. March ninth was the sort of day that sooner or later befalls all travelers--a day spent travelling. My least favorite airline produced a gleaming new Boeing 737 for a "hop on" flight. The plane came to Jaipur from Delhi and then went on to Jodhpur and Udaipur and Mumbai. So we hopped on and had a very comfortable and pleasant flight. We are now in room 102 at the Oberoi Udaivilas in Udaipur. Our room faces Lake Pichola and directly in front of us floating in the middle of the water is the Lake Palace Hotel where we shall be staying in a few days. It has frequently been called the most romantic spot in India. Behind it is the Udaipur City Palace and the town of half a million souls is spread along the lakefront. The Udaivilas is only a few years old and I have never before been in a place like it. This is an enchantment, a wonderland, a Mughal fantasy of the domes and turrets and fountains of paradise. Every last detail could not possibly be other than it is. This is an architectural masterpiece. In addition to all the fountains and pools and watercourses everywhere, there is a central cascade that tumbles down several shallow flights of stairs to lap gently over the bronze face of the sun god, Surya. Outside our room we have a small courtyard with high wooden doors that leads to our terrace with its armchairs and a table sheltered by an umbrella. The terrace is edged by a blue tiled swimming area of our own. Everything is done with such delicacy and proportionality and restraint; there is nothing here to overawe the visitor or make him or her feel insignificant or small.

The next morning we began the first of our Jain days and had our introduction to some roads which even all our travel in India had not quite prepared us for. Our new driver for the week is named Behari and he and his large Toyota Innova are both excellent. Today's destination is the temple at Ranakpur, which lies two and a half hours away through the Aravalli hills, which we are told are among the world's oldest mountains. Along our way we stopped to watch a farmer and his two bullocks working a water wheel as scores of attached clay pots poured their precious liquid into channels to irrigate nearby fields. The drive was fascinating because the inhospitable mountains were so unbelievable. Eventually we arrived not at a town or village or even a crossroads, but at the utterly isolated 15th century Jain temple at Ranakpur. Jain temples are often remote and usually have unprepossessing exteriors and this was no exception. The interior, however, was a different matter.

Ranakpur is dedicated to Adinath, the first of the 24 Jain tirthankaras. Tirthankaras are often represented as prophets or seers but this is misleading. Perhaps they are best described as ford-finders who have discovered where one can cross the waters that divide this world from eternity. Tirthankaras are larger than life; they are heroes, athletes of the spirit, examples for us all. I prefer to call them pioneers or trailblazers. Although the most important shrine at Ranakpur is devoted to Adinath, all the other heroes of the faith are represented well in 66 subordinate shrines. One's first and enduring impression of Ranakpur is of a magnificent forest all sculpted from pure white marble. There are 1,444 elaborately carved columns, no two of which are identical. The main dome as well as secondary ceilings are elaborately carved and portray tales from Hindu and Jain scriptures. There are innumerable sculptures of lotus buds and other flowers, many fine celestial beings as well as elephants and birds and various other creatures. The temple at Ranakpur is a fabulous monument to the human quest for eternal peace. We were pleased and surprised to find that we were not

RANAKPUR, Jain Temple
One of the finest Jain temples ever constructed, the one at Ranakpur has 1,444 elaborately carved white marble columns, no two of them alike.

alone in this isolated place; there were scores of other visitors, half Indians and half Westerners.

There is no question about it: travel in India is enervating at best and at worst it just defies description. We had a long day because the mountains were scarcely welcoming and all the roads were under construction. All Indian roads are always under construction and so it will remain forever and ever. Back at the Udaivilas the water channels that run outside our room and through the gardens, together with the little waterfalls and fountains, all provided music for us day and night, a soft symphony to lull us to sleep and bright bits of melody to herald the new day. Udaipur is a small, green city of enormous charm and many treasures; why in the world has it taken me 36 years to come back to a site as special and memorable as this? Unfortunately, this morning we had to say goodbye to the Udaivilas. We were told that the drive between Udaipur and Mr. Abu would require between four and five hours, winding through a hostile moonscape filled with huge boulders and steep unfriendly hillsides that are sere and dessicated at least in the month of March. The last half hour of the trip was interesting because we ascended more than 4,000 feet, and much of the time there were no guardrails of any sort and their absence was a bit disconcerting.

Mt. Abu is a small and picturesque town of about 12,000 where it is not easy to earn a livelihood unless one caters to tourists and pilgrims. Immensely popular in the days of the British Raj, it has two relics from that era, Heritage Hotels called Jaipur House and Bikaner House. We are staying in the latter, a hunting lodge built by the Maharajah of Bikaner in the late 19th century and the center of social life here for generations. The evening is still young but already we are very chilly. Hot water is simply a memory from the Udaivilas. The sparse furnishings obviously were found in some charity shop. But tomorrow we will be back in Udaipur. We came here to see more Jain temples than simply the one in Ranakpur, especially two in a complex of five that are considerably older, one from the 11th century and the other from the 13th. Both suffered the usual depradations at the hands of Muslim zealots, but both are still in astonishing condition in the light of their antiquity.

We were both thrilled and a bit disappointed by our time at Mt. Abu because we had been told that the beauty and complexity of Vimal Vasahi and Luna Vasahi clearly surpassed the finest Hindu and Mughal artisanship. This is simply not true. The exquisitely detailed sculptures of 10th century Khajuraho and 12th century Halebid and 17th century Agra are not at all excelled by the Jain artists. But that is quite beside the point. These two temples at Mt. Abu together constitute one of the great artistic and architectural monuments in India today and therefore in the contemporary world. Jains and Hindus and Mughals may take different paths to get where they are going, but they all find the same destination: sculpture and architecture as good as any in the world. Unfortunately, I must add that these shrines have no resident congregations but depend entirely on the Jain pilgrims who visit Mt. Abu every week. The reason is that no Jains live here at all because there are no commercial opportunities for them.

Vimal Vasahi Temple required 14 years to complete. The white marble for its interior had to be carried 30 miles by elephants and then the heavily burdened animals had to climb 4,000 feet to the site of the shrine. That is why each of the two major temples has a special chamber dedicated to the elephants without which the temples never could have been built. Marble was not used for

UDAIPUR, Jain temples at Mt. Abu
Vimala Vasahi and Luna Vasahi were built in the 11th and 13th centuries
and are probably the two finest Jain creations anywhere in the world.

the unimpressive exteriors, however, because Mt. Abu is prone to frequent and serious earthquakes. The interior marble is cut so that it will absorb the recurrent tremors; even the columns are fashioned of two pieces of stone. In this shrine there are 202 columns which are very richly ornamented. They are intended to be a rather comprehensive chronicle of ordinary life a thousand years ago. There are swans and goats, elephants and horses and lions, birds and flowers, musicians and dancers, a variety of celestial beings and goddesses with many arms. The wonderfully varied and exuberant panorama of life captured on these pillars is amazing. Perhaps the apsaras are not as sinuous as those at Khajuraho, perhaps the raiment is not sculpted with the rich complexity and delicacy found in the Hoysala shrines. Nonetheless, this is great art and an important part of the world's aesthetic heritage. The ceilings are certainly no less magnificent than the columns and indeed they held my attention most of all. But what is most important are not the particulars but the conception of the whole, the architect's sublime vision of the grand design of what might be created here.

It really was different, waking up in a hill station. There is a crispness in the air, an elusive smell that is alien to city streets, a muted sense of expectancy for one knows not what. As our car descended from Mt. Abu our progress was slowed because there was an incredible parade of local buses packed with Sunday trippers going up to the temples. Back in Udaipur a little launch carried us from the Lake Palace to the jetty in three or four minutes. The walls of the palace extend well beyond the rock which is their foundation and so the hotel does seem to be floating. As we look from our room windows at the water literally beneath us the power of the optical illusion of motion is very strong. After breakfast we walked in the garden outside our room and listened to the indefatigable flutist perched on the roof who played lovely melodies for hours with scarcely a break. The music reminded me of the innumerable people who have made our recent trips so pleasurable. They are uncelebrated and frequently anonymous, but without them I do not know what people like us would ever do. So I want to raise a glass to them, the uncelebrated and largely unthanked ones, without whom everything would have come unstuck. This is one lesson that travel should teach us all, although certainly not travel alone.

This was the only day we were able to devote to the city of Udaipur. Our first destination was the 17th century Jagdish Temple very near the City Palace. It is a fascinating shrine and the best thing we saw all day. The main figure of Vishnu is flanked by his consort Lakshmi and his avatar Krishna. In front of this tableau were several dozen ladies singing from dawn to dark during these last few days before the celebration of Holi and the Festival of Colors. Tomorrow night under a full moon there will be fires to burn flower-decked figures of Holika. The following morning will begin the color festival when children throw colored water on anyone in sight, young or old. I am told it has gotten rather out of hand in recent years. The exterior sculptures on the temple are wonderfully unweathered. The usual little bands of elephants and horses and lions, apsaras and musicians, and various other folk engaged in household or erotic activities are all beautifully carved and almost as fresh as they must have been more than 350 years ago when they were newly wrought.

We walked to the cavernous City Palace, where the Maharana of Mewar and his family still live. Many rooms are open to the public and two hotels occupy other parts of this immense building. Several of the courtyards are quite beautiful and some of the decoration is interesting but it is only in size that Udaipur's palace is comparable to those in Jaipur and Mysore and other places we have been. We were more fortunate at our next destination, the Garden of the Maidens, created so that the attendants of the Maharani could find a comfortable spot even on the hottest days of an Udaipur summer. From this green and tranquil refuge we went back to our jetty and a launch soon returned us to the Lake Palace.

This morning there was an editorial in The Times of India which I thought quite memorable. The title was, "Poor No More: India has more billionaires than China." In fact, India has three times as many and they are spread broadly across the economy. But the writer continues, "Billionaires form only the apex of the pyramid. How solid is the base?" The focus of the editorial lies on the divide between urban and rural, where the two nations have very different stories to tell. Rural India is being overrun by the largest late model John Deere tractors and there is a National Rural Employment Guarantee Scheme that has worked wonders in job creation. Yes, there is much terrible poverty in India but it is not simply or perhaps even primarily a rural problem. India also has many affluent farmers. Much poverty exists where urban and rural meet, on the outskirts of city slums where those who have been marginalized by the city and those who have been marginalized by the villages are thrown together in a potentially volatile situation. God knows there are endless reasons for anguish in such a Slough of Despond but this does not have much to do with endemic rural poverty.

The story about rural culture in China is very different; China "has marginalized its 900 million farmers." There is massive disquiet in the villages. Perhaps the most telling contemporary statistic is that "only 20 percent of the country's medical benefits go to the rural population even though 70 percent of the population lives in villages". How is that for lop-sided development? China has a long way to go to get to where India is today even though India still has a very long way to go. The writer then contrasts democratic and totalitarian futures and concludes, "Finally, it is not the billionaires but the billion small mutinies that take place every day and which empower the individual that really count."

Our last excursion in the neighborhood of Udaipur was very much our best. We set off on an hour's drive to Eklingji and Nagda. There is nothing memorable or charming or in any way impressive about Eklingji. But Nagda is a different story. It is a deserted site off an untraveled country lane. The precincts are meticulously maintained by the ASI. There is a large walled compound and the water from a nearby lake laps gently against the stones of the wall after the monsoon rains. The lake and the Aravalli Hills and this serene site more than a thousand years old combine in a scene of truly indescribable beauty.

I asked our guide if Nagda had many visitors. He said that it rarely had any at all because Udaipur was usually the last stop before tourists flew to their home countries from Mumbai and they had already seen more temples and ruins than they had bargained for. Although the temple suffered some vandalism at the hands of Mughal marauders in the 15th century, the building is in marvelous condition, its exterior very little weathered and its interior untouched by the passage of ten centuries. I had checked Nagda in four different guidebooks; only a single one mentioned it at all. It said baldly that this was a deserted site with the ruins of an 11th century temple. How misleading can a guidebook be? How sad it is to think that a tourist might come to visit Udaipur and never have an opportunity to ponder the glory that is Nagda. This is a temple dedicated to Vishnu, and he and his avatars appear in a great variety of graceful poses, usually with his consort Lakshmi. The portrayals of the god on the exterior walls of the shrine are especially wonderful. Perhaps Nagda does not rival the superb Hoysala temples at Belur and Somnathpur, but I think it is nonetheless one of the half dozen finest temples dedicated to Vishnu anywhere in India that I have ever seen or heard of.

Nagda is a small shrine and this is certainly part of its charm. There are only four pillars in the temple, each one alive with intricate and delicate carvings. Each column portrays different images from the Mahabharata and there seems to be not one inch anywhere that has not been adorned by the artisans' skills. The ceilings and the arches linking the columns are among the finest I have ever seen. The exterior, not surprisingly, is of the same quality. Everywhere there is vitality, dynamism, movement of enormous

UDAIPUR, Nagda
This detail of a frieze displays how little Nagda has weathered in more than a thousand years.

grace and charm. Rarely can one see stone that is so much alive. And within the living stone there are gods and goddesses, dancing girls and musicians, birds and

flowers and animals including snakes and crocodiles and scorpions and many other creatures. The virtuosity of the carvers is especially apparent in the jewelry the women wear and the ways their garments are pleated. Elaine and I agreed that the multitude of amorous couples probably captures the artisans at their very best.

This is magic. It is wonderful. It is one of the great sites of the Hindu heritage. There is also a second temple which, unlike the first, is not made entirely of marble, but it is a fitting companion nonetheless. They are called the mother-in-law and the daughter-in-law temples. Here we see more of the exuberant sculpture detailing ordinary life and its variety a millenium ago. Vishnu the Preserver can be seen everywhere. This place is truly a revelation to me because I had no idea what we would find but I certainly did not expect to find all this. We had come to Udaipur to explore the creativity of the Jain tradition. We are superlatively well rewarded for our efforts but now we are given something extra, a <u>lagniappe,</u> a gift unexpected and undeserved that expanded and enriched our acquaintance with the Hindu tradition. This is grace, such unexpected gifts, whether found on familiar or foreign soil, whether dressed in Hindu or in Christian garb. This is what India is like for many people, a land where in the midst of other things one is so often surprised by grace.

Tonight there is a splendid full moon over Udaipur to announce the arrival of Holi and the attendant Festival of Colors. Holi has to do with an old Indian legend about the triumph of good over the forces of darkness but primarily it is a celebration of the coming of spring and the relaxation of winter's dominion. The Festival of Colors celebrates the vibrant panoply of spring after the monochromatic months of winter. We had been invited along with hordes of other people to the City Palace tonight to meet the royal family, enjoy drinks and refreshments with them, and then listen to a musical evening and watch the Holi fireworks bursting above the city. We had to decline, however, and settled for watching the celebrations from our windows at the Lake Palace. We had to be up not long after four o'clock for a long day's journey to Cochin, traveling down most of India's western flank.

We arrived at Malabar House eleven hours after we began and our day was uneventful thanks to Jet Airways. I like this place because it provides a splendid change for us. It is a Raj era bungalow perhaps 100 or 150 years old and can host two dozen or so guests. Facing our commodious front verandah is a gigantic rain tree, perhaps one of the largest trees I have ever seen and reputed to be more than 400 years old. There are giant rain trees everywhere one turns in Cochin. They are all beautifully shaped like open umbrellas and my guess is their name is derived from the matchless shelter they provide in a storm. The intersection below our verandah seems more a glade than a crossroads for there is greenery everywhere, few people and less traffic. Across from us there is the great green expanse of the Maidan, once the parade ground for the troops of the British Raj and now playing fields where children frolic, for rifles and bayonets have long since yielded to cricket bats and soccer balls. We ate dinner in the courtyard of the bungalow; the catch of the day was delicious lobsters.

❀ ❀ ❀

CHAPTER EIGHT

A Journey to Hidden India

I had planned Cochin as an interlude. It is a pleasant and cosmopolitan city but not filled with important tourist attractions. Still, it seemed appropriate to stop to catch our breath and collect ourselves and Malabar House proved the perfect place to do that. After breakfasting in the courtyard we sat on our verandah and read newspapers while listening to all the happy cries of the children playing their games on the Maidan. Then the hotel florist appeared and carefully placed a large hibiscus in a small dish of water on each of our two little tables. As soon as he left a large crow appeared, knocked the blossom to the floor and drank the water in the dish. A moment later a second large crow did the same thing at our other table. Soon the blossoms and water were replaced but immediately the birds returned and the whole thing happened again. The avian message could not have been clearer: foreign matter should not be placed in our water. At ten o'clock our car and driver arrived and we set off for St. Francis Church, the first European church to be built in India. It dates from 1503. This is a very charming place; it was first Catholic, then Reformed, then Anglican, and now it is used by the ecumenical Church of South India. Vasco da Gama was buried here for 14 years before his remains were removed to Lisbon, but there is still a memorial tablet in the floor.

From the church we drove a very short distance to the shore of the Arabian Sea where we were fascinated by a dozen or so large Chinese fishing net contraptions at the water's edge. They are very picturesque, an anachronous technology largely unchanged since the 14th century. They operate by a system of weights and counterweights; each one requires a crew of four or five people. Elaine decided she wanted to participate and she was welcomed by the fishermen. But she did not bring them much luck; the catch was mainly small sardines. The next visit was to the old and quaint Dutch Palace which was in fact built by the Portuguese as a gift to the local maharajah in the 16th century. From here it was no distance at all to the Cochin Synagogue, a building that is splendidly light and bright and airy. Everything about the place soars. The floor is covered with many hundreds of antique blue and white Chinese tiles. They are remarkably beautiful and attract many visitors to this rather small but extraordinarily welcoming house of worship. The area around the synagogue is called Jewtown and it is a marvelous place for a leisurely walk. The narrow and winding byways are lined with intriguing little shops. This is the home of the thriving spice trade in this important port city where the spice trade has been the major commercial venture since the days of Kubla Khan and even earlier. We lingered in one shop, drawn by the smell of the piles of ginger drying on the floor.

On the second of the days of our Cochin interlude we had a half day cruise on the "Backwaters," which provided a pleasant change of pace. This gave us a chance to see the commercial heart of the city, Ernakulam, close at hand as well as tranquil Bolgatti Island with its many rain trees. We covered a great distance on the water and inspected a few fishing villages from close to shore. There were huge forests of tall cranes reminding us that Cochin is a major commercial port. We also saw an incredible number of deep sea fishing boats being constructed or renovated or else readied for departure. We were much impressed by the ice-making facilities in operation for the deep sea boats. There was such variety in the harbor, from massive container ships and tankers to tiny canoe-like vessels, really pirogues, that were filled with seashells that would be boiled and ground into powder for the whitewash that so much brightens the homes in Cochin. All in all, we had an instructive and relaxing day.

We were met by a car and driver in Trichy and were in Thanjavur an hour and a half later. The whole reason for coming here was to visit the Brihadeshwara Temple, built in the first decade of the 11th century and now exactly 1,000 years old. It is a UNESCO World Heritage site. I believe there are only a half dozen free-standing temple sites in all of India that have been declared World Heritage loci: Brihadeshwara and two sister Chola temples, the Sun Temple at Konarak, the Shore Temple and Five Rathas at Mahabalipuram, the western group of temples at Khajuraho and two places we have never visited but will see on the "Hidden India" part of this trip, Pattadakal and Hampi. This

Thanjavur shrine has sometimes been described as the finest temple in India. I could never endorse that sentiment. I have seen too much and in it there has been such great variety that I could never choose one active temple above all others.

Brihadeshwara is a very large compound surrounded by palm trees; the wall of the compound is surmounted by 1,008 granite Nandis so that all who approach these precincts know they belong to Siva. There are two gopurams but they do not dwarf the central shrine whose tower rises a majestic 66 meters, and the stone that caps it weighs more than 80 tons. Atop this there is a gold-covered finial that was donated by the Chola sovereign Rajaraja in 1010. There are a number of smaller buildings and they complement the main shrine rather than diverting attention from it. In front of the shrine there is a Nandi pavilion and this great beast is the second largest monolithic Nandi in India. Nearby in her own pavilion there is an utterly charming bovine mate for Nandi and she is the mount for Parvati. Within the compound there are several hundred lingas. This is very much a living temple, the destination of countless pilgrimages.

But despite the throngs at Brihadeshwara, the compound is so very large, so filled with light and air, so green with its capacious manicured lawn and neem trees, that the effect is one of serenity and calm in spite of all the bustle. Siva is portrayed in the central shrine as Lord of the Dance and he is accompanied by Parvati, his son Maruka and Ganesh, and he is also depicted here as teacher and beggar. There are graceful maidens executing 81 of the 108 positions of classical dance. There are also many handsome peacock motifs in the temple as well as countless yalis and macaras, more or less generic terms for a variety of mythological beasts. The hooded brass cobras over the linga are remarkably arresting. Columns and walls are elaborately carved and all the stone is granite. We did not leave until it was too dark to see anything more.

After an early breakfast I sat by the Parisutham's pool until I was driven inside by the three sweepers who were assiduously cleaning the area. Indian sweepers work hard, very hard, usually in uncomfortable positions, and rarely does one see them take a break for very long. This is labor for the stout-hearted. Sun and dust, this is South India, sun and dust, sun and dust. The sun bakes the water from the soil and so the soil crumbles into dust and the dust must be swept away, swept away fastidiously, and then everything must be done again the next morning until the blessed day when the monsoons begin and relief comes. Swoosh, swoosh, swoosh; the incidence of pulmonary problems must be astronomical among the sweepers and other denizens of the lower depths. The swimming pool is rather unusual. It is shaped like a good luck charm, a four leaf clover with a small island of bamboo trees, pleasingly off-center in one of the leaves. The lovely blue of the tiles was a color that I had seen elsewhere yesterday, in the Chennai airport. I watched a very little boy who had what I think were his first pair of shoes. Whenever he moved tiny electric lights on his shoes twinkled on and off in bright blue. He was clearly thrilled to have such shoes and his parents had the solace of knowing he would not be easy to lose in a crowd.

At ten we set out for the Chola temple at Darasuram; it is in a secluded area of a very small town with no signs announcing its presence and we were the only visitors. It is today included as a part of the Brihadeshwara World Heritage site. It is remarkably charming, not least of all because it is so simple and small. There are Nandis every few feet along the enclosure wall so that all and sundry will know whose property they approach and perhaps stop for puja or devotions. The vestibule has 108 wonderfully carved pillars, each one different and more elaborate than the last. The wheels and the horses carved on the sides of the temple suggest its creators envisioned it as a divine chariot. The temple tower is quite exceptional and attractive. There are superb figures of dancing girls carved very prominently on the walls and for this reason Darasuram is known as "the temple of perpetual entertainment." The granite ceilings have also been beautifully sculpted. Some of the original 12th century paint is still quite visible.

The road to Chidambaram is appalling but the destination makes the journey endurable. This Siva Nataraja temple is surely the most important in this part of India after the Brihadeshwara triple home run. I had wanted to come here because of my own long-standing interest in the notion of play, which I had used in half a dozen books to try to illuminate the nature of Christian faith and life. This notion is equally a part of the Hindu tradition. There are many differences between the two faiths and their uses of the idea of play but there are also profound and interesting affinities. I wanted to see something of the Hindu perspective set out in stone as well as in words. Where better to go than to one of the great Chola temples dedicated to Siva as the Lord of the Dance?

There are four gopurams that give access to the temple; on the walls of the eastern and western entrances there are granite panels portraying maidens in all 108 Hindu dance postures, 54 on the entry side and 54 on the exit side of the very spacious gateways. I was delighted to be here even though the temple precincts were teeming with crowds of pilgrims and other visitors. There is a dance pavilion with 1,000 pillars but unfortunately it was closed. The sacred tank at Chidambaram is huge and very beautiful. The 12th century roof of the main temple is covered with gold. There are many Nandis around, some grazing on the ground, others staring from the heights of the gopurams, all of them keeping a watchful and protective eye on the worshippers and tourists who swarm around them all day. We enjoyed ourselves, then said a reluctant farewell to Siva Nataraja at six because I wanted to reach our hotel by nightfall.

MAHAKUTA, Sacred Tank
In the hamlet of Mahakuta there are two temples facing one another across a sacred tank where village boys can play and dunk one another while the gods look down and smile.

Pondicherry belonged to the French until 1961 and today it is still a fiercely francophone culture. The Hotel de l'Orient is an 18th century French Colonial mansion that can accommodate perhaps 25 or 30 people. Its dinner menu was entirely in French and we settled for the plat du jour; it was very good and concluded with bananas flambe. This is a fine place and we like it. After dinner we walked through the dark streets of the French Quarter and marveled at the Parisian ambiance that exists even today in Pondicherry.

Our breakfast consisted entirely of croissants and brioches and very good they were. The coast road to Chennai is two lanes in both directions and has not a single pothole. It is privately maintained and therefore charges tolls, but this road is a winner. We stop several times, first to look at the salt pans where mounds of sea salt glisten in the sun. These salt flats in the backwaters cover more than 2,700 acres. We stopped again to spend more than two hours revisiting a favorite place, Mahabalipuram. Elaine bought some postcards at the ASI office and then briefly visited the Shore Temple. It was a disappointment because now there are steel gates in front of the sculpture of Vishnu and the Siva lingam. We are told this was done as protection against terrorism. So the terrorists have won again.

When we arrived at the Chola we were very warmly welcomed and ushered to a new suite directly above where we had been last year. We settled in and then went down to the residents' lounge and we met an English acquaintance we had gotten to know last year. He is a regular parishioner at St. Mary's Church in Fort St. George. We greeted one another with much pleasure and had a good conversation. Our flight tomorrow to Bangalore is scheduled for mid-afternoon so I could not plan any lengthy excursion. I decided it might be best to go to the Chennai National Museum and revisit the Bronze Gallery, mainly to see the two 11th century Chola masterpieces of Siva Nataraja and Siva the Androgyne. Unfortunately a power failure plunged the Bronze Gallery into darkness just before we arrived and so we had to go elsewhere. There was electricity in the Sculpture Gallery, however, and we had never visited there. It was a delight. The Pallava and Chola statuary were fascinating, but at least to my eyes the most mesmerizing item in the whole gallery was a Hoysala doorway, amply proportioned but not quite large enough to be called a ceremonial gateway or anything like that. The carving was unbelievably intricate.

We arrived in Bangalore in the middle of rush hour which in this city means considerably more traffic than most people have ever seen before. But it must be said that the politeness and courtliness which for me characterizes more Indians than not certainly extends to the way people drive. Our driver is named Babu. He will be with us for nine days and this pleases me very much because I have already heard that he is an excellent driver and a thoroughly reliable and amiable man. We were welcomed at the Oberoi Bangalore and given an upgrade to the sort of room we thought we had asked for. We left our two suitcases at the hotel for the next ten days and we were assured that when we returned, travel-stained and weary, our room would be awaiting us at six o'clock in the morning at no extra charge. Before leaving Bangalore for Mysore we learned that the proposed Metro for Bangalore is no longer a dream but is actually being constructed and a significant part of it should be completed within the next 12 months. I think this is really wonderful news, particularly for all of us who care that Bangalore should not lose its claim to be "The Garden City." Technological progress like the Metro need not be the enemy of old ways of life and established neighborhoods. Sometimes it can reverse the excesses of modernization. This will mean a tremendous improvement in traffic flow in the city.

Babu appeared at ten o'clock and we set off for Mysore. Last year the trip had been very difficult because of road construction everywhere. To my great surprise, this year the new road was almost entirely completed: four lanes, many lay-bys, wide verges and a median strip already planted with tens of thousands of bougainvillaea. The Lalitha Mahal is unchanged: a spectacular palace from the outside, a great disappointment from the inside, although the dining room and the food are both superb. We telephone Nagaraja Rao and he agrees to meet us for drinks and dinner at the hotel this evening.

It is grand to be with Nagaraj again. He gives us train tickets he has purchased for us, both from Mysore to Hubli and from Hospet to Bangalore nine or ten days later. They cost $100 for the two of us. He has talked with his former ASI subordinates and arranged for them to meet us and escort us around Badami,

Mahakuta, Pattadakal, Aihole, Hospet and Hampi. This escort will be especially important in Hampi because it is so vast and we will want to use roads that are closed to the public. Nagaraj will call for us tomorrow afternoon and see us to our seats or berths or whatever we have on the Dharwar Express at eight after we have a late tea.

We arise early because Babu is eager to start for Hubli around noon. We will take the overnight train while he drives our car over some very bad roads for 13 or 14 hours and then we will rendezvous at the Hubli train station at five tomorrow morning. We will leave our flight bags in the car which means we will have nothing with us except the clothes on our backs. At 8:15 we set off for the little 13th century Hoysala temple at Somnathpur. The drive is rather an education in agricultural India because we are seeing it so close up and, thanks to our vehicular progress, in such slow motion. Everyone waves to us and we always wave to them, not only the small children but even the workmen digging up the road.

For the first time ever, when we get to Somnathpur we see other tourists. There are about 20 French visitors who are also staying at the Lalitha Mahal and they seem a quite good and serious group. They have also been to Belur and Halebid to see the Hoysala temples there. Eight or ten Indians also appear during our visit. As always, everything in the large compound is meticulously cared for and the atmosphere of quietude and calm is infectious. The custodian turned on lights for us in the three diminutive shrines within the temple; even though this was my fifth or sixth visit I had never before realized there was a bit of illumination inside the little sanctuaries. We proceeded clockwise--one should never do otherwise--from Krishna with his flute in the first bay to Keshava, for whom the temple is named, and then finally Vishnu himself. This is no longer a living temple because one of the three divinities is a modern reproduction. We took our usual batch of photographs and then tried to concentrate on aspects of the temple we had not examined as carefully as we wanted to on earlier visits. The ceilings are quite spectacular and demand very careful scrutiny.

Nagaraj took us for tea to the Metropole Hotel, which we found very enjoyable. Soon after dark we went to find the Dharwar Express; Nagaraj insisted on remaining with us until we located our seats. This was fortunate because our fan did not work and the two other berths in the compartment were reserved for other people. Only 11 of the 44 spaces in the carriage had been purchased, however, so Nagaraj went off to find the conductor and ask if we could be moved to a different compartment where there would be no one in the upper berths. The conductor knew who Nagaraj was and he proved very obliging. We changed to other berths where we had some privacy; it was very quiet and pleasant and even though we did not sleep we managed to rest very comfortably on our way to "Hidden India." The Dharwar Express has no first class at all. This had caused me some real unhappiness because there are so many stories of ghastly railroad misadventures. What the train did have, however, is a single coach with real glass windows and to which there is no access from the other coaches. It is a second class air-conditioned two-tier sleeping car. All compartments had four berths. It has its own conductor and security guard and two room boys. Shortly after departure a room boy appeared with beautifully ironed sheets and pillow cases and a blanket for each of us. Later the conductor came by to ask if we were comfortable and if we would like a wake-up call 15 minutes before our arrival in Hubli.

After eight and a half hours on the train we arrived in Hubli 15 minutes ahead of schedule. So much for my apprehensions, which proved to be ridiculous. Babu was waiting for us on the platform and we were delighted to see one another again. We set out immediately for Badami, two and a half or three hours away. It was very dark until six and sunrise did not come until half an hour later. I saw so many people, mostly women, trudging along the roadside in the darkness, almost always alone. Where were they going? What were they thinking? Why were they abroad so long before there was any light? Watching them was different than watching the traffic below our windows in Chennai; this was much more stark, much more unsettling, much more strange. We seemed to be traveling amidst a company of wraiths. The Lord of the Dance unleashes more mysteries than our minds will ever fathom. We reached the Badami Court Hotel well before eight and Babu remarked that it was no Oberoi. It was hard to quarrel with that. We agreed to meet with our ASI host at nine. Badami is nothing more than a very small town perched in the middle of nowhere, even though once long ago it was an important city. But it is hugely picturesque; its winding alleys hold many interesting surprises.

The Chalukyan sacred sites in Badami consist primarily of four "cave" temples, three of which are 6th century and Hindu while the fourth is a century later and is Jain. We drove around a corner in the village and unexpectedly found ourselves at the foot of a red sandstone bluff. High above us was the first of the temples. It is devoted to Siva and it is breathtaking. I was prepared to find Badami a fascinating archeological site. I was in no way prepared to find it one of the treasures of India. But

BADAMI, Rock-cut Temple, Detail
The lowest temple at Badami is introduced by a superb statue of Siva Nataraja. Like the rest of us he has only two arms, but by the 6th century it was an artistic convention to endow him with many arms to indicate the energy and rapidity of his cosmic dance of destruction and rebirth.

Badami ranks with the cenotaphs of Gaitore and the Delwara temples of Mt. Abu and the Vishnu shrines at Nagda as the fourth wonderful highlight of this trip. At the entrance to the shrine there is a slightly more than life-size Siva Nataraja. This Lord of the Dance has 18 arms and his fingers are extended to disclose 81 of the positions of classical dance. The effect is entirely different from that at Chidambaram although complementary because there the focus lies on the Shaivite dancers exhibiting all the traditional poses while here it is entirely on the Lord of the Dance as the origin and inspiration of the motion of the cosmos. Siva holds a snake, a trident, castanets and other tokens of his identity. This is an astonishing display of sculptural virtuosity.

Just beyond this marvelous figure there is a no less impressive carving of an androgyne, Siva-and-Parvati. Facing this from the opposite side of the temple is a depiction of Harihara, half Siva and half Vishnu. The artisans at work here obviously were attempting to explore a parallel between these two figures but precisely what was in their minds now seems lost to us. In my judgment both seem to be images of wholeness and health, the unity of male and female attributes and of preserver and destroyer or of death and rebirth. The columned hall has splendid decorations that seem untouched by all the centuries since they were made. There is an icon of Durga and a beautiful peacock that are especially notable. The ceiling is simple but elegant and has some fine medallions of amorous couples.

The second shrine is devoted to Vishnu and it is high above the first. It has wonderful sculptures of groups of dwarfs. It has a very large image of Varaha, Vishnu's incarnation in the form of a boar. The boar is also a symbol of the Chalukya dynasty. There are many other avatars of Vishnu on these walls. The ceiling is quite spectacular and by the entrance there are enormous guardian figures that are awesome. The bracket carvings are extremely well done and it may well be that they influenced the artisans who created the bracket decorations at Belur and Halebid six centuries later. It is a long climb to the third temple, but this is often regarded as the finest of the four. My own choice would be the first shrine, because I found it more intellectually challenging. The sculptures here, unweathered as they are, could scarcely be excelled. Yali bracket figures and portrayals of Vishnu and his avatars are especially good. The temple also has a marvelous and very busy ceiling. The columns are splendid and above them one can see remnants of the original 6th century paint. Everything in the temple seems a bit larger and more richly decorated than the two below it. I particularly appreciated the figures of Brahma riding a swan, Siva on his Nandi and Indra astride an elephant. The principal sculptures are Vishnu seated on a coiled serpent, Varaha, Harihara, Narasimha and Vishnu with Lakshmi. There are also many beguiling dwarfs. The small Jain shrine at the top of the cliff is devoted to the first Tirthankara, Adinath, although there are images of two dozen other tirthankaras as well.

We returned to the hotel exhausted but jubilant, confident that we had seen another of the glories of India, a hidden treasure. It was a joy. It was also an ordeal. The rock-cut steps from the base to the top two caves are very uneven and slippery, some shallow and some steep, sometimes with inclines for several feet between them--and all of this a millennium and a half old. The descent can be even more arduous and dangerous than the ascent. We slept long and well. UNESCO World Heritage site it may be, but I was convinced our destination the next morning, the hamlet of Pattadakal, could wait until we were good and ready for it. I doubted that anything there could match the splendor of the Badami caves which had offered us so much even as they had demanded so much in terms of the simple exercise of climbing to them. The dozens of shrines at Pattadakal are mainly in a single enclosure on the bank of the Malprabha River, a much more domesticated scene than the stark and not entirely tamed grandeur of the red sandstone bluff guarding the Badami caves, where every prospect high or low is breathtaking.

But Pattadakal has its own persuasive claims to be a World Heritage site. First, we have an interesting juxtaposition of different sorts of roofs of the same vintage. Some are curvilinear while other shrines are capped by receding square

BADAMI, Rock-cut Temple
In the picturesque town of Badami there are four rock-cut temples carved from the side of a great red sandstone bluff, three Hindu and the topmost Jain. This temple was carved in the 6th century.

tiers that do not aspire to climb nearly so high. Second, the first half of the 8th century when most of these temples were built was a time of extraordinary ferment and innovation in Chalukyan religious architecture. We have contemporaneous temples side by side that look as though they have come from entirely different cultures. This is the climax of early Chalukyan design: we are presented with amazing variety that suggests architectural developments that will take centuries to find their final expressions, in the North as well as in the South. So Pattadakal is a prophecy of what the future holds. Like Mahabalipuram it is a text readers in the future of Indian sacred architecture and that is why today it is a World Heritage site.

The visitor proceeds to explore the east-facing shrines from north to south and from the simplest to the most complex. Galaganatha is elaborate and richly decorated. It has a fine sculpture of Siva spearing a demon. Kashivishvanatha has a particularly splendid Siva Nataraja. Then one comes to two temples that are virtually identical: Virupaksha and Mallikarjuna. They were built at the same time by two queens to celebrate a great Chalukyan victory over the Pallavas circa 745. If they are identical in conception, however, they are not at all in execution, for the latter is badly weathered externally and notably inferior in its interior carving. But both represent a great increase in size and complexity, a more sophisticated design and more ambitious multi-storeyed towers.

The columns in the great hall at Virupaksha are carved with wonderful vibrancy and delicacy; half of them have scenes from the Ramayana and the rest tell stories from the Mahabharata. There are many fine sculptures of both Siva and Vishnu, especially one of Vishnu with Durga and another of Siva springing from a lingam. The perforated stone windows are particularly remarkable. One has a snake motif and others have floral designs. There are many interesting pediments and many happily embracing couples. The temple doorkeepers are quite awesome figures. The best of the ceilings is a marvelous representation of Surya and his horse-drawn chariot high in the sky. Altogether Pattadakal is a fascinating lesson in the evolution of sacred architecture and, even if it does not quite equal the splendors of Mahabalipuram, a site worthy of its World Heritage status.

We returned to our hotel for a brief rest before visiting the small ASI museum in Badami not far from the cave temples. I had wanted to come here specifically to find two Siva icons unearthed at Pattadakal and then brought to the Badami Museum for safekeeping. I soon found them; both are splendid and probably date from the 8th century. One is Siva the archer with his muscles tensed as he readies his arrow for flight. The other is Siva defending his vulnerable human charges and spearing to death the demon of death so that people would be liberated from the tyranny of death. I was very pleased my search for these icons had ended so well. As we drove in the early morning of the next day from Badami to Aihole the landscape became much less green and cultivated and turned thoroughly forbidding. The closer we came to Aihole the fewer traces there were of any human activity at all. But the complex of temples here is beautifully tended.

The jewel in the crown is the Durga Temple, built in 742, although Durga does not refer to the goddess but to the status of the temple as a fortified outpost many centuries ago. It represents the very finest of Chalukyan art and design. The shrine is usually described as apsidal-ended and semi-circular, which

AIHOLE, Durga Temple
Built in the 8th c. the Durga Temple is the most imposing building in Aihole. Originally a military post it has a spectacular ambulatory with brilliantly conceived and executed sculptures.

I find a bit misleading. Actually it is fashioned more like the capital letter U. Its distinctive feature is a fabulous ambulatory which cradles a sanctuary and a rectangular hall. One immediately recognizes this is dedicated to Vishnu because there is a fine garuda above the entrance, where there are also sculptures of some guardian figures and amorous couples. The perforated stone windows are of different floral designs but sunflowers appear most frequently. But most important is the colonnaded ambulatory where Chalukyan sculptors created a series of masterpieces: Siva with his Nandi, Narasimha, Varaha the boar-faced avatar, Durga, Harihara and Vishnu with his garuda. This is truly superb art. The temple interior is very plain; after all, the sculptors may have thought, what more is there to say that we have not said already?

In the course of several hours we visited a good many temples but I will mention only three. First, the Surya Narayana shrine has a fine tower, a well-proportioned hall with very attractive and delicate columns and a good porch. Second, the Ladkhan shrine, which was constructed in 450 but was originally intended to be a place for town meetings. It was not until some years later that Ladkhan metamorphosed into a temple. The singularity of the stone construction clearly suggests that the builders were working with a timber model and few precedents. There are pleasing sculptures of loving couples and of river gods; the stone windows are very attractive. I was completely surprised to find a stone ladder leading to the roof leaning at perhaps a 20 degree angle against one of the walls. The reason for it is that when Ladkhan was converted into a temple there was no appropriate place for a sanctuary and so the townspeople constructed one on the roof.

We finished our time in Aihole at the Ravula Phadi cave temple, which was carved in the 6th century. Access to it is very difficult and leaving it is even more so, requiring either great agility or much assistance, which fortunately I was given. This is a remarkable and special place, as exciting to me as the Durga Temple where we began. The sculptures in this small shrine are simply wonderful. Perhaps most striking is a splendid Lord Siva with ten arms who is dancing with Parvati and Ganesh and eight quite voluptuous maidens. The temple guardian figures are majestic. Other particularly arresting and

AIHOLE, Ravula Phadi Temple
In the 6th c. Ravula Phadi Temple there is a superb frieze of Siva Nataraja dancing with eight maidens and his wife and son.

beautiful sculptures include Harihara, Varaha, Durga and Mahisha-Mardini. My own favorite is a magnificent Gangadwara depicting Siva bringing to his people the life-giving waters of the Ganges. This was a splendid way to end a visit that had begun equally well. Ravula Phadi and the Durga Temple at Aihole, the Virupaksha shrine in Pattadakal and caves one and three in Badami would be my first choices among all that we have seen of "Hidden India." But we have seen so much here in northern Karnataka, all of it worthwhile.

It was a three hour drive to Hospet but Babu pointed out so many landmarks that the time passed quickly and pleasantly. Now we are at the Malligi Tourist Home for want of anywhere else to stay. Sidewalks in Hospet do not look inviting. At eight o'clock the next morning we set out for Hampi to meet Nagaraj's two ASI subordinates who will show us something of the world of the Vijayanagar during our two day visit. The Vijayanagar empire endured for only 200 years, from the mid-14th century to the mid-16th when it fell before the onslaughts of Islamic armies that proceeded to raze most of its capital city. But for two centuries until then it flourished mightily and Hampi was a center of population and wealth and imperial power that ruled much of India and had no

AIHOLE, Ladkhan Temple
Built in 451, Ladkhan was a civic center converted to a temple with its sanctuary on the roof because there was no other place for it. As the carving indicates this is a transitional structure from rock-cut temples to wooden ones to free-standing stone structures.

rivals. In its heyday Hampi provided a home for one million people. Admiring Westerners contrasted it with the simplicity of Elizabethan London, which had very little that could match the splendor and pomp of Hampi. This World Heritage site is vast and not even ten long days would begin to exhaust all the richness it has to offer. I certainly have never seen anywhere else a moonscape such as this, crowded with enormous granite boulders carelessly strewn everywhere as though they were the relics of some mythic battle among the Titans. After we met our hosts we visited the Virupaksha and Krishna temples, marveled at a massive Ganesha about 20 feet tall and looked briefly at the hubbub of Hampi bazaar. But I had long since decided that if I could not see all or even a great deal of Hampi, there was one site I would spend all the time I needed looking at with much care, the Vitthala Temple complex, beyond question the greatest surviving glory of the Vijayanagar empire.

The Vitthala compound is very large with numerous buildings. Facing the visitor is the main sanctuary which is dedicated to Vishnu. One approaches it through a totally overwhelming Dancing Hall. There is also a Singing Hall, a

Cooking Hall, a hundred-pillared Assembly Hall and a magnificent Marriage Hall. Before one arrives at the unbelievable Dancing Hall the visitor encounters a large stone chariot that provides a home for Vishnu's garuda. The stone chariot is so exquisitely made that until recently all its parts including the wheels functioned perfectly. Before we came to Vitthala Babu turned to the ASI officers and admonished them, "Let the stones speak for themselves." Well said. These stones not only spoke eloquently for themselves, they sang. There were some musical pillars that emitted beautiful single notes when they were struck gently by the knuckles of our hosts. But the greatest music in the Dancing Hall is not audible but visible, written on each of the 56 pillars. I have never seen other

HAMPI, Vitthala Temple
The Vitthala Temple is the finest surviving complex at Hampi. This stone chariot is gorgeously carved and is dedicated to the Garuda that is Lord Vishnu's mount.

columns anywhere more elaborately and richly and exquisitely carved. Each of the 56 is different from all the others. Everything is an amazing exercise in virtuosity, genius showing as much in conception as in execution because there is nothing else anywhere that reflects the same particular imagination with which some individual has shaped this stone. Elaine and I were both at a loss for words.

The intention of these artists, or so it seems to me, is clear: simply to generate awe in every visitor. The Dancing Hall is certainly not a huge or overwhelming building but it is as awesome as anything I have ever seen. And what more fundamental religious attitude can there be among the world's great religions than a simple sense of awe? On the other hand, this is a Dancing Hall intended for play that will be pleasing both to the gods and to the dancers themselves, as well as to all their kin who watch. This is a context for rejoicing. This is one thing the hall is meant to be, impetus for joy. These were and are, at least from my perspective, the two most fundamental religious responses to the Holy that characterize all developed faiths. This is no ruin, the Vitthala complex; it articulates as well today as it did five centuries ago timeless religious truth. There is wondrous music here.

The most extraordinary sculptures in the Dancing Hall are the Yalis, wonderful mythical figures, some with the bodies of lions, others with elephantine or equine shapes. But there are also many scenes from Hindu religious epics and from daily life in Hampi in the 15th century. The city was a very cosmopolitan place then; our hosts enjoyed showing us how to distinguish between English and Portuguese and Chinese visitors by the hats they were wearing. The Marriage Hall is somewhat smaller but no less ornate; it provides a feast for the eyes that simply cannot be assimilated without much time and concentration. The other structures are less intriguing but we have already seen such rich fare that no one could possibly hunger for more. From Vitthala we went to the small but quite fine ASI museum. The curators there were preparing to pack a splendid statue of a reclining Vishnu on a coiled naga for shipment to some major exhibition in Paris. Then we made our way back to the Malligi Tourist Home; it had been a long day in fiercely enervating heat.

We left for our second day at Hampi very early in the morning to avoid the scorching midday temperatures. Altogether we probably paid attention to as many as twenty of the Vijayanagar sites but that is only a tiny fraction of what there is to see if someone has a free fortnight and can survive the Malligi Tourist Home for so long. We were quite amazed by the 22 foot high Narasimha monolith looking down upon us with a grotesque grimace of a smile. Nearby is a very small Siva shrine with a lingam in the middle of a pool. We looked at a subterranean temple that is very extensive and then at the Queen's Bath, an attractive building centered in what was once another pool. The Lotus Mahal is a two storey pleasure pavilion that is perhaps the most interesting of the secular buildings extant in Hampi. It has a number of lobed arches that are very attractive and the upper storey is capped by nine pyramidal towers, the central one being slightly higher than the others. Presumably this was used by the sovereign for special receptions. The elephant stables are also memorable. There are 11 chambers which can accommodate 22 animals chosen from the thousands in the royal herds for one or another special occasion. Within the chambers there is room to accommodate the drummers and other musicians who might accompany the caparisoned elephants. At an angle to the stables there is an arcaded building that presumably housed the attendants and in front of it is a raised verandah from which guests could watch whatever spectacle outside the stables they had been invited to view. The domes above the elephant chambers are very impressive.

Then I did what I had done yesterday with the Vitthala Temple. Once again I chose a single destination which would be the focus of our energies today. So off we went to the Hazzara Rama Temple, which along with Vitthala is the best sacred architecture at Vijayanagar. It is constructed entirely from white granite and how this recalcitrant stone could have been carved so subtly and delicately I cannot imagine. The shrine was built for the exclusive use of the royal family. The temple is guarded by a very expansive rectangular wall, the outside of which is covered with five beautifully carved bands. At the base there are elephants, then there are wonderful horses and above them various musicians and dancing female figures. Last of all there are armies drawn up to do battle. The interior of the walls begins a comprehensive portrayal of the entire

Ramayana, which is surely an extraordinary and heroic undertaking. The temple is dedicated to Vishnu and on the exterior walls there are wonderful depictions of maidens swimming with Vishnu in his form as Krishna.

A visitor to the sanctuary finds there are four astonishing black granite columns polished to a mirror-like brilliance. They have been lavishly adorned by master sculptors and are covered with figures of Vishnu in his many guises. The capitals of the pillars are also especially noteworthy. Although the four black columns are very different from one another, each is a hymn

HAMPI, Hazzara Rama Temple
The Hazzara Rama shrine at Hampi was reserved for the use of the royal family. This is a detail of one of the four great black granite pillars in the sanctuary.

in stone to God the preserver and sustainer. The narrative of the Ramayana is continued from the outer walls on the compound to the exterior of the sanctum itself, which is decorated all over by three broad bands of splendid sculpture. Hazzara Rama is the only place I have ever seen such a comprehensive exposition in stone of a whole religious epic like the Ramayana. The massive and very impressive tower that crowns the temple has been heavily restored but that certainly does not detract from its splendor.

When I awoke yesterday morning I knew that I had a major decision to make. We had been told in America that it was a very long way from Hospet to Bangalore over very difficult roads and that it would be a most uncomfortable journey requiring more than twelve hours. So we purchased berths on the night train, even though we would have to share a compartment with two or four other people. The other option was to return to Bangalore with Babu. He told us we had been woefully misled. The trip by car would be less than six hours over one of the finest new roads in India. So we threw away our train tickets and went with Babu. We were back at the Oberoi more than two hours before the night train had even left Hospet.

As I read the newspapers the next morning after ten days without seeing one, I was fascinated by the juxtaposition of two major articles in The Times of India describing the collision of two worlds. The first article reported an address to the students of the Indian Institute of Management, Bangalore, by one of India's leading entrepreneurs and richest men. Mr. Mittal said: "With a highly knowledge-based society, it's time India took on the West .... the Western world is ageing. In twenty years it will be Indian hands that will take over." There is a new mood of confidence abroad in India today that was entirely absent a generation ago. It is not aggressive or boastful; instead, it is an essential prelude to whatever comes next, because the future demands psychic as well as economic preparations. India now is a field of dreams. Many will be realized soon even though others must be deferred until another time. But aspirations are high and fierce and energy seems to have no bounds.

The second article was headlined, "France, Britain Come to Standstill." Apparently there was massive disruption yesterday when some three million people on both sides of the Channel staged a huge protest. The reason for it had to do with maintenance of European social welfare provisions in the face of the need to compete against the relatively inexpensive labor of India and China. The article reported that all transport in France was shut down while Britain had the largest public sector strike in 80 years, closing hundreds of schools and courts and disrupting trash collections and burials. The article concludes with this sentence: "The message from both Britain and France...together with the ongoing spectacle of massive public sector strikes in Germany is seen to underline 21st century Europe's reluctance to mortgage social welfare provisions in order to buy into the low-cost mantra of globalization." However greatly one's sympathies may lie with the old world, when past and future collide we usually know who the winner will be. For the moment, however, here we are at the Bangalore Oberoi, relishing our current exposure to this field of dreams far away from older developed countries that so often seem shadowed by fears that the old order will not endure and that the future is too uncertain to be embraced.

The next day at noon Babu drove us to the airport where we caught a flight to Mumbai. From there we took another plane to Bhopal, where we would stay while visiting the Buddhist shrines at Sanchi and the prehistoric cave shelters at Bhimbetka with their hundreds of paintings, before ending the trip in New Delhi. Babu is the best driver we have ever had and a most intelligent and pleasant man; he speaks seven major languages fluently. He knows of my interest in Hoysala sacred architecture and said the next time we were in India he would like to show us the 42 sites in Karnataka that are associated with the Hoysala dynasty. Apparently he once did this with someone else. We certainly hope to see him again. Jet Airways makes transfers remarkably easy, especially in Mumbai. There is always someone waiting by the plane to tell you exactly what to do and which bus to board. There is also someone waiting to carry whatever luggage you have kept with you on the plane.

We arrived in Bhopal at dusk and encountered a delightful surprise. The Noor-us-Sabah is the only hotel on the whole trip that I had not chosen. It had been selected by a travel agent. All I knew was that it had been built in the 1920s by the Nawab of Bhopal as a palace for his daughter. So I had visions of a sort of Muslim Lalitha Mahal Palace where nothing functioned and no one stirred until there was a call to prayer. In fact, the Noor-us-Sabah is a delight; our huge room and terrace greatly pleased us and Elaine was especially happy with her pink marble bathroom and shower. We had breakfast on the lawn overlooking twelve mile long Lake Bhopal. We ate all our meals on the terraces at dawn and in the darkness because all the city lights at night reflecting off the lake were as lovely as the vista during the day. We left for Sanchi at eight o'clock because we had been told it was a two hour drive each way and that much of the road was dreadful. India has three principal Buddhist pilgrimage sites. One is Bodh Gaya, where Prince Gautama found enlightenment under the Bodhi tree.

The second is Sarnath; in the deer park there Lord Buddha preached his first sermon. The third site is Sanchi, where the Buddha never came for any reason at all. But it was chosen in the third century B.C. by the Mauryan Emperor Ashoka to be an everlasting memorial to Buddhist enlightenment and the liberation it brings. The ASI complex at Sanchi is situated on a hillside surrounded by scores and scores of stupas, many of them tiny, some monastic dormitories and temples and various other buildings, in a remote location chosen as an appropriate context for meditation.

The most obvious attraction at Sanchi, of course, is the Great Stupa; nearby are the somewhat smaller but virtually identical second and third stupas and all their tiny progeny. Gertrude Stein wrote, "a rose is a rose is a rose." "A stupa is a stupa is a stupa."--or, as we would say, a cairn. There is nothing else to say, really, except that the big ones are crowned by small umbrellas. But the glory of Sanchi are the four toranas or gates to the Great Stupa, which are brilliantly and exquisitely carved, although there are some other less interesting toranas as well. All

SANCHI, Torana
Sanchi is one of the most revered Buddhist sites in India. This is one of the four toranas or gateways that lead to the Great Stupa that memorializes the life and teachings of the Buddha.

of them are approximately 25 feet tall. Each consists of two beautifully sculpted pillars which include the Ashokan emblem of four lions and which are joined high overhead by three architraves that are gracefully curved in their middles and at their ends. It seems the carvers had originally learned their craft with wood and ivory and this is the reason they were capable of such painstaking and exquisite work in this unforgiving and obdurate stone. The heavily decorated toranas include many scenes from first century B.C. life, with horses and riders and monkeys and elephants and many other creatures. But their focus really lies elsewhere, on scenes from the Jatakas which recall earlier incarnations and exploits of the young Boddhisattva Gautama and incidents from the later life of the Buddha and the subsequent history of the community of believers. But what is perhaps most notable and important of all are the Tri-ratnas which symbolize the implicit triunity that is always present in Buddhism: the Enlightened One himself, the law or Middle Way through which enlightenment is found and the community of the faithful, first entirely male and later female as well--the Buddha, the Dharma and the Sangha.

As for the Great Stupa itself, it looks as though it were built only yesterday. In fact, it is an elegant stone hemisphere that was constructed to encase the brick stupa that Ashoka himself had erected only a few decades earlier in the 3rd century B.C. Ashoka chose well. There is a pervasive serenity and peace about this place which is palpable; no attentive visitor could miss it. There are almost no images of the Buddha to be found in the whole complex, however, because in the early centuries of the faith it was thought sacrilegious to attempt to portray the face of the Enlightened One. We saw only a small number of tourists, all of them Westerners, because Buddhism really lost its grip on the subcontinent more than a millennium ago and moved to the north and east. The toranas by themselves can profitably occupy a good many days of study. By mid-afternoon, however, we wanted to be in Bhimbetka. What we went there to explore are not actually caves but simply rock shelters sculpted by the erosion of wind and water and never shaped by human hands.

The significance of these paleolithic shelters is only now being slowly grasped. They remained undiscovered until the 1950s. The site is presently in the custody of the ASI and that is fortunate. They plan to publish a book on their findings within the foreseeable future, but at this juncture it is very difficult to date many of the paintings. There are probably about a thousand of these rock shelters--I think no one really knows for certain. Perhaps half that number have paintings or at least traces of paintings. A larger number at one time or another sheltered some of our ancestors. Perhaps nowhere else in the world are there so many paleolithic shelters and paintings. Bhimbetka may be a treasure that is unique. It is thought that some of the paintings were done as early as 10,000 B.C., although others may be as recent as a millennium ago. Almost invariably, it seems, the earlier the art the finer it is. In any event, Bhimbetka has been some sort of "artists' colony" for more than ten thousand years. The earliest color seems to have been white, made from pulverized limestone and tree sap. Next came red, which was made from leaves, and black. The most recent colors are yellow and green.

The "caves" of Bhimbetka are located on the summit of a low mountain south of Bhopal in very craggy, desolate and jungle-like terrain. The ASI has constructed a concrete path that links fifteen particularly important sites and visitors would be ill-advised to stray from the route because of wild animals and

BHIMBETKA, Pre-history
Bhimbetka is about 20 miles southeast of Bhopal. There are many hundreds of prehistoric paintings in rock shelters here. The "Zoo Rock" contains horses, bison, tigers and elephants. It is not much more than 5000 years old.

many precipitous drops. Even this brief tour is more than sufficient to show why Bhimbetka today is a new UNESCO World Heritage monument. My limited vision meant that many of the paintings eluded me but many others afforded me great pleasure. There is a red picture of a hunt of epic proportions. It brims with energy and movement; there are many hunters and horses and the quarry seems to be a leopard. There is also a very crude portrayal of a four-armed Siva Nataraja of undetermined date. The "Zoo Rock" depicts elephants and tigers and horses and bison; it is probably no more than 5,000 years old. There are many other pictures of various animals and of men holding hands and dancing in a circle.

Two lone white animals especially caught my eye. One is a brilliantly white elephant that I suspect is very early. Even if it is not the progenitor of our plethora of white elephants today, its appearance so early in human history is notable. The other I will mention is a white horse, imperious and vibrant and beautiful; it may not be especially early, for horses were not introduced to India until close to 3,000 B.C. This is the finest art I found at Bhimbetka and I think it is an astonishing piece of work. Whatever its date, no one could doubt that this is truly great art. Probably all the paintings I have mentioned were done between 8,000 and 3,000 B.C., although I cannot be completely certain of that. After our lakeside breakfast the next morning we were driven to the small Bhopal airport for our flight to Delhi. Just as last year Jet Airways has given us remarkable service; I cannot imagine how this exemplary airline could be improved. We checked into the Radisson Hotel, only a few minutes from Indira Gandhi Airport, for our last Indian night of this trip. Before we went to dinner I sat by the windows in our room, watching dusk turn to darkness and thinking about all these weeks now at their end, grateful for all we had been given but sad, too, to leave behind so much we had come to cherish in this remarkable land. Below me and across the hotel garden National Highway 15 was pulsating with an incessant stream of lorries and buses and motorcycles and scooters and cars, tens of thousands of them. All these unknown people venturing into the unknown and for unknown reasons, even now that night had fallen. As always, the perennial questions crowded into my mind as I surveyed the ceaseless motion. Where were they going in the darkness and why were they going there? What do they mean to me and what do I mean to them? How can we reach out and touch one another and communicate? Why are so many all alone, even the ones on the buses? Predictably, the endless motion turns my thoughts to Siva, who began it all. Why? For what purpose? Is it all random and monadic or is there some exquisite design that escapes my vision? Modern technology makes us all solitaries, encapsulated monads speeding by one another on national highways. Our forefathers knew better, dancing around their fires and holding hands. Half of what I have seen in the subcontinent I would never have seen if I had not been offered so many supportive hands.

We went to the airport early and because this was a Sunday it was not as crowded as usual. After a pleasant time in the Virgin Atlantic lounge we boarded our plane to be met once again by Rahul, the friendly and attentive cabin steward whom we seem to meet on every flight to and from India. He always supplies us with a trove of splendid chocolates and once again he does not disappoint. I always look forward to flying over the Indian Himalayas and the equally forbidding mountains of Pakistan and Afghanistan. This is a clear day and the views are wonderful. Although it is a ten hour flight I have brought nothing to read because I know my mind is too filled with India to concentrate on anything else. So I spend my time scribbling notes about this memorable journey.

What made this trip different from the one in 2005? First, it was done largely by car, and this greatly improved our acquaintance with Indian towns and villages and with the countryside. We saw relatively little of big cities and much more of small towns. It was different in another way, too, because of the time devoted to "Hidden India"--or to one version of it chosen from a hundred possibilities with the guidance of Nagaraja Rao. Our destinations had such amazing variety; a number of them were not at all celebrated but quite obscure and gaining access to some was not very easy: tombs and cenotaphs, temples and gardens, caves and ruins and prehistoric shelters, stupas and deserted cities, churches and synagogues, palaces and forts and monasteries, the countryside and its agriculture and, most of all, ordinary life as lived by ordinary people. Despite my interest in Indian sacred architecture, this could scarcely be characterized as a temple tour. Happily, our cars and drivers were all terrific.

Perhaps the half dozen highlights of the travels for both of us were the cenotaphs of Gaitore on the outskirts of Jaipur and Amber, the Delwara temples of the Jains at Mt. Abu, the marvelous forgotten shrine at Nagda, Badami together with the Durga and Ravula Phadi shrines at Aihole, the wonders of Hampi and the paintings at Bhimbetka. It would be wrong to say these are obscure places but neither are they household names. Even Westerners who have traveled in India might be forgiven if they had never heard of these places. Most of them never see more than a handful of tourists unless some visitors have lost their way. Yet these are among the best of all the worthwhile sites in India even though, needless to say, they do not begin to exhaust the roster of the best. Unfortunately, one cannot imagine any tour that would introduce visitors to all these spots so widely separated from one another; some of them are rather remote and finding one's way to them demands time and effort. This is why India is so fascinating. There is always another "Hidden India" beckoning, asking to be explored. India requires a lifetime, far more than I have given it, because I also had other races to run and obligations to fulfill. But it has given me far more than I ever could have dreamed.

In the autumn of 1969 my life was changed. It was changed in the first place by an obscure collection of 18th century white marble cenotaphs on the outskirts of Jaipur where no one else ever came. It was changed in the second place by the overwhelming human density of the crowded bazaar in Varanasi that so disoriented me. It seemed to me the mute old stones at Gaitore had been waiting for me with a message intended for no one else. In the teeming darkness of Varanasi the communication was by touch, by the surging multitudes thrusting, jostling, pushing and shoving without ever a trace of discourtesy. I was surrounded by thousands and I was all alone, trying to catch my balance on the steps of the ghat where the bazaar's commerce ends in the embrace of the holy river that bears everything away as time is swallowed in eternity.

One lost American, a Westerner whose sense of direction had deserted him, remembering Rudyard Kipling's ballad once more, "East is East and West is

West and never the twain shall meet." East and West are strange bedfellows, but in the end it is not when they part company but when they keep company that each becomes all that it can be, just as Kipling's young brigand chief and the colonel's son become comrades forever. At both Gaitore and Varanasi I believed I had been touched by the hand of God. How curious all this is, that from such small and unremarkable beginnings there would be a whole new design added to my life. How little the Romantics understood when they proclaimed that we were masters of our destiny and captains of our fate. I was not a captain but a captive, and much more than content. As I have often said, this is what the Christian notion of grace means, a gift unexpected and undeserved. So little do we have that we have not received. Whether grace embraces us on Christian soil or half a world away, the dimensions of the grace of God are always the same. The Father to whom I pray introduced me to Siva the Lord of the Dance, and while this has not changed in any way the other religious commitments I made many years ago, it has enriched my life immeasurably and given me reason for gratitude I can never begin to adequately express. God does not kick in the door to our hearts. He speaks more softly than that and the net of my language is no match for His subtlety, using such little and unlikely things to shape a young man's life.

Nine Little Trips to see India's Grandeur

This Appendix consists of nine sketches of brief trips within India that are intended to acquaint a tourist with the best of Indian art and architecture. Some of these trips require several nights away from home. There are several omissions: there are no suggestions for either Mumbai or New Delhi because maps, guides and transportation are everywhere available. We do not pretend that these nine trips are a comprehensive guide to India. They are simply our own personal choices and have brought us much pleasure.

1. AGRA and FATEHPUR SIKRI

Perhaps the easiest excursion from New Delhi is the one to Agra, 125 miles south on the Grand Trunk Road. Agra holds most of the architectural legacy of the Mughal empire. Six miles before you enter the city you will see on your left four minarets sheltering behind an enormous sandstone entrance. Stop here for an hour, for this is the tomb of Akbar, the third and greatest of the six important Mughal rulers of India.

The Oberoi Amarvilas is a very expensive hotel but worth every penny. Each of its rooms has an unimpeded view of the Taj Mahal which is only six hundred yards away across a sea of green tree tops. At the break of day lie in your bed and watch the Taj try on a half a dozen or more pastel costumes before the sun dresses her in her business clothes. You will be ferried to and from the Taj in a golf cart because gas-powered vehicles are allowed no closer than the Amarvilas. Ideally, the Taj Mahal should be seen four times, at daybreak, noon, sunset, and in the light of the moon.

The Agra Fort is only a short distance from the Taj, although "fort" is a misnomer. Agra Fort is a whole imperial city built by Akbar in the sixteenth century behind a massive double wall. The fort was expanded by Akbar's son, Jahangir, and then radically reshaped by Jahangir's son, Shah Jahan, whose signature white marble can be seen in every direction. There are many impressive buildings within the fort, especially the wonderful Pearl Mosque, the Hall of Public Audience, the Royal Residences for Shah Jahan and his daughters, and the Mussaman Burg, a stunning octagonal tower built by Shah Jahan where the emperor spent the last seven years of his life, imprisoned there because of his profligate ways by his son and usurper Aurangzeb. Plan to spend a full half-day at the fort. But our favorite place in Agra is the tomb of Itmad-ud-Daulah, a scant three miles from the Taj and also on the bank of the Yamuna. It was built by Nur Jahan, the favorite wife of Jahangir, as a memorial to her father, who was Jahangir's chief minister.

About fifty minutes west of Agra on the road to Jaipur there is a third UNESCO World Heritage site, the desert city of Fatehpur Sikri that was once an imperial capital but abandoned forever only fourteen years after its creation. It was built by Akbar in 1571, all of red sandstone, and it remains in pristine condition. That location was chosen because it was the home of Salim Chishti, a Sufi mystic and saint who blessed Akbar and prophesied that he would soon have a male heir who would grow to manhood. The grateful emperor soon began his new capital at Sikri. There are audience halls, harem buildings, a treasury and a ladies' mosque, Akbar's own quarters, houses for his queens and much else. Architecturally most interesting, perhaps, is the Hall of Private Audience, a single tall chamber with a central column of amazing complexity.

Last but certainly not least, there is the dargah of Salim Chishti. Dargah means tomb, but by extension it can be applied to the neighboring structures: the Buland Darwaza, a massive gateway that looms over everything else in the city and celebrates Akbar's conquering of Gujarat; the beautiful Jami Masjid, a mosque built for ten thousand worshippers; and the resting place of Salim Chishti, originally red sandstone but clothed in white marble afterward by Jahangir, whose birth Salim had prophesied.

2. JAIPUR and AMBER

It is less than four hours from Fatehpur Sikri to Jaipur, the capital of Rajasthan. Our destination here is the Taj Rambagh Palace, a "Heritage Hotel" that was once a maharajah's residence. There are two principal tourist attractions in Jaipur, each of which requires so much time they are best seen on different days.

The first is Amber (or Amer), the capital of Rajputana (later Rajasthan) until Jai Singh II established Jaipur as a new capital city in 1727 a few miles away. Today the Amber fortress/palace is thronged with tourists, both Indian and Western.

The exterior of the fort is so bleak and forbidding that the visitor is unprepared to discover inside the ramparts tremendous beauty and delicacy and magic, a whole wonderland of Hindu artistry. The most dazzling part of the palace is the Hall of Private Audience; its walls are inset with myriad tiny mirrors of convex glass set at different angles so that the effect is similar to a waterfall. Below the mirrors are white marble panels with superbly carved butterflies and flowers that are no less inspired than the artisanship of the Taj Mahal. My own favorite chamber, however, is the Hall of Private Prayer, with its wonderful pastel colors and stained glass windows. There is much here to occupy a visitor for a very full half day.

On the short drive back to Jaipur, stop for an hour at the Cenotaphs of Gaitore, where there are magnificent memorials erected in the 18th century to the male members of the royal family. I have been here at least half a dozen times and I have never seen one other tourist, although I believe these cenotaphs are among the glories of Rajasthan. The finest of them is dedicated to Jai Singh II. Its many columns are slender and beautifully proportioned; the carved marble of the cenotaph is done in floral and celestial and martial patterns. The work is really exquisite, not often matched elsewhere and rarely surpassed. Near this memorial there is another, dedicated to all the male members of the royal household who died in infancy or boyhood.

The second major attraction in Jaipur is the creamy-yellow City Palace, where the former maharajah still lives although most of the palace has been converted into a series of museums. The maharani is greatly interested in education, and so part of the palace is now a school. The first museum is devoted to textiles, mainly silk and brocades, some from the 17th century, which offer a taste of the opulence of bygone days. The second museum is the armory, which holds one of the finest collections of knives and swords in India. Note the splendid painted ceiling. Then there is the Hall of Private Audience, which contains the two largest silver objects in the world, urns or water pots once filled with Ganges water, which accompanied the maharajah when he attended the coronation of Edward VII of England.

Finally there is the Hall of Public Audience, where there is an overwhelming collection of treasures; my own preference is the 17th century oriental rugs brought from Amber. Before leaving, do not fail to visit the workroom where eighteen or so artisans are busy making their splendid wares. The maharajah is determined that handicrafts will continue to flourish here.

There are two other attractions that deserve a bit of time. One is the architectronic Jantar Mantar, the observatory built by Jai Singh who was the greatest astronomer in Asia in his day. The other is the Hawa Mahal or Wind Palace, a facade with nearly 1,000 windows but which is only one room deep. It was built so the ladies of the court could watch activity in the streets outside without disclosing their own presence.

3. UDAIPUR and THE JAINS

There are many reasons to come to Udaipur, which is easily accessible by plane from Jaipur or other cities. Its Lake Pichola is very beautiful and boasts two of the world's finest hotels, the venerable Lake Palace and the new Oberoi flagship, the Udaivilas. On this trip we stayed at both and were delighted. The primary reason for our visit was to see some of the world's finest Jain architecture, the 15th century temple at Ranakpur and the 11th and 13th century temples atop Mt. Abu. Although I cannot echo the exuberance of some Indian friends who claim this is the greatest art and architecture in the subcontinent, it is a great treasure and should not be missed.

Our first day was spent at Ranakpur, which is about 60 miles from Udaipur (open to non-Jains only from 11:30 - 5 p.m.) and about a two and a half hour drive through the Aravalli Hills, some of the oldest mountains in the world. Ranakpur is a 3-storey temple; there are two small subordinate shrines as well as a small shrine dedicated to Surya, but there is no village of any sort, only the sacred buildings. The closest rest rooms are 12 miles toward Udaipur. The drive from Udaipur to Ranakpur is fascinating and care must be exercised on its many sharp curves, but the visitor will encounter little traffic.

The exteriors of Jain temples are deliberately unprepossessing, but the interiors are an entirely different matter. The temple at Ranakpur is dedicated to Adinath, the first of the 24 Tirthankaras or "enlightened ones". And to him the central shrine is dedicated although 66 subordinate shrines commemorate other religious figures. There are 1,444 columns in the temple, no two of which are identical. The carved relief decorations are often described as among the finest in India. I have found myself as much entranced by the superb ceilings as I have been by the pillars. The Ranakpur temple deserves hours of study; one should dress in a sober fashion and no leather of any sort can be worn. The visitor will leave with many indelible memories of the forbidding and fascinating ancient Aravalli Hills.

The trip to Mt. Abu to see the Vimal Vasahi and Luna Vasahi is only 115 miles but it requires four hours or so, partly because the drive ends with a 4000 foot climb to Mt. Abu along a road with no guard rails. The temples are open to non-Jains only in the afternoon and so an overnight is essential. Bikaner House and Jaipur House are old hunting lodges that offer various spartan accommodations but we did manage to sleep well because the air is pure and very fresh. The Delwara temples are glorious and their carving is even more intricate and elaborate than what is at Ranakpur.

Vimal Vasahi required more than 14 years to complete, partly because elephants had to carry all the marble for its interior 30 miles and then climb 4000 ft. This is why each major temple has a special chamber dedicated to elephants without which it could never have been built. There is an oddity about both temples: neither has a resident congregation because no Jains live in Mt. Abu, there being no opportunities for their faith to earn a livelihood there.

In Udaipur itself there was much to do. The 17th c. Jagdish Temple, near the City Palace, is extremely interesting; it is presided over by Vishnu, Lakshmi, and Krishna. The City Palace is huge but its appeal is somewhat limited. Udaipur with its dearth of beggars is a charming city in which to walk; the Garden of the Maidens with its unusual collection of fountains is a delightful place to rest and relax. No matter whether one has chosen the Lake Palace or the Udaivilas there is much to occupy the guest in either hotel and it is wise to reserve enough time to savor one's surroundings. Before we left, we drove an hour or so to see temples at Eklingji and Nagda. The Mother-in-Law and Daughter-in-Law temples at Nagda, although a thousand years old, are remarkably preserved and have almost no visitors. We look forward very much to another visit to Nagda, one of the most enchanting Vaishnavite sites we know.

4. AJANTA and ELLORA

There is one place in India that is beyond any doubt one of the wonders of the ancient world and all by itself justifies a trip to India from anywhere else on earth. It is two spots in scrub jungle not too far from the thriving industrial city of Aurangabad where there are twenty-nine rock-cut temples and monasteries at Ajanta and thirty-four nearby at Ellora, twelve of them Buddhist, seventeen Hindu, and five Jain. The work at Ajanta began in 200 B.C.; those at Ellora were sculpted between 200 and 750 A.D. The only tools used by the artisans were hammers and crude chisels. Men from different traditions worked side by side, ate together, and played together and slept together in harmony. Each complex will require a full day. It is never difficult to hire an air-conditioned car, driver and guide for two or three days. There are a number of hotels in Aurangabad that are less than spectacular, but quite satisfactory.

It is enlightening to compare the handiwork of the Hindu, Buddhist, and Jain artisans whose temples are side by side. The Buddhist work has a calm and serenity that is matchless; the human figures are ordinarily meditative and peaceful. The Hindu gods and humans are certainly recognizable as participants in Siva's cosmic dance. They move with abandon and are often in passionate embrace. On the other hand, there seems to be an extraordinary vigilance about the Jain tirthankaras, almost as though they were on sentry duty, watchful and alert and standing at attention. It is clear to even the most casual tourist that here we are walking through three different worlds.

There are many wonderful frescoes at Ajanta; perhaps your favorites will be different than ours. But I would hazard that these are among the most arresting. The two Bodhisattvas at site one, Vajrapani and Padmapani, arguably the finest figures at Ajanta; a mother and child encountering the Buddha in the guise of a beggar; the king of the gods and his retinue flying effortlessly across the sky; a swooning princess who has just been told that her husband Nanda is leaving her to become a monk; women grooming themselves with wonderful attentiveness; the Buddha calming an elephant that had run amok; the "three ominous signs" that first elicit the curiosity of Siddhartha Gautama, an old person and a sick person and a corpse; and the birth stories of the Buddha.

The greatest of the edifices at Ellora is site 16, Kailasha, a replica of Siva's legendary home in the Tibetan Himalayas. Kailasha was carved from the top down in the sense that a whole mountain was whittled away until what remained was amenable to artisanal chisels. More than three million cubic feet of solid rock were removed and disposed of before the sculptors could even start about their real business. When we left Ellora on this trip we stopped to look at the panorama if offered: thirty-four ornate entrances stretch in a single line along the mountainside for more than two miles. This was Herculean work, the labor of love. It required armies of artisans and many generations of travail, for the scale of what has been done at these two spots is astonishing. Kailasha is the largest monolithic sculpture in the world, more than twice the size of the Parthenon. Virtually every scrap of the exterior of the huge temple has been carved with astonishing delicacy and intricacy. It is a superb encyclopedia of Hinduism and Kailasha deserves to be called the greatest expression of Hindu faith in the world, its supreme articulation in art and sculpture.

One very recent commentator on Kailasha has written, "The most wonderful monument ever created by mankind on earth is the Kailasha temple. It is an illustration of one of those rare occasions when men's minds, hearts and hands, in unison, worked to build a great structure. The Kailasha represents the final stage of perfection in Hindu rock-cut architecture and constitutes a class by itself."

It was difficult to tear oneself away from such a feast for the eyes as this. What must Ellora have been like when camel caravans from the spice trade stopped here to rest? And how did they mix, the merchants and the monks? Here we have the most eloquent expression of three of the world's great religions gathered in one place where they call us to their common embrace. No longer do we encounter them as solo voices but as a magnificent troupe, an utterly astonishing ecumenical feast of faith that has no parallel elsewhere in the world.

5. MYSORE and THE HOYSALAS

I was introduced to the Hoysala legacy by my friend Nagaraja Rao, when he was Director of the Archaeological Survey of India for the State of Karnataka. On this particular trip to the Hoysala temples we began in Mysore; our driver, Krishna, brought us to the temple at Belur in three hours. Belur and its twin, Halebid, were both built in the 12th c., but today there is no trace of their lost grandeur, nothing but dust everywhere, no restaurants or hostelries, nothing but the dust and the sun and two temples.

Initially Belur is a disappointment to the visitor because it is nothing more than a flat-roofed little box. But when one draws near it is all alive, the exterior and interior walls, the columns and ceilings, everything. I had never seen such exquisite and intricate carvings in my life. There are more than 10,000 statues at Belur, so fabulously done that the bangles worn by some of the dancing girls will move if you touch them as will the stone beads from which they are made. Pay particular attention to the ceilings and columns, all different, and especially to the bracket figures.

The temple at Halebid is only a few miles distant, but it is much larger and very different because it is a double temple. There is one shrine for the ruler and a separate building for his consort; although the two are quite separate they are yoked together. Behind each of these Shaivite temples there is a superb Nandi and farther behind the king's shrine there is a lovely little Surya temple. Not surprisingly, because we have two temples we also have twice the statuary, more than 20,000 sculptures and twice as many columns, each one of them a masterpiece. I do not believe there is anything else like this in the world; if there is I haven't seen it.

From all this marvelous activity captured in stone we drove for an hour toward its antithesis, the absolute serenity and calm of Bahubali. This is one of the most important Jain pilgrimage sites in the world and is the scene of a great festival every twelve years when the statue is anointed with sandalwood paste and pots of ghee. The son of the first Tirthankara, Bahubali stood unmoving at this site for a whole year while seeking Moksha. The tenth century statue in his memory is about 57 feet tall atop a high hill and can be approached by climbing nearly 700 difficult steps. From Shrivanabelagola we returned to Mysore where we spent the next morning exploring the Keshava Temple at Somnathpur. It is only a few miles from the city but the road is truly appalling.

This temple was built in the mid-13th c., a hundred years after Belur and Halebid, and is the only one of the three that was ever entirely completed because of the repeated Muslim attacks on the other two. It has five small shikharas or towers that I think add immeasurably to its beauty. The cloister is unusually attractive, and the whole enclosure is handsomely framed by graceful palms. Unlike the other temples, Keshava has three sanctuaries, even though the whole temple could not easily accommodate more than two dozen people. For many years it has been one of my favorite places in all of India.

There is one other Hoysala monument that deserves special mention. In the National Museum at Chennai there is a Hoysala stone door frame which is absolutely breathtaking and matches anything a visitor might see at Somnathpur or Halebid. The entire afternoon was spent in the City Palace where we had access to everything because we were accompanied by Nagaraja Rao. This is certainly one of the greatest palaces in India. It is the home of the Wodeyars, long reputed to be one of the world's most enlightened ruling families. At Independence the Maharajah was elected by acclamation the first governor of Karnataka. The Palace is awesome, stupendous, unbelievable; it utterly defies description. Among the unique rooms are the Durbar Hall and the magnificent pillared corridor that borders it, the marriage hall, and its breathtaking mural and stained glass ceiling and the private Durbar Hall. There is no way to exhaust the offerings displayed before the visitor. It is the exhaustion of the visitors that will finally bring any tour of these riches to an end.

6. From BADAMI to HAMPI

There is a second trip that begins in Mysore, also arranged by my friend Nagaraja Rao. He settled us in our accommodations for the train trip on the Dharwar Express from Mysore to Hubli. There was one second-class air-conditoned car on the train, locked to prevent access to it from any other car. This night it held only nine passengers and ourselves, thirty persons short of its capacity. It had its own conductor, its own guard and two cabin boys who provided us with immaculately pressed sheets, pillowcases and a blanket. It was a very pleasant trip and we arrived at Hubli twenty minutes or so ahead of schedule to find our driver and our car waiting for us just a few feet from where we alit.

Our destination was Badami or more precisely four "cave temples" looking down upon it. This is an enchanting town, perhaps the most picturesque in which I have stayed in India. Our accommodations were at the Badami Court Hotel which we shared with a very pleasant Bollywood film crew using the town as its background. The lowest cave temple is Shaivite, where visitors are welcomed by a superb eighteen-armed Siva Nataraja. He faces an equally fine androgenous Siva-and-Parvati beyond whom there is a beautiful Harihara, Siva and Vishnu united. The temple above is dedicated to Vishnu and his avatars and includes most intriguing groups of dwarfs. The climb to the third temple is quite taxing but the rewards are many. The columns here are really splendid and the ceiling is excellent. I was very surprised to find significant remnants of the original 6th c. paint. The figures of Brahma, Siva and Indra are outstanding. These three temples are all 6th c.; the fourth is Jain and perhaps a century later. It is dedicated to Adinath but also memorializes the other two dozen tirthankaras.

The next morning we drove to the hamlet of Pattadakal, which is quite surprisingly a UNESCO World Heritage Site because it has an interesting array of very different 8th c. roofs as well as temple designs all of which were built at the same time. So it is strikingly similar, not in substance but in intent, to what is found at Mahabilipuram: a text for the sacred architecture of a whole millenium of the future, an astonishing achievement. Attention should be paid to the perforated stone windows at Pattadakal and at Aihole as well; many are done in different designs and with great delicacy. The best of the temples at Pattadakal is certainly Virupaksha. On our way back to Badami we stopped at Mahakuta, notable for its two temples facing one another across a large sacred tank. Mahakuta is a crossroads where many weddings are performed, some beneath an awesome ancient banyan tree. We watched about forty small boys dunking one another and playing ball in the sacred tank. I could imagine the gods looking down with much amusement and approval. We finished our day at the excellent little ASI museum.

In the morning we drove farther afield to Aihole where there are some truly splendid and unusual temples. As one approaches Aihole the countryside becomes ever more threatening and inhospitable. The most important temple is the Durga Temple, a fortified military outpost built in 742 and shaped like the capital letter U with a fabulous ambulatory filled with marvelous statuary - Siva and Nandi, Narasimha, Harihara, Vishnu and some avatars. The Ladkhan shrine is very early, probably built around 450, originally as a town hall. When it was converted to a temple, there was no room in it for a sanctuary so that was built on its roof. Finally, there is Ravula Phadi (cave temple) sculpted in the 6th c. This is a wonderful place with a superb Siva dancing with Parvati and their son Ganesh and many maidens. There is a Gangadwara here which is absolutely superb. And so ends the first part of a fabulous pilgrimage: Ravula Phadi and the Durga Temple at Aihole, the Virupaksha Shrine in Pattadakal and caves one and three at Badami.

It was a three hour drive from Aihole to Hospet and the Maligi Tourist Home where we stayed to visit Hampi. This is an interesting portrait of the grandeur and misery of man. The grandeur is Hampi. The misery is Hospet. At eight o'clock the next morning we set out to meet Nagaraja's ASI subordinates who would show us something of the world of the Vijayanagars during our two day visit. The Vijayanagar Empire endured for only two hundred years, from the mid-fourteenth to the mid-sixteenth centuries when it was overrun by its Islamic foes who razed Hampi. But for those two hundred years it flourished as few other places ever had, and held a million people and enormous wealth. Western visitors contrasted its opulence with the rusticity of Elizabethan London.

Because there is so much to see at the World Heritage Site I decided we should focus on just one of its riches during our first day, the Vitthala Temple. This is very large and has many buildings. It is dedicated to Vishnu. One approaches it through a dancing hall that is simply stupendous. There is also a singing hall, a cooking hall, a hundred-pillared assembly hall and a marriage hall. There is also a large stone chariot that houses Vishnu's garuda. The columns in the dancing hall simply defy description. There are fifty-six of them and it is difficult to imagine pillars more elaborately and richly sculpted. My favorite sculptures are the Yalis, some of which have the bodies of lions, others with elephantine or equine shapes. But there are also many scenes both from the Ramayana and the

Mahabharata as well as from fifteenth century life. From Vitthala we went to the small but choice ASI museum.

The next morning we left for Hampi very early to avoid the heat of the day. Once again we chose a single focus for our activities, the Hazzara Rama Temple which is the best sacred architecture at Hampi along with the huge Vitthala shrine. It is carved entirely from white granite. The bands of sculpture surrounding the whole temple are astonishing in their beauty. There are four great black granite columns covered with images of Vishnu and all his avatars, each of which is a stone hymn to God the preserver and sustainer. The narrative of the Ramayana is first carved into the outer walls of Hazzara Rama and then continued to the exterior of the sanctum itself. This comprehensive stone exposition of a religious classic may well be unique. We left Hampi after our second day thankful for our new acquaintance with so much that is so wonderful but regretful that we had not allocated far more time to this astonishing place. Our drive from Hospet to Bangalore required far less than six hours over an excellent road, half the time the night train would have taken.

7. MAHABILIPURAM and KANCHI

Mahabilipuram was an important port and commercial center between the 6th and 9th centuries, although today it is frequented only by tourists. The town lies 35 miles south of Chennai and as one draws closer there are many craftsmen's shops well worth exploration. Mahabilipuram is too much a feast to be encompassed in a single day unless one plans to spend a night. When we were last there the ravages of the great tsunami were not fully repaired.

First, Arjuna's Penance or The Descent of the Ganges. This is the world's largest bas-relief, approximately 95 ft. long and 38 ft. tall. Visit it early while you are still fresh for it richly repays careful scrutiny before the sun is at its zenith. Some commentators have said that the two great elephants are the finest ever sculpted in the sub-continent. I am greatly partial to a family of mice. Arjuna's Penance rehearses a story from the Mahabharata in which Siva is the crucial figure. Second, only a few yards from Arjuna's Penance there is Krishna's Butter Ball. This huge granitic monolith has been perched since time immemorial on the side of a steep hill from which it should have fallen long ago but it has not. Why? No one knows. There is rich mythology surrounding Krishna and butter - and milkmaids for that matter - which makes this interesting to a student of Hinduism.

Third, there are the Five Rathas. A ratha is a temple chariot; why these should be so named remains something of a mystery. The five monoliths are unfinished and represent very different south Indian architectural styles. Bring your camera for this is a fascinating display of the evolution of South Indian sacred architecture. The Five Rathas are companioned by three great and beautifully carved animals – a lion, an elephant and a bull. Fourth, at some distance there is the famed Shore Temple that has withstood all the savagery the Bay of Bengal could unleash upon it for 1300 years. The salt spray has considerably damaged its exterior but it is still remarkably well-preserved. Inside the temple there are three shrines, two dedicated to Siva and one to a reclining Vishnu engaged in his cosmic sleep. This is one of the oldest temples in South India and a model for a great deal that came later.

Fifth, there is the Krishna Mandapam. This is one of a number of cave temples at Mahabilipuram distinguished from the rest because it is an utterly unforgettable carving of a cow that is being milked while she protectively nuzzles her young calf. Sixth, and finally, there is another cave temple that is very noteworthy: the Mahishasuramardina Cave. This mandipam has a remarkable carved panel of Durga, the goddess, defeating the buffalo demon Mahishasura.

Kanchipuram today shows few traces of its grand imperial past and certainly no longer deserves its ancient boast as "the city of a thousand temples". But it is still one of the seven notable Hindu pilgrimage cities and it is a most picturesque day trip from Chennai, less than 50 miles away. Kanchi is a legendary center of the Indian silk industry. It has been said that every street in the town ends in a gopuram; it is even more accurate to say that every street ends in skeins of silk thread drying in the sun, every tint and hue imaginable. Of the plethora of temples I will mention only two: Ekambaranathar dates from the mid-9th c.; unfortunately the thousand-pillar hall of its mandipam is shrunken to half that size today but it is still most impressive. The courtyard is dominated by a mango tree thought to be more than 2500 years old, that is said to bear four different kinds of fruit every year. Legend has it that Siva and Parvati were married under this tree and that is the reason why Hindus around the world decorate with mango leaves in preparation for a wedding. I am not a fan of gopurams but the more than 10-storey 16th c. Ekambaranathar gopuram is certainly among the better that I have seen. The other temple is Kailasanatha that was commissioned by the same Pallava ruler who inspired the Shore Temple at Mahabilipuram. It is a splendid example of early Dravidian South Indian temple architecture. All temples in the city are closed from 12:30 until 4:00 in the afternoon.

8. BHUBANESHWAR and KONARAK

We flew from Chennai to Bhubaneshwar where we were soon ensconced at the Trident Hotel, one of the finest provincial hotels, perhaps, in the land. We rejoiced in the countless yellow butterflies and whirring dragonflies outside our windows, the beautiful rose gardens and mango orchard and especially the courtesy of everyone we met, for everyone seemed to regard himself as our personal host. Bhubaneshwar is another of those "towns with a thousand temples", but in this case that is not a wild exaggeration for there are at least half that number in excellent condition. To my great relief, however, I encountered not a single gopuram waiting to dwarf me into insignificance. Sooner or later Bhubaneshwar will infect you with "temple fatigue". So choose your quarries with care.

Our favorite is certainly Rajarani, an eleventh century temple in marvelous condition in the middle of a beautiful garden where two large stone snakes welcome visitors. Brahmeswar is larger, older and with more elaborate sculptures. The oldest in the city is Parasuraswara, which is also elaborately carved and exquisitely proportioned. The Mukteswara must also be included within the first group of Orissan temples; there is a distinctive stone arch over its entrance. There is a marvelous great stone cobra over the lingam in the sanctuary. Then we needed to catch our breath and so we drove in the late afternoon to a little lake around which many medieval temples are clustered. The most famous temple in the the city is Lingaraj but it is firmly closed to non-Hindus.

Early the next morning we set off for Konarak an hour and a half away; it is one of India's most notable religious sites. We stopped first just three or four miles from Bhubaneshwar, at Dhauli, at a hilltop where in 272 BCE the great Emperor Ashoka surveyed the corpse-littered battlefield where he had destroyed the armies of Kalinga. Then the great monarch repented all that he had done and all that he had been and sat down on the hillside and wept. From that day forward he was a Buddhist, the most important convert that faith ever embraced. At the site there are Ashokan edicts proclaiming the brotherhood of all men as children of Ashoka. There is also the Shanti stupa, built 40 years ago as a symbol of peace.

Suddenly in front of us reared the huge hulk of the Sun Temple, built in the mid-13th c. and dedicated to Surya. Much of it is in superb condition today because for many years the temple was buried beneath the sand of the seashore, and only after the waters of the Bay of Bengal receded were the British able to excavate it more than a century ago. It is one of the largest temples in India. Originally it stood more than 225 feet tall. It is actually two massive structures intended to portray Surya's chariot rising from beneath the waves and soaring into heavenly heights. The great chariot is drawn by seven stallions and it has 24 enormous wheels with a diameter that approaches ten feet. The spokes of each wheel are carved with incredible lavishness. There are three commanding statues of Surya on the temple wall portraying him in the morning, at noon and at dusk. The sculpture of the Sun Temple is some of the finest in India, very much comparable to the glorious 10th c. sculpture at Khajuraho and the 12th c. sculpture at Halebid. Its eroticism, by the way, matches that of Khajuraho.

Many tourists drive from Konarak to Puri, which is the site of another of India's most revered temples. This also is closed to non-Hindus. Mildew has made it utterly filthy. The beach is no cleaner and raw sewerage renders it even less salubrious. We recommend that you return from Konarak to the extraordinary comforts of the Trident Hotel. It is an Oberoi property. Enough said. We recommend flying from Bhubaneshwar to New Delhi.

9. KHAJURAHO and VARANASI

It is best to approach Khajuraho by plane rather than by train, taxi, bus or bullock cart. Khajuraho is in the middle of nowhere and, like most roads leading to nowhere, the approaches to the village are difficult. You have come here to see two dozen tenth or eleventh century temples and for no other reason. This is one of the world's great museums. The number of such great museums is limited; there are even fewer that are open-air and this is one of them. The temples are clustered in a meticulously groomed park, all of them perched on high terraces which adds to their prominence. The whole area is a UNESCO World Heritage Site. Khajuraho has been described as a world treasury of erotic carving. This is an accurate description but one must add that it is a collection of some of the world's greatest statuary. It has few rivals as a laboratory of the sculptor's art.

Beyond question this is a glorious and incomparable celebration of human flesh. But it is also something else, something that seems contradictory at first but that Khajuraho magically transforms. Everything about the temple complex is straining upward, aspiring, climbing, ascending, soaring. The whole complex is a representation of the majesty of the high Himalayas. Nowhere is the genius of the great sculptors at work here more evident than in the shikharas that crown all the temples and seem to challenge even the highest heavens. The whole place is a hymn to the transcendence that the artists themselves and their stones have achieved. So we not only celebrate the earth, we also leave it beneath us in our ascent - or better yet, - carry it with us upward. It is this unity that makes Khajuraho the magic and mystery and incomparable achievement that it is.

The greatest creation at Khajuraho is the largest and grandest temple, Kandariya-Mahadeva. Nothing else quite rivals this shrine. It is fascinating to watch the evolution of temple architecture here from the Adinatha shikhara to Visvanatha to Parsvanatha and finally to Kandariya-Mahadeva, which is roofed by eighty-some shikharas, each one climbing further into the heights than its predecessor.

It is a very brief and easy flight on Jet Airways from Khajuraho to Varanasi. It is a hugely more difficult transition to travel from this celebration of the flesh to the overwhelming sense of the mortality of the flesh. In Varanasi, the holiest city of the Hindus, every devout Hindu hopes to come to die and be cremated at the burning ghat on the bank of the Ganges. In every Indian city one encounters a plague of little beggars, but in Varanasi beggary is a religious profession honorably practiced by adepts who live comfortably on their income. You must have a city tour which will prove interesting especially when you walk through

Benares Hindu University, the largest residential institution of higher learning in this part of Asia. But soon you will be not only an onlooker but a player in the life of the city and that means you will be not simply a tourist but a pilgrim, even though this may have been far from your intention. Recently a writer said, "The streets of Varanasi throb with religious and commercial energy like no other place in India." In the evening hire a little boat and travel upstream and stop for a few minutes at the burning ghat, and then drift downstream making one's offerings of candle-lit little paper boats to Mother Ganga, and then mooring with thousands of other people to watch the Aarti ceremony as the priests cast their spells to ward off the dangers of the encroaching night. Return to Mother Ganga before dawn and watch the sunrise from your little boat and listen to the first cries and prayers as people come to wash themselves at the bathing ghat. By day or by night lose yourself in this bazaar that seems somehow different from all the others you have seen. Perhaps it is simply the astonishing numbers. Or perhaps not.